Sweet Miniatures

Also by Flo Braker

The Simple Art of Perfect Baking (1985)

Sweet Miniatures

The Art of
Making Bite-Size Desserts

Flo Braker

Color photography by Chris Shorten

Line illustrations by Laura Hartman Maestro

William Morrow and Company, Inc.

New York

Recipes for Sweet Cheese Puffs, Viennese Triangles, Miniature Pastry Tartlets, Little Gems, and Drei Augen originally appeared in *Bon Appétit,* November 1979.

Recipes for Chocolate Sushi and Meringue Bubbles originally appeared in *Chocolatier,* March 1986 and January 1990.

Recipes for Phyllo Accordions originally appeared in *Family Circle* as Phyllo Ruffles, December 1988.

The recipe for Chocolate Galaxy Petitcakes originally appeared in *The New York Times Entertaining Magazine.*

Recipes for Tiny Raspberry Cheesecakes, Four-Star Rugelach, California Rolls, and Cinnamon Twists originally appeared in slightly different versions in the *San Francisco Chronicle.*

Library of Congress Cataloging-in-Publication Data

Braker, Flo.
    Sweet miniatures: the art of making bite-size desserts / Flo Braker.
      p.   cm.
    Includes index.
    ISBN: 0-688-10539-4
    1. Cookies. 2. Pastry. 3. Cake. I. Title. II. Title: Sweet Miniatures
  TX772.B73 1991
    641.8′65—dc20   90-6594
                                                                CIP

Printed in the United States of America

First Edition

1 2 3 4 5 6 7 8 9 10

BOOK DESIGN BY RICHARD ORIOLO

For my honey, our children,
and my parents, Susie and Dick Gumberts

Contents

Acknowledgments

The one question I can always count on is, "What is your favorite dessert?" After completing *Sweet Miniatures,* the answer is clear: the generosity of my colleagues, mentors, family, and friends. I am very fortunate to have had such staunch support while I worked on this not-so-miniature project about my beloved miniatures. The efforts of all these people in behalf of me and my book are truly touching. A heartfelt thank-you with hugs and kisses seems too simple and not enough.

When *Bon Appétit* featured my miniatures in 1979, I received instant feedback, and it has never stopped. I still get letters and phone calls about the article from bakers all over the world. Thank you to the magazine and its readers for starting me off on the right foot.

Jack Lirio gave me the opportunity to teach classes on the miniatures and loves the miniatures almost as much as I do. I am indebted to him for sparking my creativity.

For her enthusiasm, helpful advice, and candor, Susan Lescher, my literary agent, was there for me through every phase.

To my editor, a keen baker herself, Maria Guarnaschelli, who always believed in this project and whose eye for detail fine-tuned the book, I offer many thanks. And many thanks to Elizabeth Portland, the best editor's assistant any author could wish for.

Shirley Rosenberg and Denise Landis have been a tremendous help. Graciously they tested and retested the recipes, only to make them better. And thanks to a fortuitous phone call from Mary Goodbody, Debbie Sachs, a jack of all trades, has been with me every step of the way.

I am forever awed by the talent, imagination, and professionalism of photographer Chris Shorten and prop stylist Roz Baker. I am sincerely grateful to Laura Hartman Maestro, whose beautiful illustrations make the recipe's techniques easy to follow.

I could not have done without the kindnesses and good humor of Michael Bauer, Casey Carsten, Marion Cunningham, Corby Kummer, and Jan Weimer, who never let me forget that I could do it—again.

Special thanks to the San Francisco Professional Food Society and the Bakers Dozen, my warm wonderful professional families of which I am so very proud to be a member.

And to Dave, whose loving actions always speak louder than any words I could ever write, I respond with words in sweet miniature: Thank you, my honey!

Flo Braker

Acknowledgments

Introduction

My fascination with cookies, pastries, and cakes in miniature started in childhood. My maternal grandmother made frequent business trips to New York and she always came back to Indiana with at least one box of cookies and small pastries from Schrafft's, the well-known tearoom. These were called Little Gems. Before these, I'd only seen candy this small. Each time I ate one of the tiny treats, I secretly dreamed of duplicating one or even creating my own someday.

Growing up, and as a young wife and mother, I often read biographies of world-renowned artists, such as Van Gogh and Rembrandt, with envy. After each book I was inspired to try the artist's medium—in the hopes that I possessed latent artistic talent.

But it was only as my interest in baking grew that my dreams became reality. Because of my fascination with every facet of baking, I baked every day, and no matter what I baked, I always focused on making it in miniature. And so, baking in miniature became my favorite creative outlet, my hobby. It made no difference whether these miniatures were cookies, pastries, or cakes—tiny proportions packed with great flavors obsessed me. Like popping corn, new miniatures kept coming. Finally, I'd found my art form.

For many years I've studied the details and designs of cakes and pastries all over the world. I've also looked at jewelry, fashion, architecture, and art for inspiration—always imagining how to apply what I saw to miniature shapes and sizes.

Soon a crossroad came in my baking. My family could not eat the cakes, cookies, and pastries that I baked daily fast enough. My production exceeded their consumption, and so, reluctantly, I froze many creations. I was grateful for occasions that allowed me to draw from the freezer's bounty. Often I arranged these sweets on plates for sick friends, or used them for Boy Scout and Brownie functions, to celebrate birthdays, or to welcome new neighbors. Word got around that if you visited me, a peek at the tortes, cakes, pies, cookies, and pastries in the freezer was a must.

The timing seemed perfect to begin baking professionally. So I began Occasional Baking, a dessert catering business. I started with no definite menu. It was solely bake-on-request for customers with advertising by word-of-mouth. I never anticipated that the majority of the orders would be for the baked items that I had personally styled: wedding cakes and miniatures.

I could understand the demand for wedding cakes, but the popularity of the miniatures was a wonderful welcome surprise. People liked them assorted on trays to adorn their tables before serving. They loved everything about them—the textures: crispy or tender; the flavors: spicy or sweet; and of course, the size. As business grew, it encouraged me to expand the miniature repertoire, which had become my trademark.

One observation I made during my catering career also holds true when I entertain in my home. No matter how much I fuss over a cake or a special dessert, when I accompany it with a tray of miniatures, the miniatures get the attention every time. Guests love to look at them, but after tasting a few—small bites of spice, tangy citrus with fresh fruit, creamy caramel and flaky pastry, bittersweet chocolate and jam, buttery coconut, pecans and tender pastry, spongy cake and honey, nutty meringue and semisweet chocolate—they become even more enthusiastic, eager to sample each variety.

After three years of business experience and hundreds of educational baking errors, I decided to teach what I had learned about the subject of baking. Of all my classes, the ones on the miniatures were in greatest demand. Some popular miniatures—Sweet Cheese Puffs (page 240), Drei Augen (page 48), and Lemon Meringue Tartlets (page 220)—became my signature miniatures.

People remember miniatures. In 1979, *Bon Appétit* magazine featured an article on my miniatures. To this day, I receive mail and telephone calls with questions and comments about the article. Readers responded to the photo of a tray of assorted miniatures that offered such a selection of textures, flavors, and shapes that you wouldn't get from a single slice of cake or pie: luscious chocolate cream, tart lemon curd, crisp florentines, pungently spicy gingersnaps, juicy strawberries on top of tartlets, and even a whimsical cookie shaped like a butterfly.

My most beloved recipes are in this book. You will find how I make them, and what works for me. What I wish for you is to enjoy them as much as I have. But the best reward for me would be if this book inspired you to invent your own memorable miniatures.

Part I

Good Things Come in Small Packages

$\mathcal{M}$iniatures have special appeal. A tray of assorted miniature cookies, pastries, and cakes offers a dazzling array of shapes, colors, flavors, and textures. Imagine a display of miniatures in all their variety. Some are round and some square. They are a delicious golden brown or brightly colored. Taste a few. Some are rich, others sweet, tart, or spicy. Their textures may be soft, chewy, crisp, crumbly, short, crunchy, or flaky.

We are attracted to miniatures. Something makes us thrill to see a familiar object scaled down to an unusually small size. And a close look at our tray reveals that each morsel is not just little, but is, in fact, a complete tiny cookie, pastry, or cake with careful, authentic decorations that give it a distinct personality. Some miniatures are elegant, others are cute, whimsical, or just plain stunning.

Before you eat a miniature, you fall in love with it. After all, it's all yours. Who would ask you to share something so small and perfect? It's never necessary to cut or alter the shape of a miniature before it is safely in your mouth.

The trim size of miniatures makes them desserts that are quite a bit less intimidating than a slice of cake or a scoop of ice cream. You can easily choose to have a portion of any size, from a single bite-sized gem to one—or two—of each of a large assortment. But I'll warn the diet-conscious right now: You may have trouble eating just one.

Making miniatures is enjoyable and rewarding. They are not difficult to make and are a great change from making cakes, pastries, and pies. Baking slips-ups don't count because the miniatures are so tiny that mistakes don't really show. It's easy to stick one in your mouth and test the taste without anyone knowing. Miniatures perfume the air while they bake with their intense and mouth-watering aromas.

Yes, I love everything about miniatures. I associate them with good will and happiness. And so, after many happy years baking miniatures, I offer a variety of

Good Things Come in Small Packages

recipes, some old favorites, some new. Whether you bake them to serve alone or to ornament other desserts, for a catered affair, a restaurant, a crowd at a tailgate, a wedding, anniversary, or birthday reception, a small dinner party, or a brunch, for holiday gifts for family or friends, or when just plain relaxing with colleagues or visiting old friends, you will help perpetuate the happiness that goes with miniatures.

These recipes are straightforward, requiring no tricky techniques to guarantee their success. In consideration of our busy lives, I have given specific information, step by step, for handling, shaping, baking, decorating, and storing with each of my recipes. In this way, you can plan your miniature making ahead according to your schedule. I have also included many shortcuts that will help you to spend time efficiently in the kitchen, to streamline your baking and ensure the best miniature results every time.

Equipment for Sweet Miniatures

Part of the fun in miniature making is that you do not need a lot of esoteric or expensive equipment. Although the equipment I recommend is basic, it does facilitate miniature making so preparation is smoother and less time-consuming.

Before You Bake

Scales

For consistent results in miniature making, a scale is invaluable for weighing dry ingredients. I prefer one that is easy to read, with markings in ounces and grams, and that can accommodate a bowl on top for holding up to 2 pounds of flour or sugar.

Food Thermometers

The mercury candy thermometer tracks the stages of cooking sugar syrups for buttercreams. When melting chocolate, I check the temperature of the water in the pan under the bowl of chocolate frequently with the instant-read thermometer since it shows results quickly.

Electric Mixers and the Food Processor

Electric mixers are invaluable for making buttercreams, doughs, batters—even flaky puff pastry. If you use a hand mixer instead of a more powerful heavy-duty mixer with the balloon whisk, dough hook, or paddle attachments, you'll need to adjust the speed given in my recipes. For instance, when a recipe says to use medium-low speed, set a hand mixer at medium.

I use the food processor when I want to make doughs quickly and easily without adding a lot of air to them (Miniature Tartlet Pastry, page 205) or crush the praline into tiny golden crumbs to flavor buttercream for the Swiss Japonais (page 100).

Nut Grinders

Nuts have a high oil content and become stale or rancid quickly, so I always grate or chop them as I need them.

How to Measure Nuts

When you're measuring whole, chopped, or finely ground nuts for a miniature recipe, pour or scoop them from the package, your hand, a serving spoon, or a metal spatula into a dry measuring cup. Do not pack them. Strange as it may seem, because you do not pack the nuts, a given volume of whole or large pieces of nuts will yield what appears to be the same volume of chopped nuts. Nougatine Cones (page 120) is a good example. The recipe calls for 4 ounces or $3/4$ cup of hazelnuts, chopped medium-fine. You will find that the nuts still measure $3/4$ cup after you chop them.

When a recipe lists a nut as an ingredient, I give the weight first, then the cup measurement before chopping or finely grinding as a matter of convenience, since you usually buy nuts in packages marked in ounces.

Finely Ground Nuts

The Mouli grater, the rotary grater you hold in your hand while you turn the handle, is fine for small amounts of nuts. For larger quantities, use a grater that attaches to the edge of a tabletop. A wooden pusher keeps the nuts against the stainless steel drum while you turn the handle.

You can use a food processor or an electric herb and spice mincer, but I recommend you grate only a few ounces of nuts at a time to prevent their high fat content from causing the finely ground nuts to become oily.

Coarsely Chopped Nuts

Chop the nuts on a chopping block with a chef's knife or use a food processor with brief on/off pulses until the desired size.

Finely Chopped Nuts

When I want nuts chopped somewhere between fine and coarse, as in the Pecan Strudel (page 265) and the Black Walnut Genoise Wafers (page 112), I use a nut mill. When chopped nuts are part of the bulk of the recipe, such as in the filling for the Pecan Strudel, rather than present simply for their texture and flavor, I use a nut mill for chopping them. Since this piece of equipment allows for no variation in speed, intensity, or length of time of chopping, the nut granules it produces will be the same proportion of slightly larger to slightly smaller pieces every time. This ensures that a given weight of nuts yields the same volume of chopped nuts every time. Chopping nuts with a chef's knife is less quick and accurate. With a nut mill the nuts go in the top hopper, you turn the handle, and the chopped nuts fall into the glass container below.

Paper Products

Waxed Paper

I keep a roll of waxed paper in every corner of my kitchen. Rolling cookie doughs between two sheets of paper into circles or rectangles before refrigerating to firm them is a technique I strongly endorse (Drei Augen, page 48).

Aluminum Foil

Aluminum foil's flexibility and strength make it easy to mold it to fit into cardboard boxes to line them before storing miniatures. When I roll up small pieces of foil to make springlike shapes to fit between spaces to cushion cookies from rattling and thereby breaking, the foil's strength and flexibility are again important. I choose foil to line cardboard boxes as well as to layer between cookies in airtight metal tins because foil won't absorb the butter from the miniatures. I line baking sheets with foil when I want cookies, such as the Florentine Squares (page 110), to be released in perfect form when cool and firm.

Parchment Paper

Lining baking sheets with parchment paper promotes even baking of many types of cookies. Parchment paper is reusable. Also, you can fashion paper cones from parchment as well as mark circles on it with pencil to make forms for piping the meringue mixture for Swiss Japonais (page 100). Rather than use waxed paper, you can roll out miniature cookie doughs between two sheets of parchment. Then it's easy to mark the paper with pencil to identify doughs with names and dates before refrigerating.

Plastic Wrap

Wrapping cylinders of dough in plastic prevents drying when refrigerated. For longer storage in the refrigerator or freezer of several dough circles stacked on one baking sheet, overwrapping with sturdy plastic wrap prevents drying out.

Baking Cup Paper Liners

Pack fluted bonbon cups with miniature cookies or cakes for serving trays or gift boxes. Cupcake liners $1^3/8$ inch across the bottom with $^3/4$-inch sides are useful for baking Dutch Minicakes (page 168).

Shaping Miniatures

Rolling Pins

Straight Wooden Pin

The rolling pin that is easiest for me to roll is a 16-inch-long straight pin, about 2 inches in diameter, without handles.

Springerle and Waffle Rollers

Both these rollers form decorative patterns when rolled over dough.

Pastry and Cookie Cutters

Sets of round graduated sizes, plain and fluted, are useful. An assortment of shapes is nice to have. Always look for them in heavy tinned steel since sturdy cutters don't bend easily and sharp ones cut doughs, especially pastry doughs, cleanly.

A set of four Japanese cutters, each one a different shape (one is a flower), can be used to cut out shapes in dough or marzipan, as in Lemon Sunflowers (page 76) and Chocolate Coins (page 182).

Cookie Stamps

Designs from clay or glass stamps can be stamped into the dough to emboss it before baking. Roll dough such as Almond Teardrop dough (page 62) into balls, roll balls of dough into sugar, and stamp. If stamp gets sticky, wash and dry thoroughly before reusing.

Ice Cream Scoops

Scoops are numbered for the number of scoops per quart of ice cream. I use scoops #70 and #100 for dropping cookie doughs and batters for miniature cookies and cakes.

Plastic Lids and Rubber Inserts

Make your own stencils from disposable plastic lids and rubber jar inserts to create reusable designs, as for Chantilly Fans (page 131) and Chocolate Fringe Cups (page 128).

Krumkake Iron

For the wafer-thin Miniature Krumkake (page 122) that I roll into small cone shapes, I prefer a cast-iron krumkake iron, though electric ones are available. Both irons imprint a pattern on the cookies.

Good Things Come in Small Packages

9

Wooden Dowels and Cornets

With a small household hand saw, I cut wooden dowels, ³⁄₈ inch in diameter, into 6-inch-long sticks to roll up cookies while warm and flexible (Crispy Corkscrews, page 124). I use a wooden cornet to roll cookies warm from the oven when I want them cone-shaped (Miniature Krumkake, page 122, and Nougatine Cones, page 120).

Wooden Decorative Molds

Doughs can be pressed into designs in wooden forms to imprint them (Speculaas, page 150).

Spritz

A metal cylinder fitted with plates with a variety of cut-out designs is filled with dough to shape it into decorative forms.

Baking Miniatures

Baking Pans

Baking Sheets

I use baking sheets for baking most miniature cookies, pastries, and cakes such as the Genoise Sheet Cake (page 289). But I also find them invaluable for holding a stack of cookie circles or cakes in the refrigerator or freezer. The two sizes that I use the most are 12- × 15½-inch and 14- × 17-inch sheets, both with a 45-degree-angle ½-inch rim on all four sides, open at the corners. When I want to remove cookies quickly while warm and flexible without fear of sticking, I use Teflon-coated baking sheets (Cigarettes, page 118, and Tuiles, page 109). And the rectangular jelly roll pan (10 × 15 × 1 inch) is perfect for glazing miniatures since drips are contained in the pan (Parisers, page 295, and Hedgehogs, page 173).

Miniature Muffin Pans

For miniatures such as the Sweet Cheese Puffs (page 240), Pumpkin Pastries (page 242), and Dutch Minicakes (page 168), the heavy-gauge aluminum pan with 12 individual cups, each measuring $1\frac{1}{4}$ inches across the bottom and $\frac{3}{4}$ inches deep, is perfect.

Tartlet Pans

To give shape to the Miniature Tartlet Pastry (page 205) and form it into an assortment of small individual tarts, I've collected over the years, from cookware shops across the country—even the world—a variety of heavy-gauge miniature tin containers with plain, fluted, or swirled sides. No matter what shape—barquette, round, square, or oval—I prefer them to measure no more than $1\frac{1}{2}$ inches to $2\frac{1}{4}$ inches across. It's nice to own at least 2 dozen of each shape, but if one shape is a particular favorite, you might want more. For example, I can fit 4 dozen $1\frac{1}{2}$-inch round Swedish tartlet tins, close together, on one 12- $\times$ $15\frac{1}{2}$-inch baking sheet. Owning this number is convenient so I can bake more at once.

Madeleine Pan

For the Sweet Seashells (page 57), I press dough into the 20 tiny shell molds in a mini madeleine pan.

After You Bake

Cooling Racks

Most miniature cookies, cakes, and pastries must be ventilated. Extra-large sturdy cooling racks, rectangular in shape, are best for miniatures. You can easily fit a batch on the rack without overlapping or crowding.

For glazing, I prefer cooling racks with wires close together to form a grid. These racks keep miniatures steady and prevent them from tilting or slipping through the wires.

Good Things Come in Small Packages

Whenever I store miniatures, my goal is to fit them as snugly as possible to avoid breakage, with as little room as possible between the miniatures and the lid of the container to prevent a lot of stale air from penetrating the miniatures.

Airtight metal containers are best for cookies that must remain crisp or age and mellow. To prevent miniatures sensitive to humidity, such as Nougatine Cones (page 120), from absorbing moisture at room temperature, I keep them in a canister called a Krispy Kan. The lid has a removable glass knob filled with nontoxic blue crystals that absorb moisture. When the crystals turn light lilac, it's time to place the knob in a hot oven to reactivate them. Many times I place this removable knob in another airtight metal container that has a more convenient shape for storing miniatures.

Sturdy plastic containers are useful when I want to ensure that moist or chewy cookies remain that way. These containers are airtight and perfect for freezing such pastries as the Sweet Cheese Puffs (page 240).

Decorative Utensils

Pastry Tips

Buttercream and whipped cream look very attractive after they have been piped through a pastry tip. But many times piping a dough, batter, or filling is the fastest and easiest way to accomplish the work of miniature making. Even though I have a drawer full of different sizes and shapes, I use just a few plain open tips ($1/4$ and $1/2$ inch) and a few open and closed star tips the most often. There are instances when the wider end of a tip (for example, the #6 $1/2$-inch plain open tip) is convenient for cutting out shapes in cakes (Parisers, page 295) or dough (Hedgehogs, page 173).

Pastry Bags

I always have 12-inch, 14-inch, and 16-inch lightweight flexible nylon pastry bags on hand. These are easy to clean. Fill the bag no more than two-thirds full, and twist the upper third tightly to prevent the mixture from coming out the top portion as you pipe.

Handmade Paper Cones

These disposable cones are great for piping small amounts of jelly, buttercream, royal icing, chocolate, and ganache. If you do not have precut triangular-shaped paper for paper cones, cut a 22-inch square from parchment paper. Fold it diagonally, and cut into two triangles. Hold a triangle in one hand with the longest side at the bottom and the thumb of your other hand in the center. Manipulate it into a cone shape so that the long side becomes the tip and the point of the triangle (opposite the long side) becomes the opening of the cone. Fold the top of the point into the cone to hold it together. Fill the cone half full, fold the tops of the two sides toward the middle, and fold the top down to enclose the mixture. Cut the tip to the desired opening before piping.

Good Things Come in Small Packages

Ingredients for Miniatures

Almost all the ingredients for the miniature recipes are straightforward and easy to acquire. Where I recommend using a more esoteric item, such as rice flour for the Shortbread Cameos (page 39), there will be a note in the recipe describing it and suggesting where to find it.

When you shop for baking ingredients, the most important criteria are that the items be good tasting and fresh. Once you get them home, store them as well as possible so as to maintain their freshness and quality and thus keep them tasting their best. Here are some brief guidelines on selecting and storing ingredients, based on what works for me in my kitchen.

I have on hand at all times the ingredients to bake several different recipes. Many of these baking ingredients go in the pantry, while in my upright freezer I've dedicated four shelves to assorted bags of nuts, one shelf to butter, with a few bags of coffee beans off to the side—everything securely wrapped. I have eggs, heavy cream, milk, cheese, and a variety of fruits in the refrigerator, and everything else I need is in kitchen cabinets or drawers.

U.S. grade AA unsalted butter smells and tastes sweet since it is made from the highest quality fresh cream. I keep a small amount of it in the refrigerator, always drawing from my ample supply in the freezer. Since butter easily picks up flavors from other foods in the refrigerator, it's a good idea to wrap securely any opened portions.

Only buy grade AA eggs that are stored in refrigerated cases at the supermarket. And always store them in their cartons in the refrigerator to avoid salmonella-contaminated eggs.

Heavy cream, sometimes called heavy whipping cream, has at least 36 percent milkfat. It is available pasteurized and ultrapasteurized. I prefer pasteurized since you might detect a cooked taste in the ultrapasteurized one.

Observe dates on packages and cartons for reference to freshness for butters, eggs, heavy creams, even packages of nuts, but also for pasteurized whole milk, buttermilk, sour cream, small curd cottage cheese, mascarpone cheese (an unripened Italian dessert cheese made from fresh cream), and cream cheese. For baking, I prefer a cream cheese with a gum arabic stabilizer. This variety is consistently less watery and gives great results after baking. Use the one without a stabilizer for no-bake recipes or spreading on English muffins or bagels.

Buy small amounts of spices because they become stale or loose their punch rapidly. Also, buy small amounts of extracts and keep them tightly capped in a cool place. I mark the date of purchase on spices and extracts and even chocolate and nuts, so that the oldest always gets used first and nothing sits on the shelf too long.

When it comes to chocolate, I always use the real thing. Whether to use bittersweet or semisweet is a matter of taste preference. Bittersweet is usually less sweet with a higher content of chocolate liquor, the nonalcoholic liquid made from the nibs of cocoa beans that is the basis of all chocolate, than semisweet. Milk chocolate has less chocolate liquor than dark chocolate and has milk solids added.

When buying white chocolate, which the U.S. Standard of Identity does not consider a pure chocolate since it contains no chocolate liquor, buy a brand that has no fats other than cocoa butter and butterfat. If you buy chocolate in bulk, overwrap it with heavy-duty aluminum foil. Store all chocolate varieties in a dark, cool, dry place. Semisweet and bittersweet chocolate keep longer than white or milk.

Unsweetened cocoa powders come in two forms: alkalized ("Dutched" to reduce bitterness and give it a darker color) or nonalkalized ("natural," which is lighter in color than alkalized, but bolder and fruitier in flavor). Either type is fine in my miniature recipes.

Always keep nuts well wrapped, whether in an airtight tin at room temperature or in storage bags in the freezer. Thaw them before using in a recipe. Choose jams and jellies based on your personal preferences. Store sugars, especially light and dark brown sugars, and flours in covered containers at room temperature.

Always store a can of solid vegetable shortening in the refrigerator. This keeps it fresh for making shiny homemade chocolate glazes, such as the Dark Satin Glaze (page 96). Since I use a lot of almond paste, I also refrigerate a large can of it to keep it fresh for an indefinite amount of time. I use store-bought marzipan when I don't have time to make my own. Always keep it well wrapped in the refrigerator so that it does not dry out.

The world of fruits, fresh and dried, is always changing. Every season a new fruit or variety appears in the produce repertoire. Dried fruits are available year-round, and even dried cherries and cranberries are more widely distributed now.

Good Things
Come in Small
Packages

The Essentials of Wonderful-Tasting Miniatures

Baking miniatures is fun and need not be complicated. Here are the essentials for smooth and easy miniature making.

Read the recipe carefully before you bake.

- Assemble all ingredients and equipment before you begin.
- Allow enough time for ingredients to reach room temperature when recipe specifies.

Trust your own judgment.

- When baking miniatures, if they test done before the time given in the recipe, remove them from the oven. Each recipe in this book tells you what to look for in a properly baked miniature and specifies a baking time. Remember, baking times are only approximate because of temperature variations in ovens.
- If you don't have time to decorate a miniature as recommended in the recipe, choose a more simple decoration, or serve unadorned.
- If you miscalculate in measuring the ingredients or the baking time, taste the dough or the baked miniature. If the flavor is OK—it's OK. Perhaps your mistake invented a new recipe.

Measure accurately.

- Use a scale or stainless steel cups for dry ingredients, Pyrex cups for liquids.

Good Things Come in Small Packages

Follow procedures in recipe closely.

- To form smooth homogeneous cookie doughs and cake batters, add the flour gradually.
- If a recipe specifies that the mixture must be baked immediately after making, be prepared to do so. For example, see Chocolate Macaroons (page 161).

Prepare baking sheets, molds, and pans as recipe specifies to ensure successful results.

- Lining baking sheets with parchment paper, which is reusable, prevents cookies from burning on the bottom and promotes even baking. It is quick and eliminates baking sheet clean-up.
- Greasing baking sheets increases spreading of cookie doughs and batters during baking, while greasing and flouring sheets inhibits spreading.

Set oven racks and temperature as each recipe specifies.

- Unless recipe specifies otherwise, always bake in the lower third of the oven to allow the heated air to circulate evenly around the baking pan or sheet.
- When using two baking sheets simultaneously, adjust two racks to divide the oven into thirds. Rotate the baking sheets from front to back and from one shelf to the other halfway through baking.
- Preheat oven for at least 15 minutes.
- Incorrect baking temperatures, whether too high or too low, ruin the taste and textures of all miniatures. Each recipe specifies the temperature for optimum results.
- Notice that many recipes in this book recommend oven temperatures lower than similar recipes from other sources. For example, my Shortbread Cameos (page 39) bake at 300 degrees and are slower to finish than most other shortbreads, which usually bake at 350 degrees. Lower temperatures prevent all cookies, tartlets, and pastries from browning too quickly and promote uniform baking.
- Notice that the Genoise Sheet Cake (page 289), a thin flexible cake, bakes at 450 degrees, which is quite hot for cakes. In this case, the hotter temperature bakes the cake more quickly and ensures a moist interior without the cake being overly dry and crisp throughout.

Bake a batch of miniature cookies or pastries on a cool baking sheet.

- Miniature doughs and batters set on hot sheets begin to spread or even bake before all the cookies or pastries are in place. Allow baking sheets hot from the oven to cool on a rack 10 to 15 minutes before baking another batch.
- If your supply of baking sheets is limited, set miniatures on parchment paper cut to fit the baking sheet while the sheet is cooling. Once the sheet is cool to the touch, slip it under the paper and set it in the oven.

Before baking a large batch, bake one miniature cookie or pastry as a sample to gauge spreading distance and cooking time in your oven.

- It only takes a few minutes to test-bake one miniature. Then you can adjust the oven temperature, recipe, or baking sheet without wasting an entire batch.
- Keep in mind that cookies brown quickly once they begin to change color, so watch them closely. It is especially easy to burn chocolate doughs because of their dark color.
- Overbaking dries cookies and spoils delicate flavors such as butter, spices, and chocolate.

Follow cooling and storing procedures each recipe specifies for best flavor and texture.

- In general, place baking sheets, molds, and pans on wire rack to cool 10 minutes before handling miniature cookies, tartlets, pastries, and cakes.
- If miniatures are still fragile after 10 minutes, wait until they are cooler to avoid breaking or distorting their form.
- If cookies or pastries are already a bit too golden, to avoid further baking on the hot-from-the-oven baking sheet, lift the parchment paper with the cookies or pastries from the sheet onto a rack.
- Cool miniatures completely before storing.

Good Things Come in Small Packages

Part II

Miniature Cookies

$\mathcal{M}$aking cookies is the most popular form of baking. Anyone can make them. They're delicious fun without taking a lot of time, effort, or skill. You can bake any size, shape, flavor, or texture. The variety is endless.

Mixing Miniature Cookie Doughs

I've discovered from years of cookie making that whether cookies are crisp, soft, chewy, brittle, sandy, short, or dense depends on a multitude of factors: the recipe's ingredients, their ratio to one another, the cookies' size and shape, baking methods, oven temperatures, and baking time.

But there is perhaps one factor that is most crucial to cookie making. I discovered it more than a decade ago, when I experienced two baking mishaps.

I cannot recall when I made my first batch of chocolate chip cookies—but I'll never forget the time I baked my most unusual batch. As always, I began making my favorite chocolate chip recipe using the electric mixer. While I was beating the butter with the sugar, the phone rang. When I returned to the kitchen five minutes later the machine was still in motion and the mixture was fluffy white. I added the egg, then the remaining ingredients, and dropped the dough on the baking sheets.

When the cookies baked sooner than I expected, I got my first indication that these were not my normal chocolate chip cookies. When I removed them from the oven, I saw that they were puffy, almost domelike. I picked one up. It was light in my hand—and in my mouth. The extra beating time had somehow modified the cookies.

The next incident occurred while I was making tartlets from a not-too-sweet cookie recipe. (See Miniature Tartlet Pastry, page 205.) I thought this recipe was ideal because it baked miniature tartlet shells firm enough to hold creamy fillings yet tender from the first bite.

I had always made the recipe dough by hand or in the food processor, but that one time I switched to the electric mixer for no reason other than to change the routine. The dough appeared smooth and homogeneous, as usual, but after the tartlets had baked and cooled in their tins, they were impossible to remove without breaking. Instead of firm and tender, they were fragile and crumbly.

The chocolate chip caper and my fateful mistake with the miniature pastry dough led me to this most important truth about cookie making: How you mix the ingredients together determines the final consistency of the dough or batter and, ultimately, the texture of the cookies after baking.

There are three basic techniques for preparing cookie doughs or batters: the simple mixing method, the creaming mixing method, and the whipping mixing method.

Understanding these methods helps me when I need to be sure that the recipes that I bake repeatedly will consistently produce what I want each time, when I want to duplicate cookies' results frequently, and even when I want to make a cookie from a recipe new to me or to improve an old one.

When you understand these simple methods, you'll be able to produce the results you want, improve and improvise your cookie making—even correct cookie errors.

Simple Mixing Method

The simple mixing method is just as its name implies: Ingredients need merely be mixed together. It's the easiest and most straightforward. You do not need to incorporate any air or work the mixture until light and creamy.

- To mix ingredients together to form smooth, homogeneous mixtures, it's important to add the ingredients in the order the recipe specifies. If the recipe calls for a fat, such as butter, it's important that it be at room temperature.
- Stir ingredients together with a rubber spatula or wooden spoon in a bowl.

- To mix ingredients together with an electric mixer, use low to medium-low speed.

This is the simplest way to make cookie doughs. Ingredients need merely be stirred together to combine them completely into a smooth, homogeneous mixture.

Since the simple mixing method is exactly as it says, it works well in combining ingredients for recipes that call for little or no fat and need not begin with an airy base. Soft batters such as Miniature Krumkake (page 122) that are moistened by sour cream, stiff batters such as Macaroon Trios (page 92) that are nut-paste or ground-nut mixtures bound and moistened by egg whites, stiff doughs such as Pains d'Amande (page 140), and soft batters such as Nougatine Cones (page 120) that begin as a warm syrupy mixture are examples. Ingredients are usually stirred together with a rubber spatula or wooden spoon in a bowl or mixed together on low to medium-low speed with an electric mixer.

Creaming Method

The creaming method is used in cookie recipes that contain an abundance of fat. Fat's job in a recipe is both to absorb dry and liquid ingredients and to trap air. A recipe using the creaming method usually begins with the phrase "cream the butter with the sugar," since it is the manipulation of the fat that causes it to incorporate air bubbles.

All recipes that use this method share in common a generous amount of fat, usually butter. Room-temperature butter is beaten with sugar (OK by hand, but easier by machine) to incorporate air, and then egg and liquid, if called for in the recipe, are beaten in before adding dry ingredients. Having the ingredients at similar temperatures makes it easier to combine them to form a smooth, homogeneous mixture.

- To cream properly, begin with room-temperature butter. Butter that is too firm requires more beating, which incorporates more air.
- Sometimes it's quicker to use a hand mixer. To beat or cream the butter with the sugar using a rotary hand mixer, cream room-temperature butter with the sugar at medium to medium-high speed just until the mixture is

smooth. When a mixture's volume is small, as in the buttercream for the Cognac Wafers (page 116), the ability afforded by a hand-held mixer to reach any part of the bowl or the bottom of a deep bowl is invaluable.

- To cream with a heavy-duty electric mixer, using the paddle, flat beater, or dough hook, begin at medium-low speed until the butter is smooth.

Within this group of recipes there are two basic types of creaming. The difference lies in how long and how vigorously the butter (or other fat) is creamed, which determines the amount of air incorporated during mixing. One method involves a minimum amount of air, and, thus, less creaming, and the other involves more air, thus more creaming. The creaming method used affects the baked cookies' texture (dense, delicate, or crumbly) and the way the cookies leaven and spread during baking (becoming thin, puffy, flat, and/or retaining their shapes).

Do not be confused by the difference between these two types of creaming. My chocolate chip cookie incident illustrates the distinction beautifully. The recipe I used started with the words "Combine the butter with the sugars until creamy." But when I inadvertently left the mixture beating for five minutes, I truly *creamed* the mixture until light and fluffy and ended up with airy, rounded cookies.

Many recipes can be made successfully starting with either a smooth and creamy mixture, pale yellow in color, or a very light and fluffy white one. The amount of mixing you choose to do depends on the degree of density or airiness you desire in your baked cookies. I have designed the recipes in this book so that if you follow my instructions exactly you will bake what I think are the best miniature cookies. But with an understanding of the creaming methods, you may freely adjust the beating of your cookie doughs to come up with cookies that suit your tastes exactly.

When you want cookies to retain their shape and bake densely—for example, with firm doughs that contain an abundance of butter but no liquid ingredients, such as Shortbread Cameos (page 39) and Drei Augen (page 48), and stiff doughs that contain a great deal of butter with small amounts of egg or other liquids, such as the Miniature Tartlet Pastry (page 205)—the minimal creaming method is useful. It also works well for cookie batters like Almond Confetti (page 78) that you want to spread thinly in the oven and bake to a delicate texture. Too much air in either type of batter and you get a crumbly texture, so only a small amount of creaming is needed.

Cookies made without incorporating a lot of air, especially those with an abundance of butter, that you slice, cut out, pipe, imprint, or mold retain their shape well during baking. Any cookie made with the minimal creaming method bakes denser than one made differently, and it can sometimes have a chewy texture as well.

The vigorous creaming method, which produces a lighter, creamier mixture, is usually recommended for dropped cookies, to support the raisins, nuts, and/or chocolate chips, and piped cookies, to make piping through a pastry bag easier.

Doughs that are creamed until light and airy can be shaped in many ways. You can pipe, roll, mold, and/or drop them, or even spread them thinly on baking sheets to make crisp wafers as in Chocolate Fringe Cups (page 128), Champagne Biscuits (page 126), Cigarettes (page 118), Crispy Corkscrews (page 124), Chocolate Pistachio Cigarettes (page 194), and Ladies' Wafers (page 114).

Hand vs. Machine

When a cookie recipe specifies "Combine ingredients until creamy," "Cream the butter until creamy," or "Cream together the butter and the sugar," you are using the creaming mixing method. When making these cookies, you can use the minimal creaming method or the vigorous creaming method to control just how much air you incorporate into the dough to make the cookies exactly the texture you prefer. Here's my guide to a spectrum of creaming methods that has evolved as baking technology has changed:

- Mixing by hand, the technique our grandparents used when making many sweet, short doughs, incorporates the least amount of air possible. On a work surface, rub or cut small pieces of fat into dry ingredients to completely coat them. This intimate blending of the fat with the flour "shortens" the flour and prevents the proteins in the flour from forming a strong bond before you add the liquid and gather the dough together. Almost no air is incorporated.
- To add slightly more air, mix the fat and sugar by hand with a wooden spoon. You can regulate aeration according to the stamina of your arm muscles.
- The next method uses the food processor, which aerates less than any other machine and simulates the hand method best, especially when you place

chilled fat, in chunks, on top of the dry ingredients in the food processor bowl before processing.

- Using the electric mixer and beating the fat with the paddle or flat beater, or even the dough hook, is the lightest and airiest end of the spectrum, since any electric mixer is capable of mixing in a lot of air. But as with any technique, how vigorously and how long you beat does influence the amount of aeration.

The amount of air incorporated into a cookie dough is not a question of right or wrong. The only thing that matters is your personal preference for a texture to serve a certain purpose, such as in my tartlet dough example, or simply the mood of your appetite, such as in my chocolate chip cookie example.

Whipping Mixing Method

The whipping method is for cookie recipes containing a lot of eggs, some sugar, and little or no fat. In these recipes, the eggs are responsible for holding air bubbles, so the method begins the same way as the one used for genoise, chiffon, or angel food cake—whipping the eggs (whole, whites, or yolks) and sugar together to trap air bubbles and expand the mixture before other ingredients are added.

Each of my recipes specifies the proper stage to which the eggs should be whipped. Stages are marked by visual clues, such as soft or thick peaks. It's the air bubbles trapped in the whipped egg, along with the eggs' moisture, that transform into steam during baking and expand, leaven, and give the cookies their characteristic textures.

Chewy Springerle (page 147), dense chewy Hahnpfeffernüse (page 144), crunchy Black Walnut Genoise Wafers (page 112), fragile crispy Chantilly Fans (page 131), and crunchy crispy Cognac Wafers (page 116) and Tuiles (page 109) are a diverse assortment of cookies with a wide variety of textures, shapes, and forms that use the whipping method.

- Use fresh eggs for best results and flavor.
- To whip properly, begin with room-temperature eggs and/or butter.
- To whip with a rotary hand mixer, begin at medium speed.

- To whip with a heavy-duty electric mixer, preferably with a whisk attachment, begin at medium-low speed.

You can modify cookies' textures from spongy to crispy by changing the amount of eggs or other liquids in the recipe to make soft to runny batters, as in Cognac Wafers (page 116) and Chantilly Fans (page 131). Any airy, spongy mixture in this group is susceptible to deflating if overmixed, so dry ingredients, such as ground nuts and flour (Japonais, page 100), and liquid ingredients, such as melted chocolate (Chocolate Macaroons, page 161) or melted butter (Genoise, page 289), must be carefully folded in.

Shaping Miniature Cookie Doughs

Please keep in mind that the benefit of mixing ingredients together correctly is that it makes a smooth dough that forms shapes easily. It's nice to shape cookies uniformly in order to promote more even baking so each cookie will taste its best.

A variety of cookie shapes creates an assortment that gives character, personality, and eye appeal to a tray of cookies. The dough's consistency, depending on the proportions of the ingredients it contains, dictates what methods you can use to shape it. Follow shaping procedures as each recipe specifies. Place all the cookies on baking sheets of the same size and thickness for uniform baking.

It's easy to classify or categorize cookies by shape. There are at least six types, each one distinct from the other: dropped, piped, rolled, hand-shaped, refrigerator, and bar. Doughs vary in their shaping versatility. For example, it's possible to mold, pipe, slice, or roll one dough (Butter Dough in Chocolate Shadows, page 196), while another dough can only be dropped (Almond Confetti, page 78). In order to produce an infinite variety of shapes and sizes, here's what you need to know.

Rolled Dough

Many cookie doughs made with a minimum of egg and a good deal of flour are firm enough to roll out easily.

- Make the dough, then roll it out between sheets of waxed paper rather than in flour. Rolling these doughs in flour changes the butter-flour balance, which can alter the cookies' delicate flavor and texture. When you roll dough between sheets of waxed paper, the scraps are always reusable. Gather the scraps into a flat disk to roll out between two waxed paper sheets again.

- Some spice doughs, such as Lebkuchen Circles (page 154), benefit from rolling out in flour. The amount of honey or molasses in a spice dough can make it too sticky to roll between waxed paper sheets. Rolling out the dough in flour does not affect its tasty bite of spice after baking.
- When rolling out the dough, it's a natural tendency to roll thicker in the middle. To compensate for this, don't roll the rolling pin off the edges. Roll with even pressure, or it will be difficult to maintain a uniform thickness.
- When cutting out shapes, dip the cookie cutter in unflavored vegetable oil rather than in flour to ensure that the cutter lifts out easily. Repeat whenever necessary to prevent dough from sticking to cutter.
- The chilled dough should not be too firm or too soft to cut out shapes easily. It's easy to compensate: Either leave it in refrigerator longer or remove from refrigerator sooner.
- If you need a special shape of cutter, make it. Form shapes in household paraffin, then mold tin or strips of heavy-duty aluminum foil around the wax.
- To cut out shapes from the dough, begin at the edges and work to the center. Cut shapes close together to keep scraps at a minimum.
- Lift shapes to a baking sheet with a metal spatula to avoid changing their form.

Bar Dough

Some doughs, usually made with egg, are soft enough to spread or pat into a baking pan. Bar cookies are convenient to bake since the whole batch goes into the oven at once.

- After making the dough, divide it into several pieces and scatter them over the baking pan. With floured fingertips, pat the dough to extend the portions to cover the pan as evenly as possible.
- It's easy to determine the quantity of bar cookies from the pan size the recipe indicates, even before baking: Decide on a standard measurement as an

appropriate portion for each bar cookie. For example, if the portion is 1½ × 1½ inches, first divide the length of the pan by 1½ inches, disregarding any fraction in your result. Do the same calculation with the width of the pan, and multiply the two resulting numbers to find the number of cookies the recipe will yield.

- Bake only until the cookies test done. If underbaked, they taste doughy, and if overbaked, they are hard and crisp. Cut portions while slightly warm, unless the recipe specifies otherwise.

Dropped Dough

Dropped cookie doughs are softer than doughs for rolling because they contain more eggs and/or other liquid or less flour. Dropped cookies are not just chocolate chip and oatmeal types; many crisp types begin as dropped cookies. Nougatine Cones (page 120) and Black Walnut Genoise Wafers (page 112) are excellent examples.

- Usually dropped cookie dough is formed and baked right after it is made. You can refrigerate the dough, covered, for several hours before baking. Chilling doughs that contain double-acting baking powder, baking soda, and/or cream of tartar does slow their chemical reaction during baking. Doughs that contain baking soda or cream of tartar do not store as well as those with baking powder. Once moistened, baking soda reacts to ingredients such as buttermilk, brown sugar, honey, molasses, unsweetened chocolate and cocoa powder, and even cream of tartar on contact and releases carbon dioxide so that the dough loses some of its potency by baking time.
- Chilling dropped cookie dough can help the cookies to maintain their shapes without spreading too much while baking. If this is the case, drop mounds of dough on parchment-lined baking sheets and refrigerate before baking to firm it up. Because the cold baking sheet might warp in the hot oven, causing the cookies to bake unevenly, lift the parchment paper onto another baking sheet just before baking.
- To form dropped cookies easily, dip two teaspoons into cold water before filling one with dough. Use the back of the other teaspoon to push the dough onto the baking sheet.

- To shape uniform mounds of dropped dough, an ice cream scoop is handy for depositing batter on the baking sheets quickly and easily. Use a size 40 scoop, with a capacity equivalent to 1 mounded tablespoon, for standard chocolate chip cookies. For smaller, daintier dropped cookies, use a size 70 scoop, with a capacity equivalent to a scant $2\frac{1}{2}$ teaspoons.
- You can form cylinders or logs of dropped dough and chill for future use.

Hand-Formed Dough

Like the dough for rolled cookies, this dough is firm enough to mold or twist into shapes.

- If the dough sticks to your fingers, chill it until you can handle it more easily before shaping.
- To aid in molding doughs more evenly, begin by pinching off teaspoonsful of dough and shaping them in the palms of your hands into smooth forms similar to the desired shape. For example, the Chevron Twists (page 60) begin with pencil-shaped ropes before the final formation; Autumn Acorns (page 70) begin as small dough balls before being formed into acorn shapes; and Miniature Tartlet Pastry (page 205) begins as small dough balls so that the dough can be pressed more evenly into tartlet tins.
- To flatten balls of dough on a baking sheet uniformly at once: Evenly space dough balls on the sheet, flour the underside of another baking sheet with similar or identical dimensions, and press down gently but firmly on balls. Carefully lift off the top baking sheet.

Piped and Pressed-Spritz Dough

These types are merely a fancier form of dropped cookies. The dough must be soft and pliable enough to pass through a pastry tip or cookie press without too much pressure but have enough body to hold a distinct form after shaping.

- A pastry bag works just as well as a cookie press for making spritz-type cookies.
- Piping forms to hold their shapes during baking requires a room-temperature dough on the stiff side. If the dough is too cold, it will be crumbly.

- Doughs or batters that are soft, sticky, or runny are easier and quicker to deposit on a baking sheet from a pastry bag than from a spoon. This method also eliminates the temptation to lick clean the finger that pushed the dough off the spoon onto the baking sheet.
- Fill the pastry bag or cookie press half full each time.
- Doughs made by the creaming mixing method are fluffier and easier to pipe than doughs made by the blending mixing method.

Refrigerator Dough

Making refrigerator doughs is great for enabling you to bake cookies when you want them at their best—fresh. Make the dough now and bake it later.

- Many doughs adapt well to being shaped into cylinders, wrapped in plastic, refrigerated for from 4 hours up to 3 days, and then sliced to make uniform cookies quickly, easily, and efficiently. Shortbread Cameos (page 39) or logs, such as Daddy Long Legs (page 74), are excellent examples.
- Patch different doughs together, such as the Apricot Medals dough (page 50) and the White Blossom Circles chocolate dough (page 188) into a cylinder or log to create a variety of shapes, patterns, and flavors.

A Word About Cookie Categories

It's popular to categorize cookies by their mixing or shaping methods. For my book, I've chosen to categorize miniature cookies in chapters according to their dominant flavor or texture, since the taste and chew of cookies after the first bite is critical to me.

Shortbread Miniatures

Shortbread Cameos

Rice flour is the secret to achieving the subtly sandy texture that sets this great shortbread apart. Because the ingredients are few, be sure to use the best-tasting butter possible to effect a clean, rich flavor.

DOUGH

- 2 cups (280 grams) unsifted all-purpose flour
- ⅓ cup unsifted rice flour
- 8 ounces (2 sticks) unsalted butter, room temperature
- ½ cup (100 grams) granulated sugar
- 1 teaspoon vanilla

DECORATION

- 1 cup (200 grams) granulated sugar

1. In a medium bowl, blend the flours briefly with a wire whisk; set aside. In the large bowl of an electric mixer, cream the butter at medium-low speed until smooth, about 1 minute. Beat in the sugar at medium speed until creamy; add the vanilla until blended, scraping down the sides of the bowl. Lower speed, and gradually add the flours, mixing only until mixture is thoroughly combined.

2. Divide dough in quarters, rolling each portion into a cylinder about ¾ inch in diameter. Wrap in plastic and refrigerate until firm, for at least 4 hours or up to 3 days; or freeze, well wrapped, up to 1 month.

3. Adjust rack to lower third of oven and preheat oven to 300 degrees. Line two large cool baking sheets with parchment paper.

4. Remove one cylinder of dough at a time from the refrigerator. Using a sharp knife, cut slices, on an exaggerated diagonal, ¼ inch thick and space them about ½ inch apart on the baking sheets.

5. Sprinkle the sugar over cookies lightly and evenly. Bake, one sheet at a time, for 12 to 15 minutes or until the cookies are no longer shiny and feel firm (lightly touch a few). Do not allow cookies to color. Using a metal spatula, transfer the cookies to a wire rack until cool.

6. Stack in an airtight metal container and store at room temperature up to 1 week.

BAKING NOTES

- To create the cookie's distinctive texture, some recipes use a combination of cornstarch and all-purpose flour while other recipes use powdered sugar instead of granulated sugar. I prefer using granulated sugar with a combination of rice flour and all-purpose flour to give the most authentic texture.
- Note that rice flour—the nonglutenous variety necessary for this recipe—is available at health food stores. You don't want to use sweet rice flour, the glutenous variety sold in Asian markets, which has a sticky characteristic and is not desirable for any type of baking.
- Pearl sugar, a larger-grain sugar than granulated sugar and a favorite choice for decorating Scandinavian cookies, may be sprinkled on top of these cookies for additional sparkle and crunch. Just combine ½ cup pearl sugar with ½ cup granulated sugar to decorate these Shortbread Cameos. You'll find pearl sugar at most confectionery or baking supply stores.

• To give these cookies a fresh spicy flavor, add 2 teaspoons finely grated lemon zest, 1 teaspoon freshly ground black pepper, and 1 teaspoon grated fresh ginger. Do not sprinkle with granulated sugar for decoration. After baking, place baking sheet on a wire rack until cookies are cool. To decorate, brush each cookie with a thin coating of Sugar Glaze: Mix $\frac{1}{2}$ cup unsifted powdered sugar with 4 teaspoons water until smooth. Return cookies to a 140-degree preheated oven until glaze is set and dry, about 10 minutes.

Shortbread Cameos

Harlequins

These simple but delicious cookies, scented with orange and lemon zest, are made elegant by an easy two-glaze decorative finish I learned at the Richemont Professional School in Lucerne, Switzerland. To achieve a sweet-and-sour flavor, brush half of each cookie with apricot jam and the other half with red currant jelly before painting a shimmery soft sugar glaze over it all.

DOUGH

8 ounces (2 sticks) unsalted butter, room temperature

⅓ cup (30 grams) unsifted powdered sugar

⅓ cup (65 grams) granulated sugar

1 egg yolk

½ teaspoon *each* finely grated lemon and orange zest

½ teaspoon vanilla

2 cups (280 grams) unsifted all-purpose flour

DECORATIVE GLAZES

Jelly Glazes

⅔ cup strained apricot jam

⅔ cup red currant jelly

Sugar Glaze

½ cup (50 grams) unsifted powdered sugar

4 teaspoons water

Additional powdered sugar for glaze

1. In the large bowl of an electric mixer, cream the butter at medium-low speed until it is smooth, about 1 minute. Beat in the sugars at medium speed until creamy. Add the egg yolk, then the citrus zests and vanilla, mixing just until mixture is well combined and slightly fluffy, scraping down the sides of the bowl.

Lower mixer speed, and gradually add the flour, mixing only until mixture is thoroughly combined.

2. Divide the dough into thirds, and roll out each portion of dough between two sheets of waxed paper to form a circle 10 inches in diameter and ⅛ inch thick. Leaving the dough circles between the waxed paper, stack them on a baking sheet and refrigerate until firm, for at least 2 hours or up to 3 days; or freeze, well wrapped, up to 1 month.

3. Adjust rack to lower third of oven and preheat oven to 325 degrees. Line two large cool baking sheets with parchment paper.

4. Remove one dough package from the refrigerator at a time. Peel off top waxed paper sheet, replace it loosely on top, and flip the entire package over. Peel off and discard the second sheet of waxed paper.

5. Using a 1½-inch cutter of any shape, cut out shapes in the dough and set them about ½ inch apart on the baking sheets. Bake, one sheet at a time, for 12 to 15 minutes, or until cookies are no longer shiny, just ivory-colored, and feel slightly firm (lightly touch a few). Place baking sheet on a wire rack until cookies are cool.

6. Keep the oven rack in the same position; preheat oven to 140 degrees. Place the apricot jam and currant jelly in two small saucepans. Simmer on low heat for 2 minutes to evaporate some liquid before decorating cookies. Cool just until warm.

7. Brush warm apricot jam over half of one cookie's surface. With a clean brush, paint the other half with the red currant jelly. Paint the remaining cookies, setting cookies as you finish about ¼ inch apart on one large clean baking sheet.

8. Sugar Glaze: Mix the sugar and water together until smooth. With a clean pastry brush, paint a thin coating of glaze over the jelly-glazed cookies. The glaze's consistency should be thin enough so that a transparent film covers the jellies. Adjust the consistency by adding 1 teaspoon water at a time if it is too thick or more sugar if it is too thin. Place cookies in preheated oven until glaze

Harlequins

43

is set and dry, about 10 minutes. Place baking sheet on a wire rack to cool for 5 minutes; then, lift cookies with a metal spatula to a rack to cool.

9. Stack undecorated cookies in an airtight metal container and store at room temperature up to 10 days. Store decorated cookies in one layer in a covered foil-lined cardboard container, such as a cake box, at room temperature up to 3 days.

$\mathcal{L}$*ittle* $\mathcal{G}$*ems*

Makes 11 dozen 1½-inch cookies

Buttery and sandy-textured, these are one of my favorite cookies and not just because they're my mother's recipe. One bite and the secret is out. The pecan halves on top hide a dot of jam. Since the recipe yields a generous amount, they're easy to make, and their flavor enhances with time, these fragrant morsels are ideal for stacking in handsome airtight metal containers to give as gifts

DOUGH

12 ounces (3 sticks) unsalted butter, room temperature

1 cup (200 grams) granulated sugar

2 egg yolks

2 teaspoons vanilla

3 cups (420 grams) unsifted all-purpose flour

DECORATION

½ cup strawberry preserves

8 ounces (about 2 cups) whole pecan halves

1. Adjust rack to lower third of oven and preheat oven to 325 degrees. Line two large cool baking sheets with parchment paper.

2. In the large bowl of an electric mixer, cream the butter at medium-low speed until smooth, about 1 minute. Beat in the sugar at medium speed until creamy. Add the egg yolks, one at a time, then the vanilla, beating until well combined and slightly fluffy, scraping down the sides of the bowl. Lower mixer speed, and add the flour, mixing only until thoroughly combined.

3. With your palms, shape the dough, 1 teaspoon at a time, into balls and drop ½ inch apart on a baking sheet. Using the end of a wooden spoon dipped in flour, gently make a small shallow indentation in the center of each cookie. Place a scant ⅛ teaspoon strawberry preserves in each indentation, and top with a pecan half, gently pressing so it will adhere and hide the preserves.

4. Bake, one sheet at a time, 13 to 15 minutes, or just until the cookies are ivory-colored and pale golden on the bottom. Transfer cookies to a wire rack to cool.

5. Stack in an airtight metal container and store at room temperature up to 10 days.

Java Sticks

These light, tender butterfingers, enhanced by flecks of walnuts, feature the fragrances of coffee and white chocolate to make a superb-tasting cookie.

DOUGH

8 ounces (2 sticks) unsalted butter, room temperature

½ cup (50 grams) unsifted powdered sugar

2 teaspoons instant coffee powder

1½ cups (210 grams) unsifted all-purpose flour

2 ounces (½ cup) walnuts, finely ground

DECORATION

⅓ cup dark corn syrup

3 ounces white chocolate, finely chopped

2 ounces (½ cup) walnuts, finely chopped

1. Adjust rack to lower third of oven and preheat oven to 325 degrees. Line two large cool baking sheets with parchment paper.

2. In the large bowl of an electric mixer, cream the butter at medium-low speed until smooth, about 1 minute. Beat in the sugar until well combined and slightly fluffy, then beat in the coffee powder, scraping down the sides of the bowl. Lower mixer speed, gradually add the flour and nuts, and mix just until the mixture is thoroughly combined.

3. Place half the dough in a 16-inch pastry bag fitted with a ½-inch plain decorating tip (such as Ateco #6). Pipe the dough into sticks 1½ inches in length and about 1 inch apart on baking sheets. To cut off the dough at the end of each piped stick, press the decorating tip down toward the baking sheet. (Piping is more efficient if you anchor the parchment paper to the baking sheet by smearing

a dab of dough in each corner of the baking sheet under the paper.) Fill the pastry bag with the remaining dough and pipe it into sticks.

4. Bake, one sheet at a time, 8 to 11 minutes or until the cookies no longer appear shiny and are pale tan or taupe in color. Place baking sheet on a wire rack and glaze cookies while warm.

5. In a small saucepan, heat the corn syrup just until warm. With a pastry brush, lightly coat cookies. Set aside until cool and the glaze is no longer sticky.

6. Melt the chocolate in a bowl set over 110-degree water. Put walnuts on a baking sheet.

7. Dip both long edges of each cookie in chocolate, then dip it into the finely chopped walnuts. To ensure that the nuts adhere to the chocolate, press them with fingertips; place each cookie on a clean baking sheet as you finish. Set sheet of cookies in a cool room or refrigerate a few minutes just to firm the chocolate.

8. Stack undecorated cookies in an airtight metal container and store at room temperature up to 10 days. Store decorated cookies in a single layer in a covered foil-lined cardboard container, such as a cake box, at room temperature up to 3 days.

Java Sticks

Drei Augen

In Germany, where they are traditional, *Drei Augen,* which translates as "three eyes," are topped with circles of dough in which three holes have been cut to reveal a jelly center. Consisting of shortbread with ground nuts and spice, these cookies taste delicious freshly baked. After a few days, the spicy nutty flavors emerge even richer.

DOUGH

2⅓ cups (325 grams) unsifted all-purpose flour

3 ounces (½ cup) unblanched almonds, finely ground

1 teaspoon ground cinnamon

10 ounces (2½ sticks) unsalted butter, room temperature

⅔ cup (130 grams) granulated sugar

DECORATION

1 cup (100 grams) unsifted powdered sugar

1 cup red currant jelly

1. In a medium bowl, blend the flour, ground nuts, and cinnamon briefly with a wire whisk; set aside. In the large bowl of an electric mixer, cream butter at medium-low speed until smooth, about 1 minute. Beat in the sugar at medium speed until well combined and slightly fluffy, scraping down the sides of the bowl. Lower mixer speed, gradually add dry ingredients, and mix just until the mixture is thoroughly combined.

2. Divide the dough in thirds. Roll out each portion of dough between two sheets of waxed paper to form a circle 11 inches in diameter and ⅛ inch thick. Leaving the dough circles between the waxed paper, stack them on a baking sheet and refrigerate until firm, for at least 2 hours or up to 3 days; or freeze, well wrapped, up to 1 month.

3. Adjust rack to lower third of oven and preheat oven to 325 degrees. Line two large cool baking sheets with parchment paper.

4. Remove one dough package at a time from refrigerator. Peel off top sheet of waxed paper, replace it loosely on top, and flip the entire package over. Peel off and discard the second sheet of waxed paper.

5. Using a 1½-inch round cutter, cut out circles in the dough. Using the narrow end of a ⅜-inch plain pastry tip (such as Ateco #3) as a cutter, cut out three small holes in each circle. Space the cookies ½ inch apart on a baking sheet. Bake for 13 to 15 minutes, or until the cookies are pale golden, no longer appear raw or shiny, and feel slightly firm (lightly touch a few). Place baking sheet on a wire rack to cool 5 minutes. Lift the cookies from the parchment with a metal spatula to a rack to cool.

6. Repeat with the other two portions of dough, cutting out holes in only one-quarter of these circles in order to sandwich the cookies later. Keep in mind that when there is a mixture of cookies with and without holes, the cookies with holes bake faster. Remove them from the oven with a metal spatula to a wire rack. Return the baking sheet to the oven until the remaining cookies are done.

7. Using a sieve, dust the powdered sugar just over the tops of cookies with holes.

8. In a small saucepan, boil the currant jelly for 2 minutes to evaporate some of its liquid. Cool just until warm. Spoon about ¼ teaspoon jelly on each plain circle, baked-bottom side up. Center a sugared circle on top of a jellied bottom, and gently press so the jelly fills in the three holes. Repeat with remaining cookies.

9. Stack undecorated cookies in an airtight metal container and store at room temperature up to 10 days. Store decorated cookies in a single layer in a covered foil-lined cardboard container, such as a cake box, at room temperature up to 3 days.

Drei Augen

Apricot Medals

Makes 4 dozen
1¾-inch pairs

This sophisticated cookie sandwich, made from buttery short dough, sparkles from a light brushing of sugar glaze and an orange crystal-clear apricot jam center.

DOUGH

1¾ cups (245 grams) unsifted all-purpose flour

⅛ teaspoon salt

8 ounces (2 sticks) unsalted butter, room temperature

⅔ cup (60 grams) unsifted powdered sugar

DECORATION

Sugar Glaze

½ cup (50 grams) unsifted powdered sugar

4 teaspoons water

½ cup strained apricot jam

1. In a medium bowl, blend the flour and salt briefly with a wire whisk; set aside. In the large bowl of an electric mixer, cream the butter at medium-low speed until smooth, about 1 minute. Add the sugar very gradually, beating at low speed to prevent sugar from flying out of the bowl, and scraping down the sides of the bowl. Gradually blend in the dry ingredients and mix just until thoroughly combined.

2. Divide the dough in half, and roll one portion of dough at a time between two sheets of waxed paper into a circle 10 inches in diameter and ⅛ inch thick. Leaving the dough circles between the waxed paper, stack on a baking sheet and refrigerate until firm, for at least 2 hours or up to 3 days; or freeze, well wrapped, up to 1 month.

3. Adjust rack to lower third of oven and preheat oven to 300 degrees. Line two large cool baking sheets with parchment paper.

Apricot Medals

50

4. Remove one dough circle package at a time from refrigerator. Peel off top sheet of waxed paper, replace it loosely on top, and flip the entire package over. Peel off and discard the second sheet of waxed paper.

5. With a 1½-inch scalloped round cutter, cut out circles in the dough. Using the narrow end of a ½-inch plain decorating tip (such as Ateco #6) as a cutter, cut out a hole in the center of each cookie. Put scalloped circles ½ inch apart on baking sheets. If the dough softens, making it difficult to transfer cutouts, refrigerate dough on its waxed paper until it is firmer.

6. Bake for 11 to 13 minutes, or until cookies no longer appear raw or shiny and feel slightly firm (lightly touch a few). Do not allow cookies to color. Place baking sheet on a wire rack to cool 5 minutes. Then lift cookies from parchment with a spatula to a rack to cool.

7. Repeat with the other portion of dough. Do not cut holes in these scalloped circles.

8. Keep the oven rack in the same position; lower the oven temperature to 140 degrees. Put the cookies with holes on a clean baking sheet.

9. Sugar Glaze: Mix the sugar and water together until smooth. With a pastry brush, spread a very thin layer of glaze on each of the cookies with holes. Return cookies to the oven until the glaze is set and dry, about 5 to 10 minutes.

10. In a small saucepan, boil the apricot jam gently for 2 minutes. Cool just until warm. Spoon about ½ teaspoon jam on each plain cookie, baked-bottom side up. Center a glazed circle on top of a jellied bottom, and gently press so the apricot jam fills the hole. Repeat with remaining cookies.

11. Stack undecorated cookies in an airtight metal container and store at room temperature up to 10 days. Store decorated cookies in a single layer in a covered foil-lined cardboard container, such as a cake box, at room temperature up to 3 days.

Apricot Medals

Pineapple Pockets

A flattened cone of butter dough with a pineapple filling laced with the pleasant taste of caramel creates an unusually scrumptious cookie.

DOUGH

6 ounces (1 ½ sticks) unsalted butter, room temperature

¼ cup (50 grams) granulated sugar

½ cup (50 grams) unsifted powdered sugar

2 egg yolks

1 teaspoon vanilla

1 ⅔ cups (235 grams) unsifted all-purpose flour

PINEAPPLE FILLING

2 tablespoons water

⅓ cup (65 grams) granulated sugar

1 8-ounce can crushed pineapple in unsweetened juice

½ tablespoon unsalted butter

1. In the large bowl of an electric mixer, cream the butter at medium-low speed until smooth, about 1 minute. Beat in the sugars on medium speed until creamy. Add the egg yolks, one at a time, then the vanilla, beating just until well combined and slightly fluffy, and scraping down the sides of the bowl. Lower mixer speed, gradually add the flour, and mix just until thoroughly combined.

2. Divide dough in half, and roll out one portion of dough at a time between two sheets of waxed paper to form a circle 11 inches in diameter and ⅛ inch thick. Leaving the dough circles between the waxed paper, transfer them to a baking sheet and refrigerate until firm, for at least 2 hours or up to 3 days; or freeze, well wrapped, up to 1 month.

3. Pineapple Filling: In a 3-cup heavy-bottomed saucepan, combine the water and the sugar over low heat. Stir occasionally, washing down any sugar crystals

clinging to the sides of the pan with a brush dipped in cold water, until the sugar is dissolved. Increase the heat to medium high and cook, without stirring, until the sugar syrup becomes thicker and amber in color, about 8 minutes. Remove from the heat, and pour in the crushed pineapple with its juice all at once. Be careful, as the mixture will foam up. Stir the mixture with a wooden spoon to distribute the heat and blend the ingredients together. Return to stove and cook over medium-high heat 4 minutes more or until mixture is golden and syrupy. Off the heat, stir in the butter. Pour the mixture into a small bowl and set aside until completely cool.

4. Adjust rack to lower third of oven and preheat oven to 325 degrees. Line two cool baking sheets with parchment paper.

5. Remove one dough circle package at a time from refrigerator. Peel off top sheet of waxed paper, replace it loosely on top, and flip the entire package over. Peel off and discard the second sheet of waxed paper.

6. Using a 2-inch round cutter, cut out circles in the dough. Place circles on cool baking sheets and spoon ½ teaspoon filling slightly off center on each. Fold over one edge of the dough, then overlap the opposite side to partially cover the filling: The cookie should look like a flattened cone with some filling showing at the wider end. Bake, one sheet at a time, for 12 to 14 minutes or until edges are light golden. Place baking sheet on a wire rack to cool 5 minutes. Then lift off cookies from parchment with a spatula to a rack to cool.

7. Stack cookies in an airtight metal container, separating the layers with strips of aluminum foil to keep them from sticking together, and store at room temperature up to 10 days.

VARIATION NOTE

Apricot Pockets

Substitute the Apricot-Pistachio Filling (page 246) for the pineapple filling.

Lemon Macaroon Triangles

The alluring contrast of tart and sweet makes these cookies unique, both in taste and presentation. Pastry dough is cut in strips and bordered with star bursts of a topping similar to an almond paste macaroon. After baking, the tender pastry with its toasty nutty-flavored topping is filled with tangy lemon curd before being cut into triangles.

DOUGH

½ recipe Miniature Tartlet Pastry (page 205)

LEMON CURD FILLING

2 large eggs

⅓ cup granulated sugar

¼ cup strained fresh lemon juice

2 teaspoons finely grated lemon zest

1 ounce (2 tablespoons) unsalted butter

MACAROON TOPPING

5 ounces (½ cup) almond paste, room temperature

⅓ cup (65 grams) granulated sugar

2 tablespoons (about 1 large) egg white, room temperature

⅛ teaspoon almond extract

1. Roll out the dough between two sheets of waxed paper to form a rectangle approximately 8 × 13½ inches and ⅛ inch thick. Leaving the dough between the waxed paper, place on a baking sheet and refrigerate until firm, for at least 2 hours or up to 3 days; or freeze, well wrapped, up to 1 month.

2. Lemon Curd Filling: Whisk the eggs in a 1½-quart saucepan to combine. Add the sugar, then the juice, and the zest, whisking to combine after each addition. Add the butter. Cook over medium heat, stirring constantly, until the

mixture begins to develop body and thicken, about 4 minutes. Remove from heat; pour into a bowl. When cool, cover the surface with plastic wrap and refrigerate.

3. Adjust rack to lower third of oven and preheat oven to 325 degrees. Line one large cool baking sheet with parchment paper.

4. Macaroon Topping: Place all the ingredients in a food processor and process just until smooth.

5. Remove the rectangular dough package from the refrigerator; peel off top sheet of waxed paper and discard it.

6. Using a ruler and pastry wheel, trim the edges of the dough. Measure and cut five 1½-inch-wide strips, each about 13 inches long. While the dough is still cool and firm, lift the strips onto the baking sheet, spacing them 1 inch apart.

7. Using a pastry bag fitted with a ¼-inch star decorating tip (such as Ateco #2), pipe lines of macaroon topping ⅛ inch from the long edges of the strips to form borders.

8. Bake for 20 to 25 minutes, or until the strips and the bottoms are light gold and the piped macaroon topping is golden in color. Place baking sheet on a wire rack until cookie strips are completely cool.

9. Remove about ½ cup of the lemon curd and spoon or pipe it over the center portions of the cookie strips inside the macaroon borders. Using a sharp chef's knife, cut diagonally across the strips in alternate directions to form triangular-shaped cookies. Cut straight down through the strips.

10. Wrap aluminum foil around unfilled strips and store, on baking sheet, at room temperature up to 1 day. Serve filled cookies within 2 hours.

VARIATION NOTES

Orange Macaroon Triangles

For an alternate filling, combine ½ cup orange marmalade with 1 tablespoon Grand Marnier.

Tiramisù Macaroon Triangles

For an alternate filling, combine 3 ounces (⅓ cup) mascarpone and 2 ounces (¼ cup) cream cheese with 3 tablespoons powdered sugar and ½ teaspoon lemon zest and beat until smooth. Pipe and spread over center of the cookie strips. Melt 2 ounces semisweet chocolate in a bowl over 120-degree water. Using a small handmade paper cone, pipe chocolate in thin lines diagonally across the filling.

Blueberry Macaroon Triangles

For an alternate filling, combine 1 egg yolk with ½ cup lemon curd. Spread it evenly over the centers of the baked cookie strips and bake in a preheated 375-degree oven for 5 minutes just to set the cream. When cool, scatter tiny fresh blueberries over the filling before cutting into wedges.

Lemon
Macaroon
Triangles

Sweet Seashells

After using what seemed like tons of flour, I discovered that potato starch was the key ingredient to these delicious sandy-textured shortbread cookies. You'll never taste the potato starch in the finished product, but it does heighten the cookies' buttery taste since it gives the illusion that there's more butter in the recipe than there actually is.

DOUGH

¾ cup (105 grams) unsifted all-purpose flour

⅓ cup (65 grams) potato starch

⅛ teaspoon salt

4 ounces (1 stick) unsalted butter, room temperature

¼ cup (50 grams) granulated sugar

1 teaspoon vanilla

DECORATION

⅓ cup strained apricot jam

1. Adjust rack to lower third of oven and preheat oven to 325 degrees.

2. In a medium bowl, blend the flour, potato starch, and salt briefly with a wire whisk; set aside. In the large bowl of an electric mixer, cream the butter at medium-low speed until smooth, about 1 minute. Beat in the sugar, then the vanilla just until well combined and slightly fluffy, scraping down the sides of the bowl. Lower speed, gradually add dry ingredients, and mix just until the mixture is thoroughly combined.

3. For each cookie, pinch off a piece of dough measuring 1 teaspoon in size. Shape into a ball with your palms, drop into ungreased tiny metal shell molds (20 shells in a pan), and press evenly into the molds with a fingertip.

4. Bake for 13 to 15 minutes or until cookies no longer appear shiny and are pale golden in color. Remove pans to a wire rack to cool 10 minutes. Tilt the pans slightly and tap them gently to loosen the cookies. Carefully lift each cookie

from its mold to a wire rack, fluted side up. Decorate while warm.

5. In a small saucepan, heat the jam just to warm and liquefy it. Using a small pastry brush, coat each cookie with a thin layer of jam. Dry on the rack until the glaze is no longer sticky to the touch, about an hour.

6. Stack undecorated cookies in an airtight metal container and store at room temperature up to 10 days. Store decorated cookies in one layer in a covered foil-lined cardboard container, such as a cake box, at room temperature up to 3 days.

VARIATION NOTE

- For a sweet-and-sour flavor, brush the Sugar Glaze (page 50) directly over the apricot jam.

$\mathcal{C}ocos$

Makes 12 dozen 1¼-inch cookies

If you're looking for the best coconut cookie, one that melts in your mouth, your search has ended. I discovered this shortbread version at Gayle's Bakery and Rotisserie in Capitola near Santa Cruz along the northern California coast. The owners, Joe and Gayle Ortiz, graciously released the recipe for this book.

DOUGH

1½ cups (210 grams) unsifted all-purpose flour

7 ounces (2½ cups) unsweetened medium-shred coconut

11 ounces (2¾ sticks) unsalted butter, room temperature

1 cup (200 grams) granulated sugar

1 egg yolk

DECORATION

2 ounces (²⁄₃ cup) unsweetened
   medium-shred coconut

1. In a medium bowl, blend the flour and the coconut briefly with a wire whisk; set aside. In the large bowl of an electric mixer, cream butter at medium-low speed until smooth, about 1 minute. Beat in the sugar at medium speed until creamy. Add the egg yolk, beating until well combined and slightly fluffy, and scraping down the sides of the bowl. Lower speed, and gradually blend in dry ingredients just until thoroughly combined.

2. Divide dough into 8 equal portions. Roll each portion back and forth in the 2 ounces coconut, on the work surface, into cylinders 9 inches long and 1 inch in diameter. Wrap in plastic and refrigerate until firm, for at least 4 hours or up to 1 week; or freeze, well wrapped, up to 1 month.

3. Adjust rack to lower third of oven and preheat oven to 325 degrees. Line two large cool baking sheets with parchment paper.

4. Using a serrated knife, and sawing the dough gently to make a clean cut, slice ¼-inch-thick rounds. Space 1 inch apart on baking sheet. Bake, one sheet at a time, for 8 minutes or until light golden around the edges. Place baking sheet on a wire rack to cool 5 minutes. Then lift cookies from parchment with a spatula to a rack to cool.

5. Stack cookies in an airtight metal container and store at room temperature up to 1 week; or freeze up to 1 month.

BAKING NOTE

• The best unsweetened medium-shred coconut is available at health food stores and specialty food markets.

Cocos

Chevron Twists

These cookies are a simpler version of the traditional pretzel shape. After tasting the buttery cookie with the maple pecan filling, you'll agree the flavors are natural companions.

DOUGH

6 ounces (1½ sticks) unsalted butter, room temperature

¼ cup (50 grams) granulated sugar

½ cup (50 grams) unsifted powdered sugar

1 egg yolk

1 teaspoon vanilla

1½ cups (210 grams) unsifted all-purpose flour

MAPLE PECAN FILLING

3¾ ounces (scant 1 cup) pecans, toasted

1 tablespoon unsalted butter, room temperature

1 teaspoon pure maple syrup

1. In the large bowl of an electric mixer, cream the butter at medium-low speed until smooth, about 1 minute. Beat in the sugars on medium speed until creamy. Add the egg yolk, and then the vanilla, beating just until well combined and slightly fluffy, and scraping down the sides of the bowl. Lower mixer speed, gradually add the flour, and mix just until thoroughly combined.

2. Adjust rack to lower third of oven and preheat oven to 300 degrees. Line two cool baking sheets with parchment paper.

3. Shape dough, 1 teaspoon at a time, into balls with your palms, and drop 1 inch apart on baking sheets. Then, with fingertips, roll each ball back and forth on work surface into a pencil-like rope about 4 to 5 inches long and ¼ inch in diameter. Place back on the baking sheet, and twist each rope of dough into a

loop, overlapping the ends, and curve the two ends. The cookie should resemble the letter "e" in lower-case script.

4. Bake, one sheet at a time, for 10 to 13 minutes or until firm when lightly touched and pale golden in color. Place baking sheet on a wire rack to cool 5 minutes. Then lift cookies from parchment with a spatula to a rack to cool.

5. Maple Pecan Filling: Finely grind the nuts in a food processor. Add the butter and maple syrup and blend until smooth. Using a 14-inch pastry bag fitted with a 1/4-inch plain decorating tip (such as Ateco #2), pipe a small dot of filling in the center hole of the loop of each "e."

6. Stack unfilled cookies in an airtight metal container and store at room temperature up to 10 days; or freeze up to 1 month. Store filled cookies in one layer in a covered foil-lined cardboard container, such as a cake box, at room temperature up to 3 days.

Chevron Twists

Almond Teardrops

Makes 5 dozen
1½-inch cookies

Almonds, ground like flour, give these cookies an extra nutty flavor. Each teardrop-shaped cookie is brushed with an egg yolk glaze and topped with a split blanched almond before baking.

DOUGH

1½ cups (210 grams) unsifted all-purpose flour

3 ounces (½ cup) blanched almonds, finely ground

⅛ teaspoon salt

5 ounces (1¼ sticks) unsalted butter, room temperature

½ cup (100 grams) granulated sugar

1 large egg

1 teaspoon finely grated lemon zest

¼ teaspoon almond extract

DECORATION

1 egg yolk

2 teaspoons heavy cream

2 ounces (about 40) blanched almonds

1. In a medium bowl, blend the flour, ground nuts, and salt briefly with a wire whisk; set aside. In the large bowl of an electric mixer, cream the butter at medium-low speed until smooth, about 1 minute. Beat in the sugar at medium speed until creamy. Add the egg, lemon zest, and almond extract, beating just until well combined and slightly fluffy, and scraping down the sides of the bowl. Lower the speed, gradually add the dry ingredients, and mix just until the mixture is thoroughly combined.

2. Divide dough in half. Roll one portion of dough at a time between two sheets of waxed paper to form a circle 11 inches in diameter and ¼ inch thick. Peel off top waxed paper sheet and roll a rolling pin with a waffle pattern over the dough once. Exert just enough pressure to flatten dough to 3/16 inch thick. If dough sticks to the pin, lightly flour dough's surface. Replace waxed paper on

top, and place on a baking sheet, waffle design up. Refrigerate until firm, for at least 2 hours or up to 3 days.

3. Adjust rack to lower third of oven and preheat oven to 325 degrees. Line two large cool baking sheets with parchment paper.

4. In a small bowl, blend the egg yolk with the cream until smooth; set aside. Put the almonds and water to cover in a small saucepan and bring to a boil. Remove from heat; let stand for 1 minute to soften. Remove nuts, one by one, and, using the tip of a small paring knife, split the almonds in half along their natural seams.

5. Remove one dough circle at a time from the refrigerator and peel off top sheet of waxed paper; discard the waxed paper. Using a pastry brush, lightly coat the waffle-patterned dough with the egg wash.

6. Pinch the wide end of a $\frac{1}{2}$-inch plain decorating tip (such as Ateco #6) into an oval shape resembling a teardrop to make a cutter. Using the cutter, cut out shapes in the dough. Space the cutouts $\frac{1}{2}$ inch apart on baking sheets. Put an almond half, rounded side up, on each cookie. Bake, one sheet at a time, until the cookies appear set and ivory-colored, about 12 to 15 minutes. Place baking sheet on a wire rack to cool 5 minutes. Then lift off cookies from parchment with a spatula to a rack to cool.

7. Stack in an airtight metal container and store at room temperature up to 10 days; freeze up to 1 month.

Macadamia Crescents

These not-overly-sweet cookies, traditionally shaped into crescents, were inspired by a recipe from my longtime friend and former baking colleague Jack Lirio. Besides savoring these cookies' nutty flavor, you will be reminded by their texture of the best short crust you ever tasted.

DOUGH

1 3/4 cups (245 grams) unsifted all-purpose flour

5 ounces (1 cup) macadamia nuts, finely ground to yield about 1 ½ cups (see Baking Note)

1/8 teaspoon salt

8 ounces (2 sticks) unsalted butter, room temperature

1/3 cup (65 grams) granulated sugar

DECORATION

2 cups (200 grams) unsifted powdered sugar

1. In a medium bowl, blend the flour, ground nuts, and salt briefly with a wire whisk; set aside. In the large bowl of an electric mixer, cream the butter at medium-low speed until smooth, about 1 minute. Beat in the sugar at medium speed until well combined and slightly fluffy, scraping down the sides of the bowl. Lower speed, gradually add the nuts and flour, and mix just until the mixture is thoroughly combined.

2. Refrigerate the dough, tightly covered, in a bowl. Chill about 1 hour or until it is partially firm but not solid, to make handling easier.

3. Adjust rack to lower third of oven and preheat oven to 325 degrees. Line two cool baking sheets with parchment paper.

4. Divide the chilled dough into several portions, each about ¼ cup. With floured fingertips roll each portion back and forth on work surface to shape ropes about ½ inch in diameter. If dough is difficult to shape, lightly flour work surface.

Cut each roll into uniform 1-inch lengths. With fingertips, shape into crescents with slightly tapered ends, and space ½ inch apart on the baking sheets.

5. Bake, one sheet at a time, for 12 to 15 minutes or until cookies are no longer shiny and their shape is set. Place baking sheet on a wire rack. Sift the powdered sugar over cookies while warm.

6. When completely cool, lift cookies with a metal spatula to an airtight metal container, arranging them in one layer. Store up to 1 week at room temperature; or freeze up to 1 month.

BAKING NOTES

- Unsalted macadamia nuts, available in health food stores and some supermarkets, are best in this recipe.
- For variety, substitute black walnuts or unblanched almonds for the macadamias.
- See How to Measure Nuts (page 6). Because the nuts provide structure as well as flavor in this recipe, it is important to measure the ground nuts.

Macadamia
Crescents

Cornmeal Batons

Dip these plump, butter cookie sticks into a cornmeal streusel before baking. These not-too-sweet treats are terrific as a snack with coffee or tea.

STREUSEL

- ½ cup (70 grams) unsifted all-purpose flour
- ⅓ cup yellow cornmeal
- ⅓ cup (65 grams) granulated sugar

- 1 teaspoon finely grated lemon zest
- 3 ounces (6 tablespoons) unsalted butter, room temperature, cut into ½-inch slices

DOUGH

- 8 ounces (2 sticks) unsalted butter, room temperature
- ½ cup (100 grams) granulated sugar
- 2 tablespoons (about 1 large) egg white

- 2 teaspoons finely grated orange zest
- 1 teaspoon vanilla
- 2 cups (280 grams) unsifted all-purpose flour

EGG WASH

- 1 egg yolk

- 2 teaspoons heavy cream

1. Streusel: In a medium bowl, combine the dry ingredients and lemon zest. With fingertips, work in the butter until the mixture resembles coarse crumbs. For a more uniform and delicate-looking streusel, push the mixture through a sieve with a rubber spatula into another bowl. Cover and refrigerate until firm, at least 2 hours.

2. In the large bowl of an electric mixer, cream the butter at medium-low speed until smooth, about 1 minute. Beat in the sugar at medium speed until creamy. Add the egg white, zest, and vanilla, beating just until fluffy, and scraping

down the sides of the bowl. Lower speed, gradually add the flour, and mix just until thoroughly combined.

3. Refrigerate the dough in a bowl, tightly covered, for 1 hour or until it is partially firm but not solid.

4. Adjust rack to lower third of oven and preheat oven to 325 degrees. Line two cool baking sheets with parchment paper.

5. With fingertips, toss the chilled streusel around gently to break up any large lumps; don't overwork.

6. Divide the chilled dough into several portions, each about ¼ cup, and with floured fingertips roll each back and forth on a lightly floured work surface to shape ropes about ½ inch in diameter. In a small bowl, blend the egg yolk with the cream for an egg wash. Using a small pastry brush, lightly coat the top of each cylinder with the egg wash. Cut each roll into 1½-inch lengths to yield uniformly shaped sticks. Dip each stick's glazed side in the streusel, then place on a baking sheet ½ inch apart.

7. Bake, one sheet at a time, about 13 to 15 minutes or until the cookies appear set and no longer shiny and are light golden on the bottom. Do not allow to color on top. Place baking sheet on a wire rack to cool 5 minutes. Then lift off cookies from parchment with a spatula to a rack to cool.

8. Stack cookies in an airtight metal container and store at room temperature up to 1 week; or freeze up to 1 month.

Cornmeal Batons

Maple Butterballs

Butter, brown sugar, vanilla, maple syrup, and heavy cream harmonize perfectly in a cookie. For gift giving at holiday time, put the Butterballs in paper candy cases.

DOUGH

- 8 ounces (2 sticks) unsalted butter, room temperature
- ¾ cup (150 grams) light brown sugar, packed
- 1 large egg

- 1 teaspoon vanilla
- 2 cups (280 grams) unsifted all-purpose flour

MAPLE CREAM FILLING

- ⅔ cup pure maple syrup
- ⅔ cup (5 ounces) heavy cream

- 1 ounce (2 tablespoons) unsalted butter

1. Adjust rack to lower third of oven and preheat oven to 325 degrees. Line two large cool baking sheets with parchment paper.

2. In the large bowl of an electric mixer, cream the butter at medium-low speed until smooth, about 1 minute. Beat in the sugar at medium speed until creamy. Add the egg, then the vanilla, beating just until well combined and slightly fluffy, and scraping down the sides of the bowl. Lower speed, gradually blend in the flour, and mix just until thoroughly combined.

3. Using a 12-inch pastry bag fitted with a ½-inch plain decorating tip (such as Ateco #6), pipe bulbs ½ to ¾ inches in diameter and ½ inch apart on baking sheets. (Piping is easier if you anchor the parchment to the baking sheet with a dab of dough in each corner under the paper.) Using a damp pastry brush, tap cookies to flatten point left from piping.

4. Bake, one sheet at a time, for 10 to 12 minutes or until firm when lightly touched and tan in color. Place baking sheet on a wire rack to cool 5 minutes.

Then lift cookies from parchment with a spatula to a rack to cool.

5. Maple Cream Filling: In a 1½-quart heavy-bottomed saucepan, gently boil the maple syrup and heavy cream over medium heat until reduced by half, about 20 minutes. Off heat, stir in the butter. Cool until filling is lukewarm and its consistency is like honey, about 30 minutes.

6. Spoon or pipe ¼ to ½ teaspoon filling on half of the cookies, flat side up. Center the remaining cookies on top of the filled bottoms, gently pressing the pairs together.

7. Stack undecorated cookies in an airtight metal container and store at room temperature up to 10 days; or freeze up to 1 month. Store decorated cookies in one layer in a covered foil-lined cardboard container, such as a cake box, at room temperature up to 3 days.

Autumn Acorns

Rich tender cookies are given a flavor and visual boost by ground hazelnuts and cinnamon. Teaspoons of dough are molded into balls and pinched on one end to create an acorn shape. The rounded end is dipped into an egg-and-nut mixture to form the acorn's cap.

DOUGH

8 ounces (2 sticks) unsalted butter, room temperature

½ cup (100 grams) granulated sugar

2⅓ cups (330 grams) unsifted all-purpose flour

DECORATION

1 large egg

1 ounce (2 tablespoons) hazelnuts, finely ground

2 tablespoons (25 grams) granulated sugar

⅛ teaspoon ground cinnamon

1. In the large bowl of an electric mixer, cream the butter at medium-low speed until smooth, about 1 minute. Beat in the sugar until well combined and slightly fluffy, scraping down the sides of the bowl. Lower speed, gradually add the flour, and mix just until thoroughly combined.

2. Adjust rack to lower third of oven and preheat oven to 325 degrees. Line two large cool baking sheets with parchment paper.

3. With your palms, shape dough, 1 teaspoon at a time, into balls. Pinch them so that each ball is pointed at the bottom to form an acorn shape, and place ½ inch apart on the baking sheet. Place baking sheet in the refrigerator for 15 minutes or just until dough is firm.

4. In a bowl, whisk the egg until smooth. In another bowl, whisk the ground nuts, sugar, and cinnamon briefly just to blend. Dip just the larger rounded end

of each acorn-shaped cookie into the beaten egg, then into the crumb mixture, returning each cookie to the baking sheet, $\frac{1}{2}$ inch apart.

5. Bake, one sheet at a time, for 12 to 15 minutes or until the cookies no longer appear shiny and feel slightly firm when lightly touched. Do not allow them to color. Place baking sheet on wire rack to cool 5 minutes. Then lift from parchment with a metal spatula to a wire rack to cool.

6. Stack cookies in an airtight metal container, separating layers with sheets of aluminum foil to keep cookies snug and the topping in place, and store at room temperature up to 10 days; or freeze up to 1 month.

Mimosa Rosettes

Shortbread dough, subtly orange-flavored, takes on an elegant look when piped into spirals and embellished with a candied mimosa in the center to resemble a flower.

DOUGH

1½ cups (210 grams) unsifted all-purpose flour

¼ teaspoon baking powder

⅛ teaspoon salt

6 ounces (1½ sticks) unsalted butter, room temperature

¾ cup (75 grams) unsifted powdered sugar

1 egg yolk

1 tablespoon Grand Marnier

1 teaspoon vanilla

1 teaspoon finely grated orange zest

3 dozen candied mimosa

DECORATION

¼ cup (25 grams) unsifted powdered sugar

1. Adjust rack to lower third of oven and preheat oven to 350 degrees. Line a large cool baking sheet with parchment paper.

2. Sift the flour, baking powder, and salt on a sheet of waxed paper; set aside. In the large bowl of an electric mixer, cream the butter at medium-low speed until smooth, about 1 minute. Beat in the sugar very gradually until creamy. Add the egg yolk, liqueur, vanilla, and zest, beating until light and fluffy, and scraping down the sides of the bowl. Lower speed, gradually blend in dry ingredients, and mix just until thoroughly combined.

3. Anchor parchment paper with a dab of dough under each corner. Using a pastry bag fitted with an open star decorating tip (such as Ateco #8), pipe soft dough onto the baking sheet. Hold the pastry tip perpendicular to the baking

sheet and $\frac{1}{2}$ inch above it, and pipe rosette shapes equivalent to $1\frac{1}{2}$ teaspoons of dough each, spaced $\frac{3}{4}$ inch apart. Each time you finish piping a rosette, twist the pastry tip in the center of the spiral. This action stops the flow of dough and makes it easy to lift the dough away from the rosette shape. Center a candied mimosa on each rosette.

4. Bake 11 to 13 minutes or until the cookies no longer appear raw or shiny, are pale golden, and feel slightly firm (lightly touch a few). Place baking sheet on a wire rack to cool 5 minutes. Then lift cookies from parchment with a spatula to a rack to cool. Sift powdered sugar over them lightly before serving.

5. Stack cookies in an airtight metal container and store at room temperature up to 10 days; or freeze up to 1 month.

Mimosa
Rosettes

Daddy Long Legs

Makes 8 dozen
2-inch cookies

Here's a great cookie to eat while sipping a cup of coffee. This crisp crunchy cookie is made with a minimum of butter and a good deal more sugar than most cookie doughs. Add a lot of nuts and you have not only an additional crunch but an intense flavor.

DOUGH

5 ounces (1 1/4 sticks) unsalted butter, room temperature

1 cup (200 grams) granulated sugar

2 large eggs, room temperature

10 ounces (2 cups) hazelnuts, toasted

2 1/4 cups (315 grams) unsifted all-purpose flour

1. In the large bowl of an electric mixer, cream the butter at medium-low speed until smooth, about 1 minute. Beat in the sugar at medium speed until well combined and slightly fluffy, scraping down the sides of the bowl. Add the eggs, one at a time, mixing until well combined. Lower speed, add the nuts all at once, then add the flour gradually. Mix just until thoroughly combined.

2. Divide dough into four equal portions. With your floured fingertips, form each portion of dough into a rectangular brick 10 inches long, 2 inches wide, and 3/4 inch high. Wrap each in plastic and refrigerate until firm, for at least 4 hours or up to 3 days; or freeze, well wrapped, up to 1 month.

3. Adjust rack to lower third of oven and preheat oven to 350 degrees. Line two large cool baking sheets with parchment paper. Remove one brick of dough at a time from the refrigerator.

4. Using a sharp knife, cut 3/8-inch-thick slices and place them, cut side down, 1/2 inch apart on baking sheet. Bake, one sheet at a time, for just 8 minutes. The cookies' surface will be dull, not shiny. Remove baking sheet from the oven and turn cookies over with a metal spatula. Return to oven and bake about 7 to

10 minutes more or until pale golden and crisp. Remove cookies with a metal spatula to a wire rack to cool.

5. Stack in airtight metal containers and store at room temperature up to 10 days.

BAKING NOTE

• Resting and chilling the dough are especially important steps in this recipe. In order to cut the dough neatly to retain chunks of nuts in each slice, you must let the dough rest and firm in the refrigerator. Resting allows time for the nuts to absorb moisture from the dough, thereby softening them for cutting. Chilling makes it easier to slice the dough precisely.

Daddy Long Legs

Lemon Sunflowers

Makes 6 dozen
1½-inch cookies

For me, these snappy, crisp, flower-shaped cookies of caramel, lemon, and butter are irresistible. Caramelized sugar fills the cookie centers to give a stained glass effect.

CARAMELIZED SUGAR

½ cup granulated sugar

DOUGH

2¼ cups (315 grams) unsifted all-purpose flour

¼ teaspoon baking powder

6 ounces (1½ sticks) unsalted butter, room temperature

1 cup (200 grams) granulated sugar

1 large egg

1 egg yolk

4 teaspoons finely grated lemon zest

1. Caramelized Sugar: Line a baking sheet with aluminum foil; set near the stove. In a 1½-quart heavy-bottomed saucepan over low heat, melt the sugar, stirring occasionally. Wash down any crystals clinging to the sides of the pan with a brush dipped in cold water. When sugar is dissolved, increase the heat to medium-high and cook the melted sugar without stirring until it becomes amber in color, about 8 minutes. Pour bubbling syrup onto the foil. Cool until firm, about 1 hour.

2. Sift the flour with the baking powder on a sheet of waxed paper; set aside. In the large bowl of an electric mixer, cream the butter at medium-low speed until smooth, about 1 minute. Beat in the sugar at medium speed until creamy. Add the egg, yolk, and lemon zest just until well combined and slightly fluffy, scraping down the sides of the bowl. Lower speed, gradually add the dry ingredients, and mix just until thoroughly combined.

3. Divide the dough in half. Roll each portion of dough between two sheets of waxed paper to form a circle 11 inches in diameter and ⅛ inch thick. Stack circles on a baking sheet and refrigerate until firm for at least 2 hours or up to 3 days; or freeze, well wrapped, up to 1 month.

4. Adjust rack to lower third of oven and preheat oven to 325 degrees. Line two large cool baking sheets with parchment paper.

5. Break the caramelized sugar into pieces. Pulverize in a food processor into golden powder crystals; set aside.

6. Remove one dough package at a time from refrigerator. Peel off top sheet of waxed paper, replace it loosely on top, and flip the entire package over. Peel off and discard the second sheet of waxed paper.

7. Using a 1½-inch scalloped round cutter, cut out circles and space ½ inch apart on baking sheets. Using the narrow end of a ½-inch plain decorating tip (such as Ateco #6) as a cutter, cut out a hole from the center of each cookie. Spoon about ½ teaspoon of the sugar crystals into each hole and lightly pat in place.

8. Bake, one sheet at a time, for 10 minutes or until edges are a delicate brown and the sugar crystals are shiny and have melted to their original amber color. Cool the cookies on the baking sheet until the caramelized sugar is firm.

9. Stack in an airtight metal container, separating layers with strips of aluminum foil to prevent rattling and sticking, and store at room temperature up to 3 days. For controlling moisture in container, see the paragraph on the nontoxic blue crystals, page 12.

BAKING NOTES

- These cookies are as crisp as the Daddy Long Legs (page 74). When a cookie recipe has a lot of sugar in relation to the amount of butter, the cookies will be crisp.

Lemon Sunflowers

- To form the cookies, use a flower-shaped cookie cutter. The one I use is from a set of Japanese cutters sold in housewares departments and cookware stores.

Almond Confetti

Makes 5 dozen
1½-inch wafers

These sweet, delicate cookies are like potato chips—you can't eat just one. Not only are they easy to make, they have a captivating almond and vanilla flavor with an unexpected tang from sour cream in the recipe.

BATTER

¼ cup (35 grams) unsifted all-purpose flour

⅛ teaspoon salt

4 ounces (1 stick) unsalted butter, softened

½ cup (100 grams) granulated sugar

½ cup (5 ounces) sour cream

½ teaspoon vanilla

⅛ teaspoon almond extract

4 ounces (¾ cup) unblanched almonds, coarsely chopped (see Baking Note)

1. Adjust rack to lower third of oven and preheat oven to 325 degrees. Unwrap an end of a chilled stick of unsalted butter and rub it over two large cool Teflon-coated baking sheets to apply a thin film of fat.

2. In a small bowl, briefly blend the flour and the salt with a wire whisk; set aside. In the large bowl of an electric mixer, cream butter at medium speed until creamy, about 1 minute. Beat in the sugar until light and very fluffy. Add the sour cream, vanilla, and almond extract, blending well. Gradually add the flour mixture, then the nuts, combining thoroughly.

3. Drop level teaspoons of the batter on baking sheets, spacing them 1 inch apart. A quick method is to pipe the soft batter from a 16-inch pastry bag fitted with a ⅝-inch plain decorating tip (such as Ateco #8). Pipe mounds about 1 inch in diameter. The decorating tip's size is large enough for the nut pieces to flow through easily.

4. Bake, one sheet at a time, for 11 to 14 minutes or until the cookies' edges and undersides are golden brown and the centers are ivory. Cool the cookies on the baking sheet only 2 minutes to firm slightly. Then, with a metal spatula, transfer cookies to a wire rack to cool.

5. Repeat baking process with any remaining batter.

6. Stack cookies in an airtight metal container and store at room temperature up to 1 week.

BAKING NOTE

- Because the nuts provide structure as well as flavor in this recipe, it is important to measure the chopped nut pieces as accurately as possible. With a food processor, through variations of brand, speed, blade, timing, and force, you can grind a given weight of nuts into widely varying volumes of chopped nuts. A nut mill grinds nuts into the same volume every time, so for this recipe use a nut mill to chop the nuts to yield a rounded ¾ cup. See How to Measure Nuts (page 6).

Almond Confetti

Chewy Miniatures

Gianduja Cubes
83

Meringue Bubbles
86

Dacquoise Cheesecake Squares
88

Panforte di Siena
90

Macaroon Trios
92

Glazed Almond Weave
94

Viennese Triangles
96

Pecan Diamonds
98

Swiss Japonais
100

Maple Japonais
104

Gianduja Cubes

Gianduja (pronounced john-doo-ya), a creamy mixture of toasted ground almonds and hazelnuts, and chocolate, is often used in French, Italian, and Swiss confectionery. In this recipe, a thin layer is spread over a thin sheet of dacquoise before it is cut into small squares. Gianduja's rich flavor and creamy texture contrast wonderfully with the dacquoise, which is simply a crisp nutty meringue.

DACQUOISE

- 3 ounces (½ cup) unblanched almonds, toasted and finely ground
- ¼ cup (50 grams) granulated sugar
- 1 tablespoon unsifted all-purpose flour

- ½ cup (about 4 large) egg whites
- ⅓ cup (65 grams) granulated sugar
- ½ teaspoon almond extract

GIANDUJA FILLING

- 2 ounces semisweet chocolate, finely chopped
- 2 ounces unsweetened chocolate, finely chopped
- 2 ounces (⅓ cup) blanched almonds, toasted

- 2 ounces (⅓ cup) hazelnuts, toasted and most skins removed
- ½ cup (50 grams) unsifted powdered sugar

DECORATION

- ¼ cup (25 grams) unsifted powdered sugar
- 24 hazelnuts, toasted and skins removed

1. Adjust rack to lower third of oven and preheat oven to 350 degrees. Line a 12- × 15½- × ½-inch baking sheet with aluminum foil, leaving a 2-inch over-

hang at each short end of the pan. Grease the foil, then flour it, tapping out excess flour.

2. Combine the nuts and ¼ cup sugar with the flour in a small bowl; set aside.

3. Using an electric mixer, preferably with a whisk attachment, whip egg whites in a large bowl at medium speed until foamy, about 30 seconds. Add the ⅓ cup sugar and continue whipping until soft glossy peaks form, about 2 to 3 minutes. Add the almond extract toward the end of whipping. Sprinkle the nut mixture over the meringue and fold the two together just until incorporated.

4. Spread the batter evenly over the baking sheet. Bake for 20 to 25 minutes, or until light brown and crisp. Remove from the oven. With a thin-bladed knife, release the edges of the dacquoise sticking to the baking sheet. Pull up on the foil overhangs to loosen the foil from the bottom of the baking sheet. Using a small paring knife, trim top edges of dacquoise to make the surface level.

5. Place a second baking sheet on top of the dacquoise, invert the dacquoise on it, lift off top baking sheet, and carefully peel the foil from the dacquoise.

6. Gianduja Filling: Melt the chocolate in a bowl set over water approximately 120 degrees. In the bowl of a food processor, whirl nuts with sugar to form a thick paste, about 4 minutes. Add chocolate to nut paste, and process just until mixture is combined and smooth. Spread evenly over the dacquoise in a very thin layer.

7. Before the creamy topping sets up, using a ruler and a paring knife, cut the gianduja-topped dacquoise into nine strips 1½ inches wide and 11½ inches long. Using a long metal spatula, lift dacquoise strips to form three stacks of three strips each on a clean baking sheet. If a strip breaks, merely fit together like pieces of a puzzle. Breaks will not be apparent when you serve the finished pastries. Crumble dacquoise trimmings into crumbs and sprinkle them over the stacks.

Gianduja Cubes

8. Set stacks, on the baking sheet, in the refrigerator for 10 minutes only, so the layers stick firmly together and absorb moisture from filling to make cutting easier and neater.

9. Lightly sift the powdered sugar over the strips. Cut into $1\frac{1}{2}$-inch squares, cutting straight down through the layers with a sharp knife and wiping the knife clean after each slice. Press a whole hazelnut on top of each square.

10. Serve at room temperature the same day they are baked.

Gianduja Cubes

Meringue Bubbles

You taste chocolate right away when you bite into these, but the appearance of a snowy white meringue "kiss" shape atop a short tender cookie gives no clue. A creative baker can have fun with these cookies: Rather than a "kiss," pipe the chocolate-flecked meringue into any shape on the cookie bases—hearts, butterflies, rosebuds, leaves, latticework—even a family coat of arms.

DOUGH

4 ounces (1 stick) unsalted butter, room temperature

¼ cup (50 grams) granulated sugar

1 cup plus 2 tablespoons (160 grams) unsifted all-purpose flour

MERINGUE

¼ cup (about 2 large) fresh egg whites

½ cup (100 grams) granulated sugar

½ teaspoon vanilla

1½ ounces semisweet chocolate, finely grated

1. In the large bowl of an electric mixer, cream the butter at medium speed until smooth, about 1 minute. Beat in the sugar until well combined and slightly fluffy, scraping down the sides. Lower speed, gradually add the flour, and mix just until thoroughly combined.

2. Divide dough in half. Roll out each portion of dough between two sheets of waxed paper to form a circle 8 inches in diameter and ¼ inch thick. Leaving the dough between the waxed paper, transfer circles to a baking sheet and refrigerate until firm, for at least 2 hours or up to 3 days; or freeze, well wrapped, up to 1 month.

3. Adjust rack to the *center* of the oven and preheat oven to 350 degrees. Line two large cool baking sheets with parchment paper.

4. Remove one dough package at a time from the refrigerator. Remove the top waxed paper sheet, and lay it loosely back on the dough. Turn the dough over and peel off and discard the second sheet of waxed paper.

5. Using the wide end of a ½-inch plain decorating tip (such as Ateco #6) as a cutter, cut out circles of dough. If the circles of dough stick to the decorating tip, use a chopstick or wooden spoon handle to gently push through the decorating tip to release the circle of dough. Place the circles of dough ½ inch apart on a baking sheet. Partially bake the cookies, one sheet at a time, for 6 to 8 minutes only or until just set. Set the baking sheet on a wire rack to cool. Reduce the oven temperature to 225 degrees.

6. When the cookies are cool, place all of them on one baking sheet lined with parchment, leaving about ¼ inch between cookies. Using an electric mixer, preferably with a whisk attachment, whip the egg whites in a large bowl on medium-low speed until surface is frothy. Increase speed to medium, then pour in half the sugar and whip until soft white peaks form, about 30 seconds. While continuing to whip, slowly add the remaining sugar and the vanilla and continue whipping until the egg whites form stiff, shiny peaks, about 1½ minutes.

7. Using a rubber spatula, fold the grated chocolate into the meringue. Immediately scoop all of the meringue into a 16-inch pastry bag fitted with a ½-inch plain decorating tip (such as Ateco #6). Pipe a bulb of meringue onto each cookie in a "kiss" shape. The bottom of the meringue "kiss" should be the diameter of the cookie circle. Bake the Meringue Bubbles an additional 60 minutes, until the meringue is firm to the touch. Place the baking sheet on a wire rack to cool. Lift cookies from parchment when cool.

8. These are best eaten the same day. To store, place them in an airtight metal container for up to 1 week.

Meringue
Bubbles

Dacquoise Cheesecake Squares

Makes 2 dozen
1½-inch squares

If you like cheesecake, you'll love these bite-size pastries. Last-minute company coming? Prepare these and the Gianduja Cubes (page 83). Both recipes are easy to prepare and make an attractive display since they are similar in shape. And your guests will enjoy the contrasting tastes.

DACQUOISE

3 ounces (½ cup) unblanched almonds, toasted and finely ground

¼ cup (50 grams) granulated sugar

1 tablespoon unsifted all-purpose flour

½ cup (about 4 large) egg whites

⅓ cup (65 grams) granulated sugar

½ teaspoon almond extract

CHEESECAKE FILLING

6 ounces cream cheese, room temperature

¼ cup (50 grams) granulated sugar

1 egg

1 teaspoon finely grated lemon zest

1. Adjust rack to lower third of oven and preheat oven to 350 degrees. Line a 12- × 15½- × ½-inch baking sheet with aluminum foil, leaving a 2-inch overhang at each short end of the pan. Grease the foil, then flour it, tapping out excess flour.

2. Combine the nuts and ¼ cup sugar with the flour in a small bowl; set aside.

3. Using an electric mixer, preferably with a whisk attachment, whip egg whites in a large bowl at medium speed until foamy, about 30 seconds. Gradually add the ⅓ cup sugar and continue whipping until soft glossy peaks form, about

2 to 3 minutes. Add the almond extract toward the end of whipping. Sprinkle the nut mixture over the meringue and fold the two together just until incorporated.

4. Spread the batter evenly over the baking sheet. Bake for 20 to 22 minutes, or until light brown and crisp. Remove from the oven, but do not turn the oven off. With a thin-bladed knife, release the edges of the dacquoise sticking to the baking sheet. Pull up on the foil overhangs to loosen the foil from the bottom of the baking sheet. Using a small paring knife, trim top edges of dacquoise to make the surface level.

5. Place a second baking sheet on top of the dacquoise, invert the dacquoise on it, lift off top baking sheet, and carefully peel the foil from the dacquoise. Invert it back, right side up, onto original baking sheet.

6. Cheesecake Filling: Beat all the ingredients in a medium bowl until creamy and smooth. Spread filling in a thin layer evenly over dacquoise.

7. Return to oven for 5 to 7 minutes or just until the cheese filling appears set. Remove from the oven. Cool for 10 minutes only.

8. Using a ruler and pastry wheel, cut the cheese-topped dacquoise into nine strips 1½ inches wide and 11½ inches long. With a long metal spatula, lift strips to form three stacks of three on a clean baking sheet. If a strip breaks, merely fit it together like pieces of a puzzle. Breaks will not be apparent when you serve the finished pastries.

9. Crumble dacquoise trimmings into crumbs and sprinkle them over the stacks. Cover with plastic wrap, and set aside at room temperature for 30 minutes to allow dacquoise to absorb moisture from the filling to make cutting easier.

10. Cut into 1½-inch squares, wiping the knife clean after each slice.

11. Serve at room temperature the same day they are baked.

Dacquoise
Cheesecake
Squares

Panforte di Siena

An Italian confection, panforte, meaning "strong bread," originated in Siena, Italy. It is a dense fruitcake of nuts, spices, and dried fruits, bound together by a sugar syrup spiked with honey. In contrast to American fruitcakes it is less cakey, more like candy, with the intense taste of the fruit and nuts. You'll enjoy it with grappa, espresso, or even freshly brewed tea. Special thanks to my friend Corby Kummer, senior editor of *The Atlantic* magazine, whose expert knowledge of and passion for Italian cuisine guided me to this recipe.

BATTER

4 ounces (½ cup packed) candied citron

4 ounces (½ cup) candied orange peel

3 ounces (⅓ cup) dried figs

1½ ounces (¼ cup) golden raisins

4 ounces (¾ cup) unblanched almonds, toasted

4 ounces (¾ cup) hazelnuts, toasted

2 ounces (½ cup) walnut halves

6 tablespoons unsifted all-purpose flour

2 teaspoons unsifted cocoa powder

1 teaspoon ground cinnamon

½ teaspoon ground coriander

¼ teaspoon ground nutmeg

1 tablespoon water

½ cup honey

⅔ cup (130 grams) granulated sugar

DECORATION

¼ cup (25 grams) unsifted powdered sugar

½ teaspoon ground cinnamon

¼ teaspoon ground coriander

1. Adjust rack to lower third of oven and preheat oven to 325 degrees. Press a sheet of heavy-duty aluminum foil to fit inside a 9-inch square baking pan. Generously grease and flour the foil.

2. Using a chef's knife, chop the candied citron and orange peel, dried figs, and golden raisins until finely minced (to yield 2 cups). In a large bowl, combine with the nuts.

3. In a small bowl, stir the flour, cocoa powder, and spices to blend.

4. In a 1½-quart heavy-bottomed saucepan, combine the water, honey, and granulated sugar over medium-low heat. Stir occasionally, washing down any sugar crystals clinging to the sides of the pan with a brush dipped in cold water, until the sugar is dissolved. Increase the heat and simmer, without stirring, until the mixture reaches 238 degrees, the soft-ball stage, on a mercury candy thermometer.

5. Immediately pour the syrup over the fruit and nuts. Pour dry ingredients on top and stir until well combined. Without delay, spoon into baking pan, spreading evenly with a rubber spatula.

6. Bake for 25 to 30 minutes or until set. Remove pan to a wire rack to cool completely. Lift up foil and remove from pan.

7. Sift the powdered sugar, cinnamon, and coriander into a small bowl. Sprinkle half the mixture over the panforte. Invert on a cutting board, peel off the foil, and sprinkle with the remaining spicy mixture. Using a sharp knife, cut into 1½-inch-square pieces. To make cutting the panforte easier and less sticky, wipe the knife between each cut with a paper towel saturated with unflavored vegetable oil.

8. Store in an airtight sturdy plastic or metal container for several months.

BAKING NOTE

• It is best to use edible rice paper to line the baking pan. If it is not available to you, you can peel away the greased and floured foil from the confection after it is completely cool, even though it is slightly sticky.

Panforte di Siena

Macaroon Trios

These cookies, easy to make quickly when time is limited, begin as clusters of three small dots of batter, which form Macaroon Trios' interesting shape after baking. Laden with a generous amount of almonds and pine nuts, these macaroons are reminiscent of Italian specialty macaroons. It's better to underbake rather than overbake them, to preserve a moist, chewy center and a nutty flavor.

BATTER

¾ cup (150 grams) granulated sugar

8 ounces (1⅓ cups) unblanched almonds, toasted and finely ground (see Baking Note)

⅓ cup (about 3 large) egg whites

1 teaspoon vanilla

¼ teaspoon almond extract

⅛ teaspoon salt

2½ ounces (½ cup) pine nuts

1. Adjust rack to lower third of oven and preheat oven to 325 degrees. Line two large cool baking sheets with parchment paper.

2. In a medium bowl, blend the sugar and the almonds briefly with a wire whisk. Pour the egg whites, flavorings, and salt over the dry ingredients, then stir just to blend together. Using a 14-inch pastry bag fitted with a ½-inch plain decorating tip (such as Ateco #6), pipe clusters of three small dots of batter, each dot about ½ inch in diameter. Space clusters about 1 inch apart. Sprinkle the pine nuts over macaroons. Gently tap macaroons with a damp pastry brush to flatten points left from piping and to secure the pine nuts in the batter.

3. Bake, one sheet at a time, for 13 to 15 minutes or until macaroons are blond and the pine nuts are golden.

4. Remove baking sheet from the oven. Lift parchment paper with macaroons to a wire rack to cool completely. The macaroons stick to the parchment while warm but when completely cool, they lift off the parchment easily.

5. Macaroons are best eaten the same day baked. Stack in airtight sturdy plastic containers and store at room temperature up to 2 days; or freeze, up to 10 days.

BAKING NOTE

• The important factor in this recipe is to begin with 2 cups finely ground almonds in order for the cookies to bake full in shape with a chewy texture. The food processor yields 2 cups finely ground almonds from 8 ounces unblanched almonds, while other nut grinders, such as electric ones, produce 2 cups finely ground almonds from 6 ounces (1 cup) unblanched almonds.

Macaroon Trios

Glazed Almond Weave

Toasted whole almonds, coated in a light honey glaze, weave into a close-fitting pattern over a buttery crust during baking. Any time you serve these stunning cookies, I guarantee you're showing off one of the best pastries you can make.

DOUGH

2 cups (280 grams) unsifted all-purpose flour

½ cup (100 grams) granulated sugar

⅛ teaspoon salt

6 ounces (1½ sticks) unsalted butter, room temperature, cut into ½-inch slices

1 large egg

1 teaspoon vanilla

TOPPING

½ cup (4 ounces) heavy cream

2 ounces (½ stick) unsalted butter

¼ cup honey

1 cup (200 grams) granulated sugar

1 pound (scant 3 cups) blanched almonds

1. Adjust rack to lower third of oven and preheat oven to 375 degrees.

2. Put the flour, sugar, and salt in a food processor bowl. Process just to blend the ingredients. Add the butter pieces all at once, and process with on/off bursts until the mixture has the consistency of cornmeal.

3. Whisk the egg and vanilla together in a small bowl. With the motor on, pour egg mixture down the feed tube. Process just until the ingredients form a ball.

4. Divide dough into eight pieces and scatter them over an ungreased 10- × 15- × 1-inch cool baking pan. With floured fingertips, pat the dough to extend the portions to cover the pan as evenly as possible.

5. Bake for 12 to 13 minutes or until crust appears set and is ivory-colored. After 5 minutes, check the dough for any lifting; if so, prick the spot(s) with a skewer to release the trapped air. When crust is set, remove it from the oven. Reduce the oven temperature to 350 degrees.

6. Topping: Combine the cream, butter, honey, and sugar in a heavy-bottomed 1½-quart saucepan. Heat over medium-low heat, stirring occasionally, until the sugar is dissolved and the butter is melted. Raise the heat to medium high, and boil the mixture until it registers 235 degrees (soft-ball stage) on a mercury candy thermometer, about 6 minutes. Off heat, stir in the almonds. Pour over crust; return crust to the oven. Bake for 15 to 17 minutes or just until the nuts are golden.

7. Place baking pan on a wire rack to cool and allow the topping to firm. With a ruler and a sharp paring knife, cut into 1- x 2½-inch sticks.

8. After cutting, cover baking pan with aluminum foil and store for up to 4 days at room temperature. Seal the foil around the rim of the pan without letting the foil touch the topping's shiny surface.

BAKING NOTE

- The dough is best made in the food processor. Besides making the dough quickly, the processor distributes the fat throughout the mixture without aerating dough too much.

Glazed Almond
Weave

95

Viennese Triangles

These Old World bar cookies, rich with almonds and a hint of spice and jam, tantalize even the most sophisticated palates. No one would guess that another appealing feature of these cookies is that this is an ideal recipe for using leftover egg whites.

DOUGH

2 cups (280 grams) unsifted all-purpose flour

1/2 cup (100 grams) granulated sugar

1/8 teaspoon salt

6 ounces (1 1/2 sticks) unsalted butter, room temperature, cut into 1/2-inch slices

1 large egg

1 teaspoon vanilla

TOPPING

1/3 cup seedless raspberry jam

3/4 cup (about 6 large) egg whites

6 1/2 ounces (2 1/2 cups) sliced almonds, toasted

1 1/2 cups (300 grams) granulated sugar

3 tablespoons all-purpose flour

1 teaspoon ground cinnamon

1 tablespoon light corn syrup

1/2 teaspoon almond extract

1/4 teaspoon baking powder

DARK CHOCOLATE SATIN GLAZE

1/4 cup (1 1/2 ounces) vegetable shortening

1 pound semisweet chocolate, chopped

1. Adjust rack to lower third of oven and preheat oven to 350 degrees.

2. Put the flour, sugar, and salt in a food processor bowl. Process just to blend the ingredients. Add the butter pieces all at once, and process with on/off bursts until the mixture has the consistency of cornmeal.

3. Whisk the egg and vanilla together in a small bowl. With the motor on, pour egg mixture down the feed tube. Process just until the ingredients form a ball.

4. Divide dough into eight pieces and scatter them over an ungreased 10- × 15- × 1-inch cool baking pan. With floured fingertips, pat the dough to extend the portions to cover the pan as evenly as possible.

5. Topping: Spread a thin layer of raspberry jam over the unbaked dough. In a 2½-quart heavy-bottomed saucepan, combine the remaining filling ingredients except the almond extract and baking powder. Stirring constantly over very low heat, bring mixture to a boil. Still stirring, allow mixture to cook for 3 to 4 minutes or until it registers 180 to 190 degrees on a mercury candy thermometer. Stir constantly to prevent any scorching. Remove from the heat and stir in the extract and baking powder.

6. Without delay, pour over unbaked crust, spreading it evenly. Bake for 20 minutes or until golden brown. Place on a wire rack to cool completely before cutting.

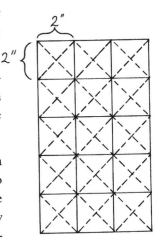

7. Using a ruler as a guide and a small sharp paring knife, cut into 2-inch-wide strips. Then cut across each strip diagonally in alternate directions to form 2-inch triangular-shaped bars. Cut these triangles in half to form 1-inch bite-size triangles.

8. Dark Chocolate Satin Glaze: Combine the shortening and chocolate in a 3-quart bowl. Place it over a saucepan filled with enough hot tap water (120 to 130 degrees) to reach the bottom of the bowl. Stir mixture occasionally until the glaze is liquid and smooth and registers close to 110 degrees on a mercury candy thermometer. If water cools while melting the chocolate, maintain the water's 120-degree temperature over very low heat.

9. Dip just the edges of each triangle in the chocolate glaze. Put the coated cookies on a strip of aluminum foil in a cool room until the chocolate sets.

10. Store in a covered foil-lined cardboard box, such as a cake box, at room temperature up to 4 days.

Viennese Triangles

- Dipping the edges into chocolate is decorative, adds flavor, and holds any crumbs from the cookie base in place.

Pecan Diamonds

Treat yourself to mouth-watering bar cookies of crunchy pecans covered with creamy, honey-flavored, brown sugar caramel on a butter crust. This luscious topping is an adaptation of a recipe given to me by Myrtle Singer of Manalapan, Florida.

DOUGH

- 2 cups (280 grams) unsifted all-purpose flour
- ½ cup (100 grams) granulated sugar
- ⅛ teaspoon salt
- 6 ounces (1½ sticks) unsalted butter, room temperature, cut into ½-inch slices
- 1 large egg
- 1 teaspoon vanilla

TOPPING

- 8 ounces (2 sticks) unsalted butter
- ½ cup honey
- ¼ cup (50 grams) granulated sugar
- 1¼ cups (250 grams) light brown sugar, packed
- ¼ cup heavy cream
- 8 ounces (2 cups) whole pecans
- 8 ounces (2 cups) whole pecans, coarsely chopped
- 1 teaspoon finely grated orange zest

1. Adjust rack to lower third of oven and preheat oven to 375 degrees.

2. Put the flour, sugar, and salt in a food processor bowl. Process just to blend the ingredients. Add the butter pieces all at once, and process with on/off bursts until the mixture has the consistency of cornmeal.

3. Whisk the egg and vanilla together in a small bowl. With the motor on, pour egg mixture down the feed tube. Process just until the ingredients form a ball.

4. Divide dough into eight pieces and scatter them over an ungreased 10- × 15- × 1-inch cool baking pan. With floured fingertips, pat the dough to extend the portions to cover the pan as evenly as possible.

5. Bake for 10 minutes. Don't allow the dough to color. Remove from oven. Reduce oven temperature to 350 degrees.

6. Topping: Combine the butter, honey, and sugars in a heavy-bottomed 1½-quart saucepan. Heat over medium-low heat until butter melts; then raise heat to medium and bring mixture to a boil. Without stirring, allow mixture to boil only 1 minute. Off heat, stir in the cream, nuts, and zest. Pour over bottom crust; return crust to oven. Bake for 30 to 35 minutes or until the topping is an amber color. Topping will bubble toward the end of baking.

7. Place on a wire rack to cool to allow the topping to firm before cutting. Using a ruler as a guide and a small paring knife, make marks at 2-inch intervals on the long sides and 1½-inch intervals on the short sides. Cut along the diagonals as shown in the illustration to form diamond-shaped bars.

8. After cutting, cover baking pan with aluminum foil and store up to 4 days at room temperature. Seal the foil around the rim of the pan without letting the foil touch and disrupt the topping's glossy shiny surface.

BAKING NOTE

- Mild-tasting clover and light, delicate, citrus-tasting orange blossom honeys are best suited for baking since their flavors will enhance rather than overpower the baked items. But if you're partial to another variety of honey, feel free to use it in this recipe.

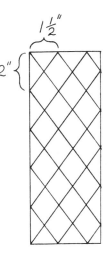

Pecan
Diamonds

99

Swiss Japonais

Swiss Japonais (pronounced zhah-po-nay), two almond meringue disks filled and frosted with a praline buttercream, then coated with meringue dust, makes an incredibly delicious two bites.

JAPONAIS MERINGUE

2 ounces (¹/₃ cup) unblanched almonds, finely ground

¼ cup (50 grams) granulated sugar

²/₃ cup (5 large) egg whites, room temperature

2 tablespoons granulated sugar

²/₃ cup (130 grams) granulated sugar

DECORATION
Praline

½ cup (100 grams) granulated sugar

1 ounce (2 tablespoons) whole blanched almonds, roasted

1 ounce (2 tablespoons) whole hazelnuts, roasted and most skins removed

Praline Buttercream

4 egg yolks

¼ cup water

½ cup (100 grams) granulated sugar

8 ounces (2 sticks) unsalted butter, room temperature

1 recipe Praline Powder (page 102)

1. Adjust one rack to lower third of oven and second rack to upper third; preheat oven to 225 degrees. Line two large cool baking sheets with parchment paper to fit. Trace 1½-inch-diameter circles on the parchment with a pencil, using a cutter as a guide; cover both sheets with circles, spacing circles about ¼ inch

apart. Fit a 16-inch pastry bag with a ¹/₂-inch plain decorating tip (such as Ateco #6).

2. In a small bowl, blend the ground nuts and the ¹/₄ cup sugar briefly with a wire whisk; set aside. Using an electric mixer, preferably with a whisk attachment, whip the egg whites in a large mixing bowl on low speed for 30 seconds or until the surface is frothy. Increase speed to medium, pour in the 2 tablespoons sugar, and continue whipping until soft peaks form, 45 seconds.

3. Maintaining medium speed, add the ²/₃ cup sugar in a steady stream. Continue whipping until a small amount rubbed between your thumb and forefinger feels smooth, not granular, about 2 minutes. Tap whisk against the side of the bowl. Sprinkle the almond-sugar mixture over the meringue, and, using a rubber spatula, fold the two together.

4. Scoop all the mixture into the pastry bag. Pipe spirals to fit the traced circles on the parchment. Bake for 60 to 75 minutes, or until spiral disks are flat, lightly colored, and dry. As they cool, they will crisp. Remove one meringue from oven as a sample to test if drying time in oven is enough. Place baking sheet on a wire rack to cool. Gently lift meringues from parchment when cool.

5. Praline: Lightly grease a baking sheet with vegetable oil. Place the sugar in a 1¹/₂-quart heavy-bottomed saucepan or 10-inch skillet. Place over low heat until sugar dissolves; swirl to distribute the heat evenly. When sugar has dissolved, raise the heat to medium-high and cook until the melted sugar reaches an amber color, about 8 to 10 minutes. Pour in the nuts, remove from heat, and swirl; then pour out onto the baking sheet. Set aside to cool and firm for about 1 hour.

6. Crumble enough of the meringue disks to make 1¹/₂ cups of fine crumbs. You can grind them through a nut mill or chop with a chef's knife on a cutting board. Put the crumbs on a plate.

Swiss Japonais

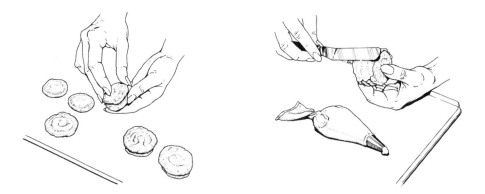

7. Match the remaining disks to make pairs: The base of the bottom disk is the flat baked surface, while the disk on top has its baked flat side up. Gently rub the curved sides of each pair together to ensure a more even, level fit. Place each matched pair on a baking sheet.

8. Praline Buttercream: In the large bowl of an electric mixer, whip the egg yolks until light and fluffy, about 4 minutes. Remove bowl from mixer stand. Combine the water and sugar in a 1-quart saucepan over low heat. Stir occasionally, washing down any crystals clinging to the sides of the pan with a brush dipped in cold water, until the sugar is dissolved. Increase the heat and cook syrup, without stirring, until it reaches 238 degrees on a mercury candy thermometer. Pour into the center of the yolks and quickly whisk vigorously to combine. Return bowl to mixer, and whip at medium speed until the egg yolk mixture thickens and cools to body temperature, about 5 minutes. Maintaining speed, add the butter to the cooled mixture, 2 tablespoons at a time. Continue mixing until all the butter has been incorporated and the buttercream is smooth and homogeneous.

9. Praline Powder: Break the cool, firm praline into small pieces, and place them in food processor bowl. Process until the praline has the consistency of fine crumbs. Pour crumbs through a sieve to strain out any larger lumps. Stir $1/2$ cup praline powder into the buttercream and store the remaining powder in an airtight container at room temperature for another use.

10. Using a pastry bag fitted with a $1/4$-inch plain decorating tip (such as Ateco #2), pipe a scant teaspoon of the buttercream, spiral fashion, on top of

each bottom disk. Fit the top disk on the buttercream, and press it gently to level. Then refrigerate the sandwiched disks for about 30 to 60 minutes, just to firm the buttercream to facilitate handling when you frost them. Set the filled pastry bag aside at room temperature.

11. To frost the Japonais, stack one on top of another, and pipe about 3 or 4 rows of buttercream around the outside of the two sandwiched pastries. Using a small flexible metal icing spatula, smooth the buttercream around them in a thin layer. Then roll them in the meringue crumbs, wheel fashion, as illustrated. Put them back on the baking sheet, separating the two.

12. Any excess buttercream left on the spatula after smoothing sides of Japonais may be used to refill the pastry bag as necessary. After frosting and coating the pastries, return the baking sheet to the refrigerator again to firm the buttercream around the Japonais, about 30 minutes.

13. Pipe a spiral of buttercream on top of each Japonais; sprinkle it with meringue crumbs, and press lightly so they adhere. Finish each pastry by piping a small dot of buttercream on top for decoration. Return the baking sheet with the Japonais to the refrigerator to firm the buttercream, then cover the sheet with plastic wrap.

14. Stack undecorated disks in an airtight metal container and store at room temperature up to 3 days. The decorated Japonais are best served the next day; or freeze, well wrapped, in an airtight plastic container up to 1 week.

TECHNIQUE NOTE

• This recipe illustrates several time-saving techniques of assembling, filling, frosting, and coating round petits fours whether meringue disks, short dough, or cake. See step 11 in the recipe.

STORING NOTE

• During overnight storage in the refrigerator, the crisp Japonais meringue disks absorb moisture from the buttercream, thereby softening the disks to a pleasant chewy consistency.

Swiss Japonais

Maple Japonais

An alternative to the traditional meringue sandwich with praline buttercream, these pastries are given an American twist with maple syrup. These crisp, cloud-like cookies, blended with ground almonds, and layered with chocolate ganache and maple syrup whipped cream, are a lighter, somewhat chewy version of the Swiss Japonais. This recipe was inspired by a dessert that pastry chef Phil Ogiela serves at Restaurant 231 Ellsworth, in San Mateo, California.

JAPONAIS MERINGUE

- 2 ounces (⅓ cup) unblanched almonds, finely ground
- ¼ cup (50 grams) granulated sugar
- ⅔ cup (5 large) egg whites, room temperature

- 2 tablespoons granulated sugar
- ⅔ cup (130 grams) granulated sugar

CHOCOLATE BUTTER GANACHE

- 6 ounces semisweet chocolate, chopped
- ½ cup (4 ounces) heavy cream

- 1½ ounces (3 tablespoons) unsalted butter, soft

MAPLE FILLING

- ⅓ cup pure maple syrup

- 2 cups (1 pint) heavy cream

DECORATION

- ½ cup (50 grams) unsifted powdered sugar

1. Adjust one rack to lower third of oven and second rack to upper third, and preheat oven to 225 degrees. Line two large cool baking sheets with parchment paper. Trace 1½-inch-diameter circles on the parchment with a pencil, using

a cutter as a guide; cover both sheets with circles, spacing circles about ¼ inch apart. Fit a 16-inch pastry bag with a ½-inch plain decorating tip (such as Ateco #6).

2. In a small bowl, blend the ground nuts and the ¼ cup sugar briefly with a wire whisk; set aside. Using an electric mixer, preferably with a whisk attachment, whip the egg whites in a large mixing bowl on low speed for 30 seconds or until the surface is frothy. Increase speed to medium, gradually add the 2 tablespoons sugar, and continue whipping until soft peaks form, about 45 seconds.

3. Maintaining medium speed, add the ⅔ cup sugar in a steady stream. Continue whipping until a small amount rubbed between your thumb and forefinger feels smooth, not granular, about 2 minutes. Tap whisk against the side of the bowl. Sprinkle the almond-sugar mixture over the meringue, and, using a rubber spatula, fold the two together.

4. Scoop all the mixture into the pastry bag. Pipe spirals to fit the traced circles on the parchment. Bake for 60 to 75 minutes, or until spiral disks are flat, lightly colored, and dry. As they cool, they crisp. Remove one meringue from oven as a sample to test if drying time in oven is enough. Place baking sheet on a wire rack to cool. Gently lift off meringues from parchment when cool.

5. Chocolate Butter Ganache: Put the chocolate in a large bowl. In a small saucepan, heat the cream just to the boil. Pour over the chocolate, and stir until completely dissolved. Whisk in the butter until smooth and glossy. Set aside until ganache is cool and begins to take some shape when lifted with a spoon.

6. In a small saucepan, boil the maple syrup until reduced to ¼ cup. Refrigerate until cool.

7. Match the disks to make pairs: The base of the bottom disk is the flat baked surface, and the disk on top has its baked flat side up. Gently rub the curved sides of each pair together to ensure a more even, level fit. Place each matched pair on a clean baking sheet.

8. Using a pastry bag fitted with a ½-inch plain decorating tip (such as Ateco #6), pipe a chocolate ganache dot in the center of each bottom disk.

Maple Japonais

9. Blend the chilled maple syrup with the heavy cream; whip until soft peaks form. Using a pastry bag fitted with a ¼-inch plain decorating tip (such as Ateco #2), pipe it, spiral fashion, on top of each bottom disk around the chocolate. Fit the top disk on the chocolate and whipped cream, and press it gently to level.

10. With one hand, stack two pastries together between your forefinger and thumb. With the other hand, using a small flexible metal icing spatula, smooth the whipped cream around them in a thin layer. Put them back on the baking sheet, separating the two. Sprinkle tops with the powdered sugar.

11. These are best eaten the same day.

Maple Japonais

Crispy Miniatures

Tuiles

What I like best about these crispy thin cookies is that their delicate texture and subtle nutty flavor do not overpower but instead complement any fruit, fresh or poached.

BATTER

- ⅓ cup (about 3 large) egg whites
- ½ cup (100 grams) granulated sugar
- ⅓ cup (45 grams) unsifted all-purpose flour

- 2½ ounces (5 tablespoons) unsalted butter, melted and cooled to lukewarm
- 1 teaspoon vanilla
- 2 ounces (⅔ cup) sliced almonds, preferably blanched

1. Adjust rack to lower third of oven and preheat oven to 325 degrees. Unwrap an end of a chilled stick of unsalted butter and rub it over two large cool Teflon-coated baking sheets to apply a very thin film of fat.

2. In a large mixing bowl, whisk the whites with the sugar just until foamy, about 30 seconds. Whisk in the flour, and then the butter and vanilla until well blended.

3. Drop teaspoonsful of batter 1½ inches apart on a baking sheet. Rap the baking sheet on the work surface to spread the batter slightly. Sprinkle a few sliced almonds on each disk.

4. Bake, one sheet at a time, 8 minutes or just until the edges are golden with ivory-colored centers. Place baking sheet on a wire rack to cool for only 15 seconds. With a metal spatula, lift the cookies one at a time, and lay over a rolling pin to curve each cookie while it is still pliable. Cookies crisp as they cool.

5. Repeat the baking and shaping process with the remaining batter.

6. Stack in an airtight metal container and store at room temperature up to 1 week. Keep tuiles in container until serving since they are very susceptible to any moisture in the air. See Storage Containers in the equipment section (page 12).

Florentine Squares

I love these crunchy, candy-like cookies so much that often I don't even coat them with chocolate, though it really is an important feature. Without sacrificing any of their rich flavor, it's easier to decorate them with just a few zigzags of chocolate. If you want to follow tradition, add finely grated zest or small pieces of candied orange peel to the mixture before baking.

BATTER

⅓ cup heavy cream

2½ tablespoons light corn syrup

¾ cup (150 grams) granulated sugar

3 ounces (3 tablespoons) unsalted butter

5 ounces (1½ cups) sliced almonds

DECORATION

4 ounces semisweet chocolate, finely chopped

1. Adjust rack to lower third of oven and preheat oven to 400 degrees. Line a 12- × 15½- × ½-inch baking sheet with aluminum foil, leaving a 2-inch overhang at each short end.

2. Pour the cream, corn syrup, and sugar into a 1½-quart heavy-bottomed saucepan. Stir to combine, then add the butter. Stir over medium-low heat until the butter melts. Then raise the heat to medium, and stir constantly with a wooden spoon—especially toward the end of cooking—to prevent scorching. Cook until the mixture reaches 238 degrees, the soft-ball stage, on a mercury candy thermometer, about 10 minutes; the mixture will appear between ivory- and straw-colored. Remove from heat, and stir in the almonds.

3. Pour the mixture onto the center of the foil-lined baking sheet, and spread it in as thin a layer as possible. A pool about 8 inches in diameter is fine. Bake for 3 minutes; then spread the more liquid mixture evenly over the baking sheet.

If the mixture still does not completely cover the baking sheet, bake another minute, then tilt the baking sheet to allow the mixture to spread evenly. Bake for about 5 to 6 minutes total, or until golden but not dark brown. Though the mixture bubbles while baking, the bubbles form more slowly toward the end of the baking time than at the beginning.

4. Place baking sheet on a wire rack and cool for 2 to 3 minutes. While the mixture is still warm but no longer liquid, cut 1½-inch squares using a ruler and pastry wheel. If the mixture is too warm, it will not cut cleanly. If it is too cool, it will splinter or not cut; in that case return it to the oven for a few seconds to soften it a bit.

5. When the squares are completely cool, melt the chocolate in a bowl set over water at approximately 120 degrees. Fill a small handmade paper cone with chocolate and snip off the tip. Pipe thin lines of chocolate back and forth over the squares' surface. Set aside in a cool, dry place until chocolate sets.

6. Remove squares from the foil and store them in an airtight metal container at room temperature up to 1 week.

VARIATION NOTE

- Using a food processor, whirl the baked Florentine Squares (without any chocolate decoration) to make coarse or fine crumbs. Then sprinkle these crumbs over unbaked cookies, or even fill cutouts in cookies with them before baking. These bits and pieces can also be incorporated in cookie doughs before slicing and baking.

Florentine
Squares

Black Walnut Genoise Wafers

Makes 3 dozen
1³/₄-inch
sandwiches

The batter for these thin nutty cookies, crispy outside, soft and chewy inside, reminds me of a genoise that you bake in cookie form. Black walnuts have a distinctive taste, more dominant and pungent than the English walnut.

BATTER

¹/₃ cup (45 grams) unsifted all-purpose flour

¹/₈ teaspoon salt

2 large eggs

1 cup (200 grams) light brown sugar, packed

4 ounces (1 scant cup) black walnuts, finely chopped (see Baking Note)

FILLING

3 ounces white chocolate, finely chopped

1. Adjust rack to the lower third of the oven and preheat oven to 375 degrees. Grease and flour two large baking sheets, tapping out excess flour.

2. Blend the flour and salt briefly in a small bowl with a wire whisk; set aside. In the large bowl of an electric mixer, preferably with a whisk attachment, whip the eggs and sugar at medium speed until mixture is thick and taupe-colored, about 3 minutes. Batter should still flow freely when the beaters are lifted. Avoid whipping the mixture too thick or stiff, or the baked result will be a crisp rather than a chewy texture. Now, with a rubber spatula, fold in the salted flour, then the nuts.

3. Spoon or pipe, using a 16-inch pastry bag fitted with a ⁵/₈-inch plain decorating tip (such as Ateco #8), rounded ¹/₂ teaspoonsful of batter on baking sheets, placing them 1¹/₂ inches apart to leave space for spreading while baking.

4. Bake, one sheet at a time, for about 4 minutes or until lightly browned around the edges. Cookies puff at the beginning of baking but deflate toward the

end. Do not overbake. Place baking sheet on a wire rack to cool 2 minutes only. With a metal spatula, transfer the cookies to another wire rack to cool completely.

5. Turn half the cooled cookies baked-bottom side up on a clean baking sheet. In a small bowl, melt chocolate over water at approximately 110 degrees. Using a small handmade paper cone, its tip snipped off, pipe a dot of white chocolate similar in size to a chocolate chip in the center of each disk. Place remaining cookie disks on top, baked-bottom side down, to form pairs.

6. With a rubber spatula, spread the remaining melted white chocolate over a sheet of aluminum foil into a layer about $\frac{1}{8}$ inch deep. Roll each sandwiched cookie in the chocolate, wheel fashion, just to coat the edge. Place on a clean baking sheet as each cookie is decorated. Refrigerate on the baking sheet just long enough to set the white chocolate, about 10 minutes.

7. These are best when eaten the same day baked; or freeze, stacked in an airtight sturdy plastic container, up to 1 week.

BAKING NOTE

- Because the nuts provide structure as well as flavor in this recipe, it is important to measure the chopped nut pieces as accurately as possible. With a food processor, through variations of brand, speed, blade, timing, and force, you can grind a given weight of whole or even coarsely chopped nuts into widely varying volumes of chopped nuts. A nut mill grinds nuts into the same volume every time, so for this recipe use a nut mill to chop the nuts to yield 1 cup. See How to Measure Nuts (page 6).

Black Walnut Genoise Wafers

Ladies' Wafers

Makes 7 dozen
1½-inch cookies

Flavored with cognac and tiny currants, these classic coin-sized French cookies, known as Palets de Dames, sparkle after a light brushing with a sugar glaze.

BATTER

1¾ ounces (⅓ cup) dried currants

1 tablespoon cognac

1 cup (140 grams) unsifted all-purpose flour

⅛ teaspoon salt

4 ounces (1 stick) unsalted butter, room temperature

⅔ cup (130 grams) granulated sugar

3 large eggs, room temperature

1 teaspoon vanilla

COGNAC SUGAR GLAZE

½ cup (50 grams) unsifted powdered sugar

4 teaspoons cognac

1. Adjust rack to lower third of oven and preheat oven to 375 degrees. Unwrap an end of a chilled stick of unsalted butter and rub it over three large cool baking sheets, preferably Teflon-coated, to apply a very thin film of fat.

2. Toss the currants with the cognac in a small bowl; set aside. Briefly blend the flour and the salt in another bowl; set aside.

3. In a large bowl of an electric mixer, cream the butter at medium-low speed until creamy, about 1 minute. Increase to medium speed and beat in the sugar until the mixture is light and fluffy. Add the eggs, one at a time, scraping down the sides of the bowl. Add the vanilla and continue mixing until mixture is smooth. Reduce to low speed, and add all the flour mixture at once, blending just until smooth. With a rubber spatula, stir in the macerated currants.

4. Using a 16-inch pastry bag fitted with a ½-inch plain decorating tip (such as Ateco #6), pipe small mounds about 1 inch in diameter and 1½ inches apart on baking sheets.

5. Bake, one sheet at a time, just until the edges are golden brown with ivory-colored centers, about 10 minutes. Place baking sheet on a wire rack and decorate while warm. Reduce oven temperature to 200 degrees.

6. Cognac Sugar Glaze: Mix the sugar and cognac together until smooth. With a pastry brush, apply a thin coating of glaze to each cookie. Return the cookies, one baking sheet at a time, to the oven for about 3 to 4 minutes or until the glaze is set. Using a metal spatula, remove cookies to a wire rack to cool.

7. Stack in an airtight metal container and store at room temperature up to 1 week.

VARIATION NOTE

• For a contemporary touch, substitute dried cherries or dried cranberries for the currants and kirsch for the cognac in the sugar glaze. Using a chef's knife, chop them coarsely on a cutting board before adding them to the batter.

Ladies' Wafers

Cognac Wafers

These simple but sophisticated cookies are perfect at the end of the meal, either alone with a cup of coffee or served three on a plate with fresh blackberries and ollalie berries. Light, crisp wafers are layered with tiny dots of cognac buttercream to create a glamorous miniature.

BATTER

⅓ cup (about 3 large) egg whites

½ cup (100 grams) granulated sugar

⅓ cup (45 grams) unsifted all-purpose flour

2½ ounces (5 tablespoons) unsalted butter, melted and cooled to lukewarm

1 teaspoon vanilla

COGNAC BUTTERCREAM FILLING

2 egg yolks

2 tablespoons water

¼ cup (50 grams) granulated sugar

4 ounces (1 stick) unsalted butter, room temperature

1 tablespoon cognac

DECORATION

¼ cup (25 grams) unsifted powdered sugar

1. Adjust rack to lower third of oven and preheat oven to 325 degrees. Unwrap an end of a chilled stick of unsalted butter and rub it over two large cool Teflon-coated baking sheets to apply a very thin film of fat.

2. In a large mixing bowl, using an electric mixer on medium speed, whisk the egg whites with the sugar just until foamy, about 1 minute. Maintaining the same speed, whisk in the flour, scraping mixture down the sides of the bowl. Add the butter and vanilla and whisk until well blended.

3. Drop about twelve ½ teaspoonsful of batter 1½ inches apart on the baking sheet. Rap the baking sheet on the work surface to spread the batter slightly.

4. Bake, one sheet at a time, about 8 minutes or just until the edges are golden with ivory-colored centers. Place baking sheet on a wire rack and cool just 5 seconds. With a metal spatula, remove wafers to a rack to cool. If wafers are too crisp to remove from the baking sheet, return to the oven for a few seconds to soften again.

5. Repeat the baking and shaping process with the remaining batter.

6. Cognac Buttercream: Using an electric mixer, whip the yolks in a medium bowl until light and fluffy, about 4 minutes. Combine the water and the sugar in a 1-quart heavy saucepan over low heat. Stir occasionally, washing down any sugar crystals clinging to the sides of the pan with a brush dipped in cold water, until the sugar is dissolved. Increase the heat and cook the syrup, without stirring, until it reaches 238 degrees on a mercury candy thermometer. Pour into the center of the egg yolks and quickly whisk vigorously to combine. Continue mixing at medium speed until the egg yolk mixture thickens and cools to body temperature, about 5 minutes. At same speed, add the butter, 2 tablespoons at a time. Continue mixing until all the butter has been incorporated and the buttercream is smooth and homogeneous. Whip in cognac until smooth.

7. Set two-thirds of the cookies, baked-bottom side up, on a large clean baking sheet. Using a handmade paper cone, its tip snipped off, pipe tiny dots of cognac buttercream similar in size to a chocolate chip in the center of each disk. Put one cookie on top of another, then place a plain cookie on top; press each stack gently to spread the buttercream evenly between the cookie layers. Finish the cookies with a light dusting of the powdered sugar.

8. Stack undecorated cookies in an airtight metal container and store at room temperature up to 3 days. Store decorated cookies in one layer in a covered foil-lined cardboard container, such as a cake box, at room temperature up to 1 day.

Cognac Wafers

$\mathcal{C}$*igarettes*

What I especially like about this batter is that you can bake it in any shape and size you wish: cones, cups, cigars, cylinders, cigarettes, or cornucopias. When I wanted to mark a milestone birthday for my husband, I fashioned cigar-shaped cookies from this classic batter as one of the grand finale desserts. Stacked on a large silver tray, the faux cigars had slender cellophane strips tucked into one end to simulate smoke. Similar to a fortune cookie, each rolled cookie had a narrow strip of paper with a humorous quote about aging from such notables as Miss Piggy and Bernard Baruch inside it.

BATTER

7 tablespoons (100 grams) unsalted butter, room temperature

1¼ cups (125 grams) unsifted powdered sugar

½ cup (about 4 large) egg whites, room temperature

12 tablespoons (100 grams) unsifted all-purpose flour

1. Adjust rack to lower third of oven and preheat oven to 350 degrees. Unwrap an end of a chilled stick of unsalted butter and rub it over two large cool Teflon-coated baking sheets to apply a very thin film of fat.

2. In the large bowl of an electric mixer, cream the butter at medium speed until it has the consistency of mayonnaise. Add the powdered sugar, 2 tablespoons at a time, and beat until each addition of sugar is absorbed by the butter before you add more. Whip until light and fluffy.

3. Maintaining the same speed, gradually add the egg whites. Wait for each portion of whites to be incorporated before adding the next. Last, add the vanilla. Don't worry if the mixture appears curdled at this point. Lower speed and add the flour, combining thoroughly.

4. Drop 3 or 4 teaspoonsful of batter on each baking sheet. Using a small offset metal spatula, spread each mound into paper-thin squares approximately

$1\frac{1}{2} \times 1\frac{1}{2}$ inches. Bake for 2 to 3 minutes, or until pale gold. Remove baking sheet from oven to a wire rack. Turn each cookie over with a spatula, and quickly roll, baked-bottom side in, around a chopstick or wooden dowel 6 inches long and $\frac{3}{8}$ inch in diameter. Remove from the wooden form to another wire rack until cool. If the cookies become too brittle to shape, return them to the oven just until they soften, a few seconds.

5. Repeat the baking and shaping process with the remaining batter.

6. Stack in an airtight metal container and store at room temperature up to 1 week.

SHAPING NOTE

- Here's a way to make a reusable template for easily shaping the batter uniformly, quickly, and efficiently: With a pencil or felt pen, trace a form such as a circle, triangle, or butterfly on the surface of a thin plastic lid from a storage container similar to those used to cover nuts and cheese. Use a utility knife to cut out the shape you traced. Trim the outside edge from the lid.

  To use the stencil, drop a teaspoon of batter inside it and using a small offset metal spatula, spread the batter across it. Lift the stencil and continue shaping cookies on baking sheet as recipe specifies. When you're finished shaping a batch of cookies, simply wash and dry the stencil.

Cigarettes

Nougatine Cones

These thin lacy wafers, rolled into tiny cones while hot from the oven, make perfect receptacles for chocolate ganache or coffee buttercream. When I want a simpler, less rich cookie, I dip just the edges of the cone's wide end in melted chocolate.

BATTER

2 ounces (4 tablespoons) unsalted butter

¼ cup light corn syrup

¼ cup (50 grams) granulated sugar

4 ounces (¾ cup) hazelnuts, chopped medium fine to yield ¾ cup (see Baking Note)

¼ cup (35 grams) unsifted all-purpose flour

1. Adjust rack to lower third of oven and preheat oven to 350 degrees. Unwrap an end of a chilled stick of unsalted butter and rub it over two large cool Teflon-coated baking sheets to apply a very thin film of fat.

2. Put the butter, corn syrup, and sugar in a 1-quart heavy-bottomed sauce-pan. Stir over low heat until the butter is melted. Remove from the heat, and stir in the nuts and flour.

3. Drop five or six ½ teaspoonsful of batter 1½ inches apart on each baking sheet. A quick and easy method is to pipe the soft dough from a 14-inch pastry bag fitted with a ½-inch plain decorating tip (such as Ateco #6). Bake, one sheet at a time, for 6 to 7 minutes, or until golden brown. While baking, the cookies bubble; a clue that they are finished baking is when the bubbling subsides.

4. Place baking sheet on a wire rack to cool for just 15 seconds. With a metal spatula, lift one wafer at a time and roll it around a wooden cornet to shape the cookie while it is still flexible. Remove cone from the form, and place it on a wire rack to cool; continue rolling the remaining cookies.

5. Repeat the baking and shaping process with the remaining batter.

6. When the cookies are cool and firm, stack them in an airtight metal container and store at room temperature up to 1 week.

BAKING NOTES

- Hazelnuts or almonds, blanched or unblanched, are fine for this cookie. If you prefer the flavor of toasted nuts, put them on a baking sheet in a 325-degree preheated oven for about 10 minutes or until pale gold.
- See How to Measure Nuts (page 6).

SERVING NOTE

- For entertaining, I bake tiny 1-inch wafers without rolling them. Before serving, pipe a dramatic rosette of whipped cream in the center of each dessert plate; then, stick several wafers in the cream, rose petal–fashion.

Nougatine Cones

Miniature Krumkake

These crunchy cone-shaped cookies, with their embossed pattern, bake one at a time in cookie irons. These irons, traditional in Italy, Norway, and France, have a variety of names—*cialde, pizelle, krumkake,* and *gaufrette.* No matter which iron you use, making these cookies is a festive occasion.

BATTER

½ cup (70 grams) unsifted all-purpose flour

½ cup (50 grams) unsifted powdered sugar

1 tablespoon sesame seeds

½ cup (5 ounces) sour cream

1 teaspoon vanilla

1. In a 3-quart bowl, blend the flour, powdered sugar, and sesame seeds briefly with a wire whisk. Mix in the sour cream and vanilla until thoroughly combined.

2. Open iron and spray nonstick cooking spray lightly on both sides of the iron. Place over medium heat. Alternating sides of the iron, heat until water dripped inside the iron sizzles. Open iron and spoon 1 level measuring teaspoonful batter into the center of the iron. Close it and bake over heat, first on one side, then on the other, turning every 10 to 15 seconds until the cookie is light golden brown. It's fine to open the iron occasionally to check doneness.

3. With a small metal spatula, lift cookie while warm and, while still pliable, wrap around a wooden cornet to form a cone shape or roll into a cylinder around a wooden dowel ½ inch in diameter. Slip the cookie off the wooden form to cool.

4. Return iron to heat; repeat the baking and shaping process with the remaining batter. If at any time the cookies brown too quickly or burn, adjust the heat.

5. When the cookies are cool and firm, store them in an airtight metal container at room temperature up to 1 week.

• Cookie irons without nonstick surfaces work best. You need to season them when new. To season, place over medium heat until a drop of water dripped inside sizzles. Open iron and brush amply with vegetable oil. Close and return to heat just until oil smokes. Remove from heat and let iron cool in open position. Wipe clean with a paper towel.

SERVING NOTE

• After shaping, these krumkake look like tiny ice cream cones. When the weather is sunny and warm, stage an ice cream festival: With a tiny ice cream scoop, fill several krumkake cones with a variety of ice creams and sorbets, such as vanilla, orange, chocolate, strawberry, and coffee. Arrange three or five cones fan-fashion on each dessert plate.

Miniature
Krumkake

Crispy Corkscrews

Makes 3 dozen
2-inch-long spirals

The corkscrew spiral shape is what gives this cookie its name. Forming them takes some patience, but the payoff is evident when you see the delicate spirals on a tray of assorted cookies. The cookies' simple flavors of butter and sugar balance perfectly with a glass of dry champagne.

BATTER

3 ounces (6 tablespoons) unsalted butter, softened

1/2 cup granulated sugar

1/3 cup (about 3 large) egg whites, room temperature

3/4 cup plus 1 tablespoon (114 grams) unsifted all-purpose flour

1. Adjust rack to lower third of oven and preheat oven to 375 degrees. Unwrap an end of a chilled stick of unsalted butter and rub it over two large cool Teflon-coated baking sheets to apply a very thin film of fat.

2. In the large bowl of an electric mixer, cream the butter at medium speed until smooth, about 45 seconds. Beat in the sugar until fluffy. Add the egg whites, a tablespoon at a time, blending well after each addition. With a rubber spatula, scrape down the sides of the bowl. Add the flour, combining thoroughly.

3. Using a 14-inch pastry bag fitted with a 1/4-inch plain decorating tip (such as Ateco #2), pipe only three strings about 1/4 inch wide, 3 inches long, and at least 1 1/2 inches apart on each baking sheet. Bake, one sheet at a time, for about 4 minutes or just until edges are light golden brown.

4. Place baking sheet on a wire rack. Without delay, lift the end of one string at a time with a metal spatula, and wrap the cookie spiral fashion around a 6-inch wooden dowel or wooden spoon handle about 3/8 inch in diameter. After shaping a cookie, gently slip it off the dowel to a wire rack until cool. Repeat the baking and shaping process with the remaining batter.

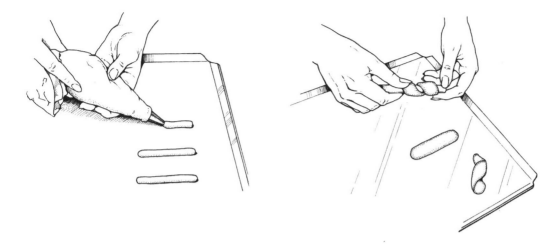

5. When firm, store in an airtight metal container at room temperature up to 1 week.

BAKING NOTE

- For maximum results with a minimum amount of effort, I bake these cookies relay-fashion. When I remove one baking sheet from the oven, replace it with another, then I shape the just-baked cookies into spirals while they are warm, then I prepare another baking sheet to exchange with the one in the oven when the time is right. In this way, you can make a batch very quickly.

Crispy
Corkscrews

Champagne Biscuits

Makes 6 dozen
3-inch-long
cookies

These crispy, finger-length cookies are ideal with fresh fruit, ice cream, and sorbet. I think they are even more delicious with a decorative zigzag of white chocolate drizzled over half the cookie.

BATTER

- 4 ounces (1 stick) unsalted butter, softened
- 1/2 cup (100 grams) granulated sugar
- 1 large egg, room temperature
- 2 tablespoons (about 1 large) egg white, room temperature

- 1 teaspoon vanilla
- 1/4 teaspoon almond extract
- 3/4 cup (105 grams) unsifted all-purpose flour

DECORATION

- 2 ounces white chocolate, finely chopped

1. Adjust rack to lower third of oven and preheat oven to 375 degrees. Unwrap an end of a chilled stick of unsalted butter and rub it over two large cool Teflon-coated baking sheets to apply a very thin film of fat.

2. In the large bowl of an electric mixer, cream the butter on medium speed until smooth, about 45 seconds. Beat in the sugar until fluffy. Beat in the whole egg, blending thoroughly, then add the egg white. With a rubber spatula, scrape down the sides of the bowl. Lower speed and add the flavorings, then the flour, combining thoroughly.

3. Using a 16-inch pastry bag fitted with a 1/4-inch plain decorating tip (such as Ateco #2), pipe strings about 1/4 inch wide, 3 inches long, and at least 1 1/2 inches apart. Bake, one sheet at a time, for about 5 to 6 minutes or just until edges and bottoms are light golden brown.

4. Place the baking sheet on a wire rack and lift the cookies with a metal spatula to another wire rack to cool. If cookies become difficult to remove, return baking sheet to the oven a few seconds until they soften.

5. When firm, put cookies on a baking sheet lined with waxed paper. Melt the chocolate in a bowl set over water at approximately 105 degrees. Using a small paper cone, its tip snipped off, pipe thin lines of chocolate zigzag fashion across half of each cookie. Set aside in a cool place or refrigerate just until the chocolate firms, about 10 minutes.

6. Stack undecorated cookies in an airtight metal container and store at room temperature up to 1 week. Store decorated cookies in a single layer in a covered foil-lined cardboard container, such as a cake box, at room temperature up to 2 days.

Champagne
Biscuits

Chocolate Fringe Cups

Circles of thinly spread batter are piped with chocolate around the edge, baked, and shaped while warm from the oven. They come out looking like wavy swatches of fabric, making a delightful and unusual cup for fresh raspberries or other fruits.

BATTER

2 ounces (4 tablespoons) unsalted butter, room temperature

2/3 cup (130 grams) granulated sugar

1/3 cup (about 3 large) egg whites, room temperature

1 teaspoon vanilla

1/2 cup (70 grams) unsifted all-purpose flour

DECORATION

2 ounces semisweet chocolate

1. Adjust rack to lower third of oven and preheat oven to 375 degrees. Unwrap an end of a chilled stick of unsalted butter and rub it over two large cool Teflon-coated baking sheets to apply a very thin film of fat.

2. To streamline shaping these cookies, make a reusable 3-inch round plastic template. With a pencil or felt pen, trace a 3-inch circle on a thin plastic lid (as thin as a playing card) from a storage container. Use a utility knife to cut out the traced shape from the template.

3. In the large bowl of an electric mixer, cream the butter at medium speed until it has the consistency of mayonnaise. Add the sugar and beat until mixture is well combined. Scrape down the sides of the bowl.

4. Maintaining the same speed, gradually add the egg whites. Wait for each portion of whites to be incorporated before adding the next. Add the vanilla. Lower mixer speed and add the flour, combining thoroughly.

5. Melt the chocolate in a small bowl that fits snugly over a pan of water at approximately 120 degrees; set aside.

6. Set the reusable template on the baking sheet and drop a small amount of batter inside it. With a small offset metal spatula, spread the batter very thinly and evenly within the template.

7. Carefully lift the template. Repeat this procedure until four round cookies are formed on each baking sheet.

8. Fill a small handmade paper cone with the chocolate. Snip its tip off and pipe a thin string of chocolate ¼ inch in from the edges of the unbaked rounds of batter.

9. Bake, one sheet at a time, for 3 to 5 minutes, or until pale golden. Place baking sheet on a wire rack and, without delay, lift one cookie at a time with a metal spatula and drape each cookie, baked-bottom side up, over the top of a spice jar or vinegar bottle (see Baking Note). Using a ⅓-cup measuring cup as a mold, place it over each cookie just long enough to shape it into a cup. Remove cookies from jar or bottle tops and set them in empty egg carton cups until cool and set. If any cookies become brittle before molding, return to oven for a few seconds until pliable again.

10. Repeat this procedure with the remaining batter.

Chocolate Fringe
Cups

129

11. Stack in an airtight metal container and store at room temperature up to 1 week. Fill with fresh fruit or a favorite cream filling close to serving time.

BAKING NOTES

- Shaping the pliable cookies into cups begins over 1-inch-diameter vinegar or $1^3/_4$-inch-diameter spice bottle caps. To set their shape, the cookies are put in egg carton cups while cooling. Later, the egg carton becomes handy again. It cradles these fragile cookies with just enough support to prevent their breaking when filling them with small pieces of fresh seasonal fruit.
- I recommend a low oven temperature here so these very thin cookies won't bake too dark and crisp too soon.

Chocolate Fringe
Cups

130

Chantilly Fans

The name of this cookie comes from its interesting shape. A creamy batter, flecked with ground hazelnuts, is thinly spread over a circular mold. While warm from the oven, it is folded into quarters, creating a fan. This technique produces four thin, crispy layers with a delicate texture that crumbles with each bite, releasing a sweet, nutty flavor. If the first cookie you fold isn't perfect, don't worry. The next one is easier and the third time, you'll feel like a pro.

BATTER

⅓ cup heavy cream	¼ cup (about 2 large) egg whites
1¾ ounces (scant ⅓ cup) hazelnuts, toasted and finely ground	⅓ cup (65 grams) granulated sugar
2 tablespoons potato starch	

1. Adjust rack to lower third of oven and preheat oven to 350 degrees. Unwrap an end of a chilled stick of unsalted butter and rub it over two large cool Teflon-coated baking sheets to apply a very thin film of fat.

2. For a reusable template, use the removable rubber ring (⅛ inch thick, 2½ inches in diameter) from a canning or old-fashioned-type storage jar. Its proportions make it easy to form uniformly shaped cookies quickly.

3. In a deep 1½-quart mixing bowl, whip heavy cream until soft peaks form. Refrigerate it. In another small bowl, blend the nuts and the potato starch briefly with a wire whisk. Using an electric mixer at medium speed, preferably with the whisk attachment, whip the egg whites in a large bowl until small bubbles appear, about 30 seconds. Gradually add the sugar, about a half tablespoon at a time, and continue whipping until thick, stiff, glossy peaks form, about 3 minutes. With a rubber spatula, fold in the dry ingredients alternately with the whipped heavy cream, beginning and ending with the dry ingredients.

4. Put the reusable template on the baking sheet and drop a small amount

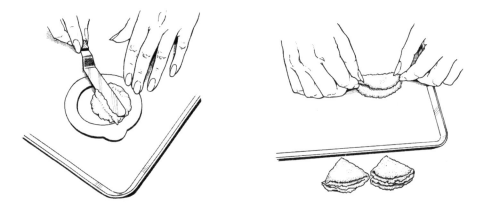

of batter, about 1 mounded teaspoon, inside it. Using a small offset metal spatula, spread the batter evenly across the ring.

5. Carefully lift the template. Repeat this procedure until five wafers are formed on each baking sheet. Bake, one sheet at a time, for 5 minutes only or just until edges are golden brown, the centers are ivory-colored, and cookies no longer appear shiny or wet on top. Don't overbake. Place baking sheet on a wire rack. While cookies are warm, using a small metal spatula, lift one wafer at a time and flip it over (baked-bottom side up) back onto the hot baking sheet. Fold it in half, then in half again to form a quarter-circle wedge. Set the wedges on another wire rack until cool. Repeat the baking and shaping process with the remaining batter.

6. Gently stack these delicate cookies in an airtight metal container and store at room temperature up to 3 days.

BAKING NOTES

- After toasting the hazelnuts, remove just the dark brown skins that come off easily after rubbing them together in the palms of your hands. (Too many skins can cause a bitter taste.)
- If cookies crisp before you can fold them, return for a few seconds to the oven until pliable, and don't bake the next batch as long.

Chantilly Fans

132

Spicy Miniatures

Creamy Ginger Squares

The spicy dough, flavored with ginger, ground black pepper, and lemon zest, is tamed with a creamy topping. Like the traditional Italian duet in which spicy black pepper is paired with sweet fresh strawberries, these unusual cookie squares will bring out the sweetness in a bowl of fresh fruit.

Makes 4 dozen 1½-inch bars

SPICY DOUGH

- 2 cups (280 grams) unsifted all-purpose flour
- ⅔ cup (130 grams) brown sugar, packed
- 1 teaspoon ground ginger
- ¾ teaspoon freshly ground black pepper
- ¼ teaspoon ground cinnamon
- ⅛ teaspoon *each* allspice and salt
- ½ teaspoon *each* cocoa powder and baking soda
- 8 ounces (2 sticks) unsalted butter, room temperature, cut into ½-inch slices
- 1 tablespoon water
- 1 teaspoon vanilla
- 1 teaspoon finely grated lemon zest

TOPPING

- ½ cup raspberry jam
- 2 cups heavy cream
- ½ cup granulated sugar
- Pinch of salt

DECORATION

- Ground cinnamon
- Crystallized ginger, optional

1. Adjust rack to lower third of oven and preheat oven to 350 degrees.

2. Put the flour, sugar, spices, salt, cocoa powder, and soda in food processor bowl. Process just to blend ingredients. Add the butter pieces all at once, and process with on/off bursts until mixture has the consistency of cornmeal.

3. Whisk the water with the vanilla and lemon zest in a small bowl. With the motor running, pour mixture down the feed tube and process just until ingredients form a ball.

4. Divide dough into eight pieces and scatter them over a 15- × 10- × 1-inch ungreased baking pan. With floured fingertips, pat the dough to extend the portions to cover the pan as evenly as possible.

5. Bake about 20 minutes or until crust appears set and feels slightly firm. Remove to a wire rack while preparing the topping.

6. Topping: Spread jam evenly over the baked crust. In a 2½-quart heavy-bottomed saucepan, mix the cream, sugar, and salt to blend. Over medium heat, bring mixture to a continuous boil, stirring occasionally to prevent scorching. If it threatens to boil over, reduce the heat and continue to let it bubble lightly until it is thicker and has a very pale ivory color. This procedure takes about 20 minutes. The mixture reduces to about 1½ cups. Pour over the cooled cookie crust and spread evenly with a rubber spatula. Let the cream cool completely at room temperature before decorating and cutting.

7. Lay ½-inch-wide strips of parchment or waxed paper 1 inch apart over topping in a lattice design and sprinkle cinnamon lightly to create a pattern. Remove waxed paper strips. With a ruler and sharp knife, cut 1½-inch squares, wiping the knife clean between each slice. Set an ⅛-inch-thick slice of crystallized ginger on top of each square for decoration, if desired.

8. Store in baking pan, uncovered, at room temperature up to 1 day.

VARIATION NOTES
- Sprinkle 1 cup toasted coconut over the cream topping. Or, perhaps, scatter stemmed fresh red currants, Candied Cranberries (page 222), pomegranate seeds, or fresh raspberries over the creamy topping before cutting.
- In place of the parchment or waxed paper strips, decorate the batch of Creamy Ginger Squares with a stencil design. Using a large piece of cardboard slightly bigger than the baking pan, cut a stencil in it of any pattern you wish. Hold it closely over the cream topping in the pan and sprinkle the cinnamon to create the pattern. You can use a large cake box for the stencil.

Creamy Ginger Squares

Spicy Twin Thins

Here's another intriguing spicy shortbread-like dough with a twist—literally. This cookie is formed by putting two five-point star-shaped cookies together to create a ten-point star. The technique is simple, but the results are stunning. While the cookies are still warm from baking, sprinkle finely chopped white chocolate over the tops. Place one cookie on top of the other and rotate to form the ten-point star. Then accent each of the star sandwiches with chopped pistachio nuts.

DOUGH

- 2 cups (280 grams) unsifted all-purpose flour
- ⅔ cup (130 grams) granulated sugar
- ½ teaspoon *each* ground ginger and freshly ground black pepper
- ¼ teaspoon *each* ground cinnamon and allspice
- ⅛ teaspoon salt
- 8 ounces (2 sticks) unsalted butter, room temperature, cut into ½-inch slices
- 1 egg yolk
- 1 teaspoon vanilla
- 2 teaspoons finely grated lemon zest

DECORATION

- 4 ounces white chocolate, finely chopped
- 1 ounce pistachio nuts, blanched, roasted, and finely chopped

1. Put the flour, sugar, spices, and salt in a food processor bowl. Process just to blend ingredients. Add the butter pieces all at once, and process with on/off bursts until the mixture has the consistency of cornmeal.

2. Whisk the egg yolk with the vanilla and zest in a small bowl. With the motor running, pour egg mixture down the feed tube and process just until ingredients form a ball.

3. Divide the dough in half and roll out each portion between two sheets of waxed paper to form $\frac{1}{8}$-inch-thick rounds about 11 inches in diameter. Leaving the dough circles between the waxed paper sheets, stack them on a baking sheet and refrigerate until firm, for at least 2 hours or up to 3 days; or freeze, well wrapped, up to 1 month.

4. Adjust rack to lower third of oven and preheat oven to 325 degrees. Line two cool baking sheets with parchment paper.

5. Remove one dough circle package at a time from the refrigerator. Peel off top sheet of waxed paper, replace it loosely on top, and flip the entire package over. Peel off and discard the second sheet of waxed paper.

6. Using a $1\frac{1}{2}$-inch star cutter, cut out shapes in the dough and set them $\frac{1}{2}$ inch apart on the baking sheets.

7. Bake, one sheet at a time, for 8 to 10 minutes, or until cookies are no longer shiny and feel slightly firm when lightly touched. Place baking sheet on a wire rack.

8. While the cookies are still hot, sprinkle the finely chopped chocolate on them. Sprinkle pistachio nuts over only half of the chocolate-coated cookies.

9. The heat from the cooling cookies melts the chocolate and makes it easy to sandwich two cookies together. Using a small metal spatula, center a pistachio–white chocolate-topped cookie on top of a white chocolate–topped cookie. Twist the cookie on top so the star points are between the bottom cookie's star points. Now gently press the pair together to form a ten-point star. Repeat with remaining cookies while chocolate is soft.

10. Transfer cookies to a clean baking sheet and put in a cool room to allow the chocolate to set, about 1 hour.

11. Stack cookies in an airtight metal container, separating the layers with strips of aluminum foil, and store at room temperature up to 1 week.

Eight-Spice Twists

This cookie utilizes the doughs used in the Creamy Ginger Squares and the Spicy Twin Thins. Twist two thin strings of dough together to form a rope. After baking, brush each one with an almond glaze. It's simple, but delicious.

Makes 8 dozen
2½- × 1¼-inch
twists

½ recipe Spicy Dough (page 135)

½ recipe Spicy Twin Thins dough (page 137)

ALMOND SUGAR GLAZE

½ cup (50 grams) unsifted powdered sugar

¼ teaspoon almond extract

3 teaspoons water

1. Adjust rack to lower third of oven and preheat oven to 325 degrees. Line a large cool baking sheet with parchment paper.

2. For each cookie, shape ½ teaspoon of each dough into a ball with your palms. With your fingertips roll each ball back and forth on a lightly floured work surface into a pencil-like rope about 2 inches long. Twist the two ropes together once or twice, without extending them any longer. Continue shaping the cookie twists, spacing them about ½ inch apart on the baking sheet.

3. Bake for 10 to 12 minutes or until firm (lightly touch a few). Place baking sheet on a wire rack and glaze while warm. The double spiral will have become a single spiral, the two colors melting into one.

4. Almond Sugar Glaze: Mix the sugar, water, and extract together until smooth. Brush lightly over warm cookies.

5. Stack cookies in an airtight metal container, separating the layers with strips of aluminum foil, and store at room temperature up to 1 week.

Eight-Spice Twists

Pains d'Amande

This traditional Belgian cookie, known as almond bread, is one of my favorites. The raw sugar's light golden color and distinctly old-fashioned flavor, similar to that of turbinado-style sugar, gives this cookie its unique taste, texture, and appearance. A slow baking develops a crispy texture and toasty flavor. Though the dough is pale in color, it becomes honey-colored and delicious when baked.

DOUGH

2⅓ cups (325 grams) unsifted all-purpose flour

¼ teaspoon baking soda

4 ounces (1 stick) unsalted butter, chilled and cut into quarters

1⅓ cups (280 grams) Hawaiian washed raw sugar

½ teaspoon ground cinnamon

⅓ cup water

3 ounces (1 cup) sliced almonds

1. Sift flour and baking soda onto a sheet of waxed paper; set aside.

2. In a 1½-quart saucepan over low heat, combine the butter, sugar, cinnamon, and water. Stir occasionally just until the butter melts. Do not allow the mixture to boil. Don't be concerned if some of the sugar has not dissolved by the time the butter has melted. Remove from the heat and stir in the almonds. Pour this mixture into a 3-quart mixing bowl; set aside for about 30 minutes at room temperature until lukewarm, about 90 degrees.

3. Add dry ingredients all at once; stir until thoroughly blended.

4. Press the soft dough into an 8½- × 4½-inch straight-sided pan (such as a 1½-quart Pyrex loaf pan) lined with plastic wrap. Cover surface with plastic wrap and refrigerate until firm, for at least 4 hours or up to 3 days; or freeze, well wrapped, up to 1 month.

5. Adjust rack to lower third of oven and preheat oven to 325 degrees. Line two large cool baking sheets with parchment paper.

6. Lift out the firm dough from the pan, on its plastic, to a cutting board. Using a sharp chef's knife, cut it in half crosswise and then cut the halves lengthwise into thirds. Using a sharp knife, cut each bar into ⅛-inch or thinner slices, and space them, cut sides down, ¼ inch apart on the baking sheets. (The dough slices as though it were fudge.) You can use a sawing action with a serrated knife in order to cut through the nuts to make very thin slices.

7. Bake, one sheet at a time, 8 to 10 minutes or until the undersides are light golden; then turn cookies over and bake an additional 8 to 10 minutes or until crisp and honey-colored. Place baking sheet on a wire rack to cool. Lift off cookies from parchment when cool.

8. Stack cookies in an airtight metal container and store at room temperature up to 10 days.

BAKING NOTE

- Hawaiian washed raw sugar is available in supermarkets in 2-pound plastic bags. If you cannot locate it, you can substitute turbinado sugar.

VARIATION NOTE

- For a more intense almond flavor, use 4 ounces (⅔ cup) whole blanched almonds instead of the sliced almonds. Slicing the dough into thin slices is trickier though, since the larger almond pieces can cause the dough to fall apart.

Pains
d'Amande

Sesame Spice Chips

Makes 8 dozen
1½-inch cookies

I fondly remember this molasses-cinnamon cookie from my childhood. However, I've made them even better by adding sesame seeds. These round, cinnamon-brown cookies are great served with baked apples. I've even concluded a formal dinner party by arranging them on a silver plate and passing them when coffee was served. Substitute these cookies for graham crackers in your next pie for the best crumb crust ever.

DOUGH

- 2 cups (240 grams) unsifted all-purpose flour
- 2 teaspoons baking soda
- 1 teaspoon ground cinnamon
- ¼ teaspoon *each* ground ginger, allspice, and salt

- 6 ounces (1½ sticks) unsalted butter, room temperature
- 1 cup (200 grams) granulated sugar
- 1 large egg
- ¼ cup light molasses

DECORATION

- 5 ounces (⅔ cup) sesame seeds

1. Adjust rack to lower third of oven and preheat oven to 350 degrees. Line two large cool baking sheets with parchment paper.

2. Sift the flour, baking soda, spices, and salt on a sheet of waxed paper; set aside. In the large bowl of an electric mixer, cream the butter at medium-low speed until smooth, about 1 minute. Beat in the sugar at medium speed until creamy. Add the egg and beat just until fluffy, then gradually add the molasses until incorporated, scraping down the sides of the bowl. Lower speed, gradually blend in the dry ingredients, and mix just until thoroughly combined.

3. Using a 16-inch pastry bag fitted with a ½-inch plain decorating tip (such as Ateco #6), pipe ½ teaspoons of dough 1 inch apart on cool baking sheets.

4. Using a damp pastry brush, flatten cookies slightly to remove tip left from piping. Generously sprinkle the sesame seeds over cookies. With another baking sheet, press down evenly on cookies to flatten them all at once.

5. Bake, one sheet at a time, for 8 minutes or until cookies are flat, feel slightly firm to the touch, and are cinnamon brown. Place baking sheet on a wire rack to cool. Lift off cookies from parchment when cool.

6. Stack in an airtight metal container at room temperature and store for up to 1 week.

BAKING NOTES

- If you want more sesame seed flavor, shape teaspoons of soft dough, 1 teaspoon at a time, into balls, then roll in sesame seeds to coat before flattening and baking them.
- You'll enjoy serving these cookies with baked apples, poached pears, or simply homemade applesauce. For a special hostess gift, package these along with a pound of toasted unsalted macadamia nuts—perfect partners.

Sesame Spice Chips

Hahnpfeffernüsse

Just as you wouldn't think of eating the crust of an apple pie without the apples, you must not eat these cookies without the sugar glaze. The glaze works together with the cookie, enclosing its spiciness and adding good taste.

Barbara Hahn, from my hometown, Evansville, Indiana, gave me this old-fashioned German cookie recipe that in many ways resembles many other pfeffernüsse recipes. *Pfeffernüsse* means "peppernut" in German, suggesting the cookies' healthy dose of spices and resemblance to unshelled walnuts. Their small thick shapes and abundant assortment of spices are two characteristics most recipes share in common. However, Hahnpfeffernüsse, with no fat and lots of flour, bake hard with a spirited peppery pungent flavor. But the texture softens and the fragrant flavor heightens and improves after the cookies have been stored in an airtight metal container at least one week.

Baking powder, a modern addition to the recipe, produces a softer texture. Anise flavoring is customary in pfeffernüsse glazes. Use anise oil rather than anise extract for a richer, more authentic, intense flavor. Anise oil is available at well-stocked pharmacies. Citron and nuts provide additional texture and flavor.

DOUGH

- 3 cups (420 grams) unsifted all-purpose flour
- 1 teaspoon baking powder
- 2 teaspoons ground cinnamon
- 1/2 teaspoon allspice
- 1/4 teaspoon *each* freshly ground black pepper, mace, and nutmeg
- 1/8 teaspoon *each* ground cardamom and cloves
- 1/4 teaspoon salt
- 2 large eggs, room temperature

- 1 egg yolk, room temperature
- 1 cup (200 grams) dark brown sugar, packed
- 1 1/2 tablespoons cold brewed black coffee
- 1 teaspoon finely grated lemon zest
- 1 1/2 ounces (1/4 cup) blanched almonds, finely ground
- 1 1/2 ounces (1/4 cup) finely chopped citron

PFEFFERNÜSSE ICING

1 cup water

3 cups granulated sugar

⅛ teaspoon anise oil

1. Adjust rack to lower third of oven and preheat oven to 350 degrees. Line two large cool baking sheets with parchment paper.

2. Sift the flour, baking powder, spices, and salt on a sheet of waxed paper; set aside. In the large bowl of an electric mixer, preferably with a whisk attachment, whip the eggs and yolk with the sugar at medium speed until thick and taupe-colored, about 2 minutes. Lower speed and mix in the coffee. By hand, using a rubber spatula, gradually blend in the zest, the dry ingredients, and then the nuts and citron. Mix just until thoroughly combined.

3. For each cookie, pinch off a piece of dough measuring 1 teaspoon in size, and drop 1 inch apart on cool baking sheets. Then, shape into balls with your palms.

4. Bake, one sheet at a time, for 10 to 12 minutes or until firm to the touch and lightly browned on the bottom. Place the baking sheet on a wire rack until the cookies are cool. Repeat the shaping and baking process with the remaining dough.

5. Adjust rack to lower third of oven and preheat oven to 200 degrees. Line two large baking sheets with aluminum foil.

6. Pfeffernüsse Icing: In a 1½-quart heavy-bottomed saucepan, combine the water and sugar over low heat. Stir occasionally, washing down any sugar crystals clinging to the sides of the pan with a brush dipped in cold water, until the sugar is dissolved. Increase the heat and, without stirring, gently boil to 230 degrees, the thread stage, on a mercury candy thermometer. Remove from the heat, pour in the anise oil, and swirl the pan to blend.

7. While syrup is hot, drop about 20 cookies at a time in the icing and completely cover with the syrup. Lift one at a time from the icing with a fork. Tap the fork on the pan to remove excess. Place cookies ½ inch apart on foil-lined baking sheets. Put baking sheets in oven about 7 minutes to dry the glaze.

Hahnpfeffernüsse

145

Place baking sheets on wire racks, and lift off cookies to another wire rack to cool and dry cookies' undersides.

8. When icing is dry and set, stack cookies in an airtight sturdy plastic container and store at room temperature for at least 1 week or up to 2 months before serving. During this time, the cookies soften while the flavors mellow. If the cookies remain hard, add some apple wedges to the container and cover tightly for one day or until cookies are soft; then discard apple pieces.

Shortbread Miniatures

Chewy
Miniatures

Crispy Miniatures

Spicy Miniatures

Chocolate Miniatures

Tartlet Miniatures

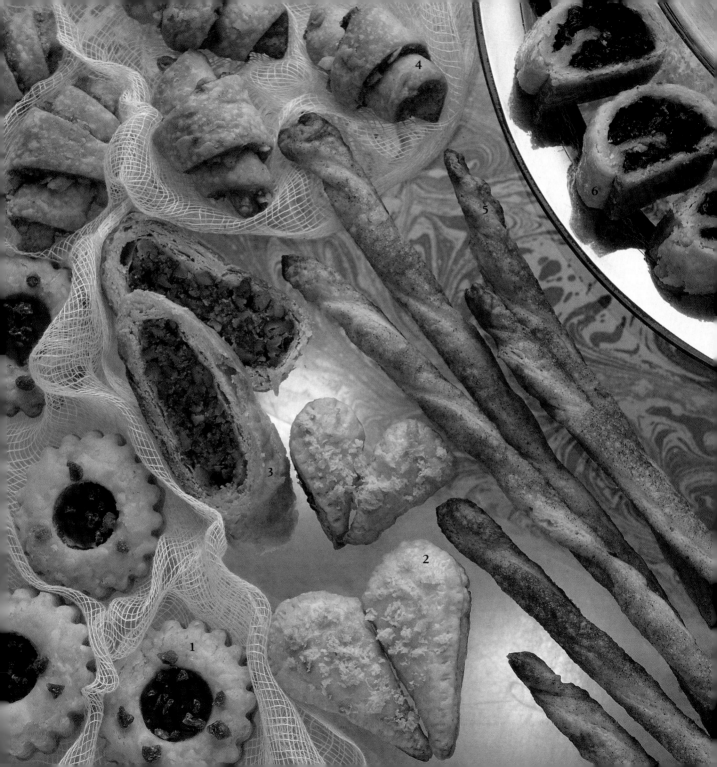

Flaky Miniatures

Cake Miniatures

Shortbread
Miniatures

Springerle

These ivory-colored cookies, crunchy and chewy in texture and embossed with designs from a special mold, remind me of the holidays in Indiana when I was a child. Though the anise flavor was too sophisticated for me then, I savor its powerful flavor now.

Springerle are especially appealing with any tangy fruit, such as fresh currants or raspberries, or even with lemon curd. As simple as it may seem, a cup of coffee and a Springerle perk up anyone's workday.

If you don't like the crunch of anise seeds on the surface of the cookies, roll a rolling pin over seeds to crush them. Use ¼ teaspoon anise oil in the dough if you prefer to eliminate using them altogether.

DOUGH

⅓ cup anise seed

3½ cups (490 grams) unsifted all-purpose flour

⅛ teaspoon salt

4 large eggs

3¾ cups (1 pound) unsifted powdered sugar

1 ounce (2 tablespoons) unsalted butter, softened

2 teaspoons finely grated lemon zest

1. Unwrap an end of a stick of unsalted butter and rub it over two large cool baking sheets to apply a film of fat. Sprinkle anise seeds evenly over them; set aside.

2. Sift the flour and salt onto waxed paper; set aside. In the large bowl of an electric mixer, preferably with a whisk attachment, whip the eggs at medium speed until fluffy, thick, and ivory in color, about 2 minutes. Gradually add the sugar and whip until the mixture is thick enough that when the whisk is lifted, the batter flows back into the bowl in ribbons, about 10 minutes. Whisk in the soft butter.

3. Lower the speed and gradually whisk in the flour mixture and zest. Scoop mixture out onto a floured surface and knead just until dough is smooth and cohesive. Cover the dough's surface with waxed paper and let rest at room temperature for 1 hour.

4. To imprint designs in the dough, roll out half of the dough at a time on a lightly floured surface into a 10½-inch square about ¼ inch thick. Dust a wooden springerle board with flour, and tap it to remove the excess. Press the springerle board firmly into dough to imprint the designs as deeply and clearly as possible. Remove board and, using a pastry wheel, cut the designs apart and place them an inch apart on top of the anise seeds on the baking sheets. Brush any excess flour from cookies with a clean dry pastry brush. Reflour mold before imprinting again. Set the cookies aside uncovered at room temperature for at least 8 hours or up to 24 hours to surface dry and set the embossed impressions before baking.

5. Adjust rack to lower third of oven and preheat oven to 250 degrees. Bake 27 to 30 minutes or until barely straw-colored and firm (lightly touch a few). Do not allow cookies to color. Transfer the cookies to a wire rack to cool.

6. Stack in sturdy airtight plastic containers and store at room temperature up to 1 month. If cookies get too hard, add some apple wedges to the container, and cover tightly for one day or until cookies are softer; then discard apple pieces.

Chrabeli

If you don't have wooden molds or a wooden rolling pin to imprint designs in the Springerle dough, it's easy to make these leaf-shaped cookies with the same dough.

Makes 12 dozen
1½-inch cookies

DOUGH

1 recipe Springerle dough (page 147)

⅓ cup anise seeds

1. Adjust rack to lower third of oven and preheat oven to 250 degrees. Unwrap an end of a stick of unsalted butter and rub it over two large cool baking sheets to apply a film of fat. Sprinkle anise seeds evenly over them; set aside.

2. Divide the dough equally into 8 portions, about ¼ cup each. With fingertips, roll each portion of dough back and forth on a lightly floured surface into a 15-inch-long rope about ⅜ inch in diameter. Cut each rope into 2-inch lengths to yield uniformly shaped pieces. With fingertips, bend each shape on the anise seed-coated baking sheet into a crescent; space crescents ½ inch apart. With the pointed tip of a scissors, snip three short slashes in the upper side of each crescent along the curve.

3. Bake for 15 minutes or until cookies feel firm (lightly touch a few). Do not allow them to color. Transfer the cookies to a wire rack to cool.

4. Stack in sturdy airtight plastic containers and store at room temperature up to 1 month. If cookies get too hard, add some apple wedges to the container, and cover tightly for one day or until cookies are softer; then discard apple pieces.

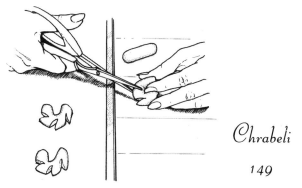

Chrabeli

Speculaas

Makes 3 to 4
dozen, depending
on size of
cutter or molds

These thin, mildly spicy, crunchy cookies with a dusting of nuts on top are traditionally presented as shaped figures printed from decorative wooden molds. Though I include instructions for making impressions from any decorative mold, I prefer cutting out round shapes from chilled dough circles. This allows you to make Speculaas at your convenience. A low oven temperature ensures even baking and at the same time imparts a toasty flavor.

DOUGH

2 cups (280 grams) unsifted all-purpose flour

½ teaspoon baking soda

1½ teaspoons ground cinnamon

¼ teaspoon freshly ground black pepper

⅛ teaspoon *each* ground cloves and nutmeg

⅛ teaspoon salt

1 dash cayenne pepper

½ cup (100 grams) granulated sugar

½ cup (100 grams) light brown sugar, packed

5 ounces (1¼ sticks) unsalted butter, softened

3 tablespoons cold water

1½ ounces (½ cup) sliced almonds

1. Sift the flour, baking soda, spices, and salt into a large mixing bowl. Add the sugars and, using an electric mixer on low speed, beat just until combined. Increase mixer speed to medium-low, add the butter, and blend until mixture is crumbly and resembles a streusel. Maintaining same speed, blend in the water, 1 tablespoon at a time. Mix just until ingredients come together in a cohesive ball.

2. Divide dough in half, and roll each portion between two sheets of waxed paper to form a circle 12 inches in diameter and ⅛ inch thick. Leaving the dough circles between the waxed paper, transfer to a baking sheet and refrigerate until firm, for at least 2 hours or up to 3 days; or freeze, well wrapped, up to 1 month.

3. Adjust rack to lower third of oven and preheat oven to 300 degrees. Line two large cool baking sheets with parchment paper; sprinkle just enough sliced almonds over to cover each sheet.

4. Remove one dough package at a time from the refrigerator. Remove the top waxed paper sheet, and lay it loosely back on the dough. Turn the dough over, peel off second waxed paper sheet, and discard the waxed paper.

5. Using a 1½-inch round cutter, cut out shapes in the dough. Place cutouts about ½ inch apart on nut-covered baking sheets, lightly pressing cookies into nuts. Bake, one sheet at a time, for about 20 minutes or until golden brown on the bottom. With a metal spatula, remove cookies to a wire rack to firm as they cool.

6. Stack the cookies in an airtight metal container and store at room temperature up to 10 days. Serve the cookies nutty side up.

SHAPING NOTES

- If you're using wooden molds, dust them well with flour, then tap out excess before making an imprint. Press pieces of dough into molds, and roll a rolling pin over dough to ensure filling the crevices. With the tip of a small knife, trim excess dough to shape it neatly. Tap the mold on work surface to release the forms. If necessary, ease the dough's release with tip of knife. Put each cookie, imprinted side up, on nut-covered cool baking sheets. With a clean dry pastry brush, brush off excess flour and lightly press cookies into almonds without disturbing the imprint.
- Before baking, set aside the cookies, uncovered, at room temperature for at least 8 hours or up to 24 hours to surface dry and set the embossed impressions.

Speculaas

Gingersnaps

Makes 8 dozen
1½-inch cookies

These are the best Gingersnaps I've found, given an additional depth of flavor with dark molasses and a few tablespoons of cold coffee. The cookies are even better drizzled with lemon icing.

DOUGH

2½ cups (350 grams) unsifted all-purpose flour

1 teaspoon baking soda

¼ teaspoon salt

⅓ cup dark molasses

2 tablespoons cold brewed black coffee

7 ounces (1¾ sticks) unsalted butter, softened

¾ cup (150 grams) granulated sugar

1 tablespoon ground ginger

1 teaspoon ground cinnamon

½ teaspoon ground cloves

LEMON ICING

1 ounce (2 tablespoons) unsalted butter, soft

2 tablespoons lemon juice

1 cup (100 grams) unsifted powdered sugar

1. Sift the flour, baking soda, and salt on a sheet of waxed paper. Set aside. In a small bowl, combine the molasses and coffee. Set aside.

2. In the large bowl of an electric mixer, cream the butter at medium-low speed until smooth, about 1 minute. Increase speed to medium, add the sugar, and mix until well combined and slightly fluffy. Blend in the spices. Maintaining the same speed, add the flour mixture in three additions, alternating with the liquid, until thoroughly combined.

3. Cover dough's surface with plastic wrap and refrigerate until the soft dough is firmer, about 1 hour. Then divide dough into 4 equal parts; roll each portion on a lightly floured surface into a cylinder about 7 inches long and 1¼ inches in diameter. Wrap each log in plastic wrap and refrigerate until the dough

Gingersnaps

152

is firm, for at least 4 hours or up to 1 week; or freeze, well wrapped, up to 1 month.

4. Adjust rack to lower third of oven and preheat oven to 350 degrees. Line two large cool baking sheets with parchment paper.

5. Remove one dough cylinder at a time from the refrigerator. With a sharp knife, slice the dough into thin slices less than $1/8$ inch thick. Place the slices about $1/2$ inch apart on the cool baking sheets. Bake, one sheet at a time, until cookies are no longer shiny and appear set, about 8 to 10 minutes. With a metal spatula, remove cookies to a wire rack to cool.

6. Lemon Icing: Beat ingredients in a small bowl until smooth. Using a small handmade paper cone, its tip snipped off, pipe thin lines of lemon icing over the cookies in one direction. Then pipe lines perpendicular to the original lines, making a crisscross pattern.

7. Stack undecorated cookies in an airtight metal container and store at room temperature up to 10 days. Store decorated cookies in one layer in an airtight container at room temperature up to 3 days.

Lebkuchen Circles

Lebkuchen, a spicy cake-like honey-flavored dough, soft and chewy to eat, is Europe's gingerbread. I bake these in late November before the holiday season becomes frantic. While the cookies are stored in airtight containers, the honey draws in moisture and improves the flavor and texture. For Valentine's Day, you can cut out heart shapes and decorate them along the edges with royal-icing scribbling to resemble lace.

DOUGH

2/3 cup honey

1 cup granulated sugar

2 ounces (1/2 stick) unsalted butter

1 tablespoon fresh lemon juice

2 teaspoons finely grated lemon zest

1 tablespoon ground cinnamon

1/4 teaspoon *each* ground cardamom, cloves, ginger, and nutmeg

3 cups (420 grams) unsifted all-purpose flour

1/2 teaspoon baking powder

1/2 teaspoon baking soda

1/4 teaspoon salt

1 1/2 ounces (1/4 cup) blanched almonds, finely ground

1 large egg

3 ounces (1/2 cup) finely chopped citron

40 blanched almonds, split (see Technique Note)

COGNAC SUGAR GLAZE

1/2 cup (50 grams) unsifted powdered sugar

4 teaspoons cognac

1. In a 1 1/2-quart saucepan over low heat, heat the honey, sugar, and butter just until butter is melted and sugar is almost dissolved. Do not boil. Add the lemon juice, zest, and spices, blending completely. Transfer mixture to a large bowl and set aside at room temperature to cool, about 30 minutes.

2. Sift the flour, baking powder, baking soda, and salt on a sheet of waxed paper. Add the nuts, egg, and citron to cooled honey mixture, blending well. Stir in flour mixture in three additions, blending thoroughly into a soft dough. Cover surface of dough with plastic wrap, and refrigerate until it is firmer, for at least 4 hours or up to 3 days. A cold, firm dough is less sticky than a soft one so less flour is needed for rolling.

3. Adjust rack to lower third of oven and preheat oven to 350 degrees. Line two large cool baking sheets with parchment paper.

4. Work with a third of the dough at a time; keep unused portion covered in the refrigerator. On a floured work surface, roll out dough ⅜ inch thick. Using a 1-inch round cutter, cut out circles and space 1 inch apart on baking sheets. Press a split almond on top of each cookie.

5. Bake, one sheet at a time, for 10 to 12 minutes or until golden brown. Place baking sheet on a wire rack and glaze cookies while warm.

6. Cognac Sugar Glaze: Mix the sugar and cognac together until smooth. Using a pastry brush, coat the cookies lightly. With a metal spatula, transfer cookies to wire racks to cool completely. To seal in as much moisture as possible for a lengthy storage, apply the glaze over bottoms as soon as top coating dries.

7. Store in an airtight sturdy plastic container at room temperature for at least 2 weeks or up to several months before serving. If cookies get too hard, add some apple wedges to the container and cover tightly for one day or until cookies are soft again; then, discard apple pieces.

TECHNIQUE NOTES

- Put almonds and water to cover in a small saucepan, and bring to a boil. Remove from heat; let stand for 1 minute to soften. Using a slotted spoon, remove nuts, one at a time, and using the tip of a small paring knife, split the almonds in half along their natural seams.
- You roll this dough in flour rather than between two sheets of waxed paper because this honey-rich dough is sticky and would only adhere to the waxed paper.

Lebkuchen
Circles

155

- Using fat in the recipe, in this instance butter, adds flavor and makes the cookie softer and less brittle than those made from a recipe without fat.
- Besides using it to make cookies for festive Christmas decorations, you can also roll this dough less than $1/4$ inch thick and cut out assorted shapes for friends as housewarming, engagement, or birthday presents. You can even personalize them with royal icing.

Biberli

A thin layer of Lebkucken dough without the ground nuts and citron is wrapped around a lemon-scented almond paste filling to showcase this versatile dough at its best. It's a good idea to plan ahead when baking Biberli since aging develops their proper flavor and texture.

Makes 6 dozen 1½-inch cookies

DOUGH

- ⅔ cup honey
- 1 cup granulated sugar
- 2 ounces (½ stick) unsalted butter
- 1 tablespoon fresh lemon juice
- 2 teaspoons finely grated lemon zest
- 1 tablespoon ground cinnamon
- ¼ teaspoon *each* ground cardamom, cloves, ginger, and nutmeg
- 3 cups (420 grams) unsifted all-purpose flour
- ½ teaspoon baking powder
- ½ teaspoon baking soda
- ¼ teaspoon salt
- 1 large egg

FILLING

- 8 ounces (1 scant cup) almond paste, room temperature
- ¼ cup (50 grams) granulated sugar
- Zest of 1 lemon
- 1 egg white

LEMON SUGAR GLAZE

- ½ cup (50 grams) unsifted powdered sugar
- 2 teaspoons fresh lemon juice, strained
- 2 teaspoons water

Biberli

157

1. In a 1½-quart saucepan over low heat, heat the honey, sugar, and butter just until butter is melted and sugar is almost dissolved. Do not boil. Add the lemon juice, zest, and spices, blending completely. Transfer mixture to a large bowl and set aside at room temperature to cool, about 30 minutes.

2. Sift the flour, baking powder, baking soda, and salt on a sheet of waxed paper. Add the egg. Stir the flour mixture into the cooled honey mixture in three additions, blending thoroughly into a soft dough.

3. Cover surface of dough with plastic wrap and refrigerate until it is partially chilled, about 2 hours. If longer storage is necessary, refrigerate for up to 3 days.

4. Filling: In food processor bowl fitted with steel blade, process all the ingredients just until blended smoothly. Set aside.

5. Adjust rack to *center* of the oven and preheat oven to 350 degrees. Line two large cool baking sheets with parchment paper.

6. On a floured work surface, roll dough to form a 12-inch square, ¼ inch thick. Using a ruler and pastry wheel, cut into six strips, each 2 inches wide.

7. Using a 14-inch pastry bag fitted with a ½-inch plain decorating tip (such as Ateco #6), pipe a rope of filling down the center of each strip. (The filling will be about ½ inch thick.) Bring the two edges of dough together to wrap around the filling. Pinch the edges together to seal the seam. Then, roll each rope back and forth to smooth its surface and even out its thickness to ¾ inch. Cut each roll into ¾-inch-wide slices. As you lift each cookie between your thumb and index finger to set seam side down on a baking sheet, reshape its round top since slicing the cookies flattens and distorts their shape. Space ½ inch apart.

8. Bake, one sheet at a time, for about 10 minutes or until the cookies are no longer shiny and feel slightly firm (lightly touch a few). Place baking sheet on a wire rack to cool. Lift cookies from parchment when cool.

9. Lemon Sugar Glaze: Mix the sugar, lemon juice, and water until smooth. Using a pastry brush, coat cookies lightly with glaze. Set aside to dry.

10. Store in an airtight container at room temperature up to 1 month. For best flavor and texture, store at least one day before serving.

Chocolate Miniatures

Chocolate Macaroons

Years ago while touring in France, I discovered a cookie unlike any other I had ever tasted. One bite filled my mouth with more chocolate flavor than a double chocolate sundae. The French call these delicately textured, intensely flavored cookies Chocolate Macaroons, but they do not resemble the American version at all. The French version sandwiches two chocolate cookies with a creamy dark chocolate filling. A heart full of thanks to the Christophe Patisserie in Roanne, France, for this recipe.

BATTER

3¾ cups (1-pound box) unsifted powdered sugar

9 ounces (1⅔ cups) unblanched almonds, finely ground (see Baking Note)

½ cup (50 grams) unsifted cocoa powder

1 cup (about 7 to 8 large) egg whites, room temperature

½ cup (50 grams) unsifted powdered sugar

1 teaspoon honey

DARK CHOCOLATE GANACHE

6 ounces semisweet chocolate, finely chopped

¾ cup (6 ounces) heavy cream

1. Adjust rack to *upper* third of oven and preheat oven to 475 degrees. Line two large cool baking sheets, each measuring 14- × 17- × ½-inch, with parchment paper. Place two additional pieces of parchment paper, identical in size to the ones on the baking sheets, on the work surface near the baking sheets. Fit a 16-inch pastry bag with a ⁵⁄₁₆-inch plain decorating tip (such as Ateco #5).

2. Pour half the pound of powdered sugar and half the nuts and cocoa into a large medium-mesh sieve. Shake over a sheet of waxed paper to blend the ingredients. Sieve the remaining half-pound of powdered sugar and nuts and cocoa

over the waxed paper. Add to the sifted mixture any nut particles that remain in the sieve.

3. In the large bowl of an electric mixer, preferably with a whisk attachment, whip the egg whites at medium-low speed until the whites form soft frothy peaks, about 2 minutes. Increase to medium speed, add the ½ cup powdered sugar and the honey, and whip just until billowy, thick, but not dry, peaks form, about 3 minutes.

4. Using a rubber spatula, fold in all the dry ingredients. As you fold, the mixture will deflate somewhat to resemble a brownie batter. Without delay, scoop all of the mixture into the pastry bag. Piping the batter may be easier if you anchor the parchment by smearing some batter on each corner under the paper. Pipe kiss shapes, ¾ to 1 inch in diameter, on the cool baking sheets. The kiss pattern will dissolve before baking, leaving a smooth surface. Pipe the remaining batter on the additional sheets of parchment paper.

5. Allow to dry at room temperature for 30 minutes to prevent the cookies' surface from cracking during baking.

6. Just before baking each batch, double-pan the cookies: place the baking sheet on a second sheet of the same size. This will diffuse the flow of heat on the baking sheet. Place one baking sheet of cookies in the oven, and immediately reduce the temperature to 425 degrees. Reduce the temperature 25 degrees every 2 minutes. Bake, one sheet of cookies at a time, for *8 minutes only,* finishing at 350 degrees. Lowering the temperature in this way maintains a constant flow of heat but prevents the cookies from overbaking, inflating, and cracking.

7. Place baking sheet on a wire rack until cookies are completely cool. With a metal spatula, carefully lift the cookies from the paper.

8. Continue to bake the other batches in the same manner. Each time be certain to preheat the oven to 475 degrees. To bake the cookies piped on the two sheets of parchment, merely slide the paper onto a cool baking sheet.

9. Dark Chocolate Ganache: Put chocolate in a medium bowl. In a small saucepan, heat the heavy cream just to the boil. Remove from heat. Pour over

*Chocolate
Macaroons*

162

chocolate; whisk until chocolate melts and mixture is smooth and shiny. Set aside to cool until it develops enough body to pipe.

10. Turn half the macarooons baked-bottom side up. Using a 14-inch pastry bag fitted with a ¼-inch plain decorating tip (such as Ateco #2), pipe a bulb of filling equivalent to ½ teaspoon. Place plain macaroons, dome side up, on top of the filled ones; press gently to fit the pair together.

11. These are best eaten the same day; or freeze, separating the layers with strips of waxed paper, in airtight sturdy plastic containers up to 1 month.

BAKING NOTE

- Because the nuts provide structure as well as flavor in this recipe, it is important to grind the nuts to yield 2⅓ cups. The food processor does this with no problem.

TECHNIQUE NOTE

- It's easier to fill the pastry bag with all the mixture at once when you set the bag, fitted with its decorative tip, into a deep 1½-quart bowl for support. To hold the bag open for filling, fold a portion of the bag's top edges over the bowl.

Double Kisses

These cookies aim to surprise. A delicious, simple chocolate–peanut butter short-bread wraps around a chocolate candy. The balance of ingredients makes it possible for the cookies to hold their kiss shape after baking. Individual foil wrapping makes these cookies all the more fun and special, and perfect for handing out to your friends or packing in a decorated box to give to your special someone.

DOUGH

- 1½ cups (210 grams) unsifted all-purpose flour
- ¼ cup (25 grams) unsifted cocoa powder
- 4 ounces (1 stick) unsalted butter, room temperature
- ¼ cup creamy peanut butter
- ⅔ cup (130 grams) granulated sugar
- 2 tablespoons (1 large) egg white
- 42 milk chocolate candy kisses, foil removed

1. Adjust rack to lower third of oven and preheat oven to 350 degrees. Line a large cool baking sheet with parchment paper.

2. In a small bowl blend flour and cocoa powder briefly with a wire whisk; set aside. In the large bowl of an electric mixer on medium-low speed, cream butter until smooth, about 1 minute. Increase speed to medium, add the peanut butter, then the sugar, and mix until well combined and slightly fluffy. Lower speed, add the egg white, then the flour mixture in two additions, scraping down the sides of the bowl, and combine ingredients thoroughly.

3. Using 2 level teaspoons of dough, form a flat disk in the palm of your hand. Center a candy kiss on dough and bring dough up to cover completely, keeping kiss upright. Pinch dough on top to resemble kiss shape. Space cookies an inch apart on baking sheet.

4. Bake 8 to 10 minutes or until the cookies are no longer shiny and the bottoms are brown. Don't overbake. Place baking sheet on a wire rack to cool.

Lift off cookies from parchment when completely cool. The cookies' structure remains fragile only while warm.

5. To make individual kisses, center each cookie on a 5-inch square of aluminum foil, bring up edges, and twist them to enclose cookie completely. If desired, before twisting the foil, insert a name or personal message on a narrow paper strip.

6. Store in an airtight metal container at room temperature up to 10 days.

Double Kisses

Chocolate Thimbles

Here's the ultimate chocolate miniature, since chocolate is the only ingredient used to mold these tiny cases that resemble the shape of a thimble. You can fill them with my Punsch Cakelets (page 319), a favorite creamy vanilla mousse, a rich chocolate bavarian cream—or simply tiny fresh stemmed strawberries.

For this recipe, you need to bring the melted chocolate to the temperature at which it is stable and will set properly since the chocolate must be firm and shiny after molding. This process is known as tempering. I've developed a short-cut tempering method that will guide you successfully through the process.

1 ½ pounds semisweet or
    bittersweet chocolate

1. Cut twenty-four 4-inch squares of waxed paper. Press one paper square at a time over the base of a glass spice jar that measures about 1½ inches in diameter or any other cylindrical object with a smaller diameter. Set these molded paper forms near the stove.

2. Chop the chocolate into matchstick pieces, reserving one chunk of chocolate that weighs approximately 2 ounces.

3. Fill the bottom vessel of a double boiler with enough 125-degree water just to touch the bottom and sides of the top container without floating it. Maintain this temperature throughout the melting process by reheating the water from time to time over very low heat. An instant-reading thermometer is the quickest way to check the water's temperature. Fill the top of the double boiler with half the chopped chocolate.

4. Stir the chocolate occasionally and, as it melts, gradually add the remaining chopped chocolate. When the melted chocolate reaches 115 to 120 degrees, replace the 125-degree water with 95-degree water. Let the melted chocolate sit over the cooler water and stir the chocolate frequently until the chocolate reaches 98 degrees. Be sure to wipe the stem of the thermometer after each measurement.

5. Remove the top half of the double boiler. Add the reserved chunk of

chocolate to the melted chocolate. Stir the chocolate slowly and evenly with a dry rubber spatula. The chunk of chocolate helps lower the temperature gradually and evenly as it melts into the chocolate. It also "seeds" the melted chocolate with stable cocoa butter crystals, which help keep it in good temper as the chocolate hardens.

Dark chocolate must be cooled to 86 to 90 degrees. If the melted chocolate cools too much and loses its fluidity, simply replace the top vessel of the double boiler over hot tap water to reheat the chocolate. Never let the chocolate's temperature exceed 90 degrees or the stable cocoa butter crystals will start to melt and the temper will be lost.

6. When the chocolate has cooled to the correct temperature (86 to 90 degrees), remove what is left of the chunk of chocolate and set it aside. Replace the water with 86- to 90-degree water to maintain the chocolate's correct temperature.

7. Hold the molded paper cups by the edges and dip them, one by one, into the chocolate, coating the outside. Place them on a foil-lined tray, right side up.

8. Repeat the dipping process. Another coat of chocolate strengthens the cup and makes it less fragile. Place in a cool room or refrigerate until chocolate sets.

9. Grasping the edges of the waxed paper, gingerly twist it until it releases from the chocolate cup. Don't fret if the chocolate chips a bit around the edges—it gives each cup individual charm. After all, they are handmade, not machine made.

10. Store in one layer in an airtight metal container in a cool room up to 1 week.

Chocolate Thimbles

Dutch Minicakes

With the taste and texture of rich, chewy brownies, these bite-sized baby cakes were a signature pastry when I owned my baking business. Baked in miniature muffin cups, the batter is given added zing by hazelnuts, cocoa powder, and semisweet chocolate.

BATTER

⅓ cup (46 grams) unsifted all-purpose flour

1 tablespoon unsifted cocoa powder

½ teaspoon baking powder

3 ounces (6 tablespoons) unsalted butter

6 ounces semisweet chocolate, chopped

½ cup (100 grams) granulated sugar

2 large eggs

1 teaspoon vanilla

4 ounces (1 scant cup) toasted hazelnuts, coarsely chopped to yield 1 cup

DECORATION

¼ cup (25 grams) unsifted powdered sugar

1. Adjust rack to lower third of oven and preheat oven to 350 degrees. Line 2½ dozen miniature muffin cups that measure 1½ inches × ¾ inch with miniature cupcake liners.

2. Sift the flour, cocoa powder, and baking powder on a sheet of waxed paper; set aside. In a small saucepan, melt the butter and chocolate over very low heat. Remove from heat; stir in the sugar. Pour into a 3-quart mixing bowl; set aside to cool slightly, about 5 minutes. Add the eggs and vanilla, stirring just until blended. Stir in the flour mixture, then the nuts.

3. Fill each paper-lined muffin cup three-quarters full. Bake in preheated oven 10 minutes only. Don't overbake. Remove pans to wire racks to cool 5 minutes to allow cakes to firm a bit. Carefully remove cakes to other racks to cool. Sprinkle with powdered sugar before serving.

4. These are best eaten the same day they are baked; or freeze, in airtight sturdy plastic containers, up to 1 month.

SERVING NOTE

• I think these are prettier without the muffin papers. If the minicakes are not already frozen, freeze them for 30 minutes. Then the papers can be lifted quickly and easily from the rich sticky surfaces without altering the shape of the cakes.

Dutch
Minicakes

Neapolitan Wedges

The glazing and cutting techniques transform simple cookies into dazzling petits fours. The instructions given here are detailed but not time-consuming. Following them will reward you with a generous amount of trapezoid-shaped wedges with layers of short dough and red currant jelly buttercream, topped with a modernistic marble effect in the thin chocolate glaze.

DOUGH

1 recipe Miniature Tartlet Pastry
(page 205)

BUTTERCREAM

4 ounces (1 stick) unsalted
butter, softened

2 tablespoons red currant jelly

ROYAL ICING

1 cup (100 grams) unsifted
powdered sugar

2 tablespoons (1 large) egg white

1/8 teaspoon cream of tartar

Red food coloring

GLOSSY CHOCOLATE GANACHE GLAZE

1/4 cup heavy cream

1 tablespoon light corn syrup

4 ounces semisweet chocolate,
finely chopped

1. Divide the dough in half. Roll out each portion between two sheets of waxed paper to form a rectangle 8 × 14 inches and 1/8 inch thick. Leaving the dough between the waxed paper, transfer the rectangles to a baking sheet and refrigerate until firm, for at least 2 hours or up to 3 days; or freeze, well wrapped, up to 1 month.

2. Adjust rack to lower third of oven and preheat oven to 325 degrees. Line two large cool baking sheets with parchment paper.

Neapolitan
Wedges

3. Remove one dough package at a time from the refrigerator. Peel off top waxed paper sheet, replace it loosely on top, and flip the entire package over. Peel off and discard the second sheet of waxed paper.

4. Using a ruler and pastry wheel, trim the edges of the dough. Measure and cut three 2-inch-wide strips, each about 13½ inches long. While the dough is still cool and firm, lift the strips onto one of the baking sheets, spacing them ½ inch apart.

5. Bake, one sheet at a time, for 13 to 16 minutes, or until the strips are pale blond, are no longer shiny, and feel slightly firm when lightly touched. Place baking sheet on a wire rack to cool the cookie strips completely. While warm, they're more fragile than when cool.

6. Buttercream: Using a rubber spatula, stir the butter in a 1½-quart mixing bowl until it looks like mayonnaise. Stir in the jelly until smooth.

7. Place three of the strips close together, baked-bottom side up, preferably on a portable plastic or polyethylene cutting board. With a flexible metal icing spatula, spread a total of 3 tablespoons of the buttercream in a very thin, even coating over two of the cookie layers.

8. With a long metal icing spatula, lift the layers one at a time, and stack them to form one strip. If a layer should break when being lifted, just fit it in place as though it were a jigsaw puzzle piece. When the strip is sliced into individual wedges, there will be no evidence of the break.

Neapolitan
Wedges

9. Assemble the other strip in the same manner. Refrigerate until the filling is firm, for at least 2 hours or, well covered, up to 2 days. The advantage of a longer chilling time is that it firms the buttercream and allows moisture from the buttercream to soften the cookie strips and make slicing into wedges easier.

10. Remove the two cookie strips from the refrigerator.

11. Royal Icing: Mix the sugar, egg white, and cream of tartar together in a 1½-quart mixing bowl. With a hand mixer on medium speed, whip until the mixture is thick and has a marshmallow-like consistency, about 5 minutes. Add 1 drop of red food coloring to tint the icing a pastel pink. Fill a small handmade paper cone with 3 tablespoons of the icing; set it aside. Cover the remaining icing's surface with plastic wrap to prevent drying.

12. Glossy Chocolate Ganache Glaze: Combine the heavy cream and corn syrup in 1-quart heavy-bottomed saucepan. Heat just to boiling. Off heat, stir in chocolate just until melted and smooth.

13. While the glaze is warm and liquid, spoon about 2 tablespoons of it over the top of one of the pastry strips. With a long flexible metal icing spatula spread a thin, even layer over its surface. Try to contain the glaze on top of the strip, guiding it with the spatula and preventing it from flowing down the sides. Repeat the procedure to glaze the second strip.

14. Without delay, cut a small tip from the paper cone, and pipe four evenly spaced lengthwise lines over the glazed surface of one strip. Repeat on the other strip. Then draw the tip of a small paring knife back and forth across the lines, pulling the chocolate slightly to create a marbling effect. Wipe the knife tip clean between each stroke. Allow the glaze to dry at room temperature, about 1 hour.

15. With a sharp knife, slice each strip diagonally in alternate directions to form wedges, about 1 inch wide at the base and 1¼ inches wide at the top. Use a two-handed chopping motion, cutting straight down, rather than a sawing motion.

16. Store wedges in one layer in a covered foil-lined cardboard container, such as a cake box, at room temperature up to 2 days.

Hedgehogs

These charming chocolate and rum buttercream creatures, each with its own personality, are known as Igels in Austria. They captured my heart in Belgium and Germany and I know you'll love them too. Include them on an assorted miniature tray for a touch of delicious whimsy.

Makes 4 dozen 1½-inch edible pets

DOUGH

1 ¾ cup (245 grams) unsifted all-purpose flour

⅓ cup (35 grams) unsifted cocoa powder

¼ cup (45 grams) rice flour

7 ounces (1 ¾ sticks) unsalted butter, room temperature

⅔ cup (130 grams) granulated sugar

FILLING
Rum Silk Buttercream

4 egg yolks

¼ cup water

½ cup (100 grams) granulated sugar

8 ounces (2 sticks) unsalted butter, room temperature

1 tablespoon dark rum

2½ ounces (½ cup) pine nuts

DECORATION
Dark Chocolate Satin Glaze

¼ cup (1½ ounces) solid vegetable shortening

1 pound semisweet chocolate, chopped

Royal Icing

1 cup (100 grams) unsifted powdered sugar

2 tablespoons (1 large) egg white

⅛ teaspoon cream of tartar

Hedgehogs

173

1. In a medium bowl, briefly blend the flour, cocoa powder, and rice flour with a wire whisk; set aside. In the large bowl of an electric mixer, cream the butter at medium-low speed until smooth, about 1 minute. Beat in the sugar at medium speed until fluffy, scraping down the sides of the bowl. Lower speed and gradually add the flour mixture, combining thoroughly.

2. Divide the dough in half; roll one portion at a time between two sheets of waxed paper to form a circle 10 inches in diameter and ⅛ inch thick. Leaving the dough between the waxed paper, transfer the circles to a baking sheet and refrigerate until firm, for at least 2 hours or up to 3 days; or freeze, well wrapped, up to 1 month.

3. Adjust rack to lower third of oven and preheat oven to 350 degrees. Line two large cool baking sheets with parchment paper.

4. Remove one dough circle at a time from the refrigerator. Peel off top waxed paper sheet, replace it loosely on top, and flip the entire package over. Peel off and discard the second sheet of waxed paper.

5. Pinch the wide end of a ½-inch plain decorating tip (such as Ateco #6) into an oval to make an oval cutter. Using the cutter, cut out oval shapes in the dough, and space them ½ inch apart on baking sheets. Bake, one sheet at a time, for 10 to 13 minutes, or until cookies appear dull brown and feel slightly firm (lightly touch a few). Place baking sheet on a wire rack until cookies are completely cool. To store, stack in an airtight metal container at room temperature up to 1 week.

6. Rum Silk Buttercream: In the large bowl of an electric mixer, whip the egg yolks until light and fluffy, about 4 minutes. Remove bowl from mixer stand. In a 1-quart heavy-bottomed saucepan, combine the water and the sugar over low heat. Stir occasionally, washing down any sugar crystals clinging to the sides of the pan with a brush dipped in cold water, until the sugar is dissolved. Increase the heat and cook, without stirring, until the syrup reaches 238 degrees on a mercury candy thermometer. Pour into the center of the yolks and quickly whisk vigorously to combine. Return bowl to mixer, and whip at medium speed until the egg yolk mixture thickens and cools to body temperature, about 5 minutes. Main-

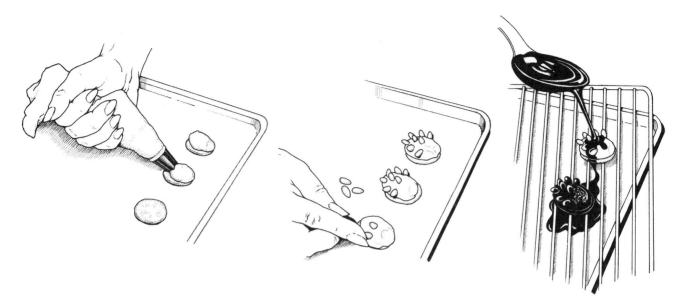

taining medium speed, gradually add the butter to the cooled egg yolk mixture, a tablespoon at a time. Continue mixing until all the butter has been incorporated and the buttercream is smooth and homogeneous. Add the rum, whipping until thoroughly combined.

7. Set the cookies close together on one large clean baking sheet. Using a 14-inch pastry bag fitted with a ½-inch plain decorating tip (such as Ateco #6), pipe an oval bulb of buttercream on each cookie. Hold a cookie in one hand as you pipe with the other. Then stick 8 pine nuts into each buttercream oval as illustrated. Refrigerate to firm the buttercream, at least 2 hours.

8. Dark Chocolate Satin Glaze: Combine the shortening and chocolate in a 3-quart mixing bowl. Place it over a saucepan filled with enough hot tap water (120 to 130 degrees) to reach the bottom of the bowl. Stir mixture occasionally until the glaze is liquid and smooth and registers close to 110 degrees on a candy thermometer. If water begins to cool while melting the chocolate, maintain the 120-degree temperature over very low heat.

9. Place the chilled Hedgehogs an inch apart on two wire racks set over shallow baking pans to catch drips. Ladle about 2 tablespoons glaze over each Hedgehog, to cover completely. After masking the pastries, gently move each one slightly on the rack with a small metal spatula while the glaze is liquid, to remove chocolate drippings from its underside. This neat finish also keeps the pastries from sticking to the rack.

10. Pour the glaze from the baking pans back into the saucepan, and reheat. Pour through a sieve in case any cookie crumbs have fallen into it.

11. The warm glaze sets up quickly after touching the cold, firm buttercream, leaving a gorgeous sheen. Do not refrigerate the pastries after they have been glazed.

12. Royal Icing: When the glaze has set, mix royal icing ingredients together in a 1½-quart mixing bowl. With a hand mixer on medium speed, whip until the mixture is thick and has a marshmallow-like consistency, about 5 minutes. Fill a small handmade paper cone with 2 tablespoons of icing and pipe three tiny dots on each Hedgehog. Then, dip a toothpick into some of the remaining liquid chocolate glaze, and place a dot of it on two of the icing dots, forming the Hedgehog's eyes. Now their true personalities will be evident.

13. Gently lift each pastry with a small metal spatula, and arrange in a single layer in a foil-lined cardboard container, such as a cake box. Cover and store at room temperature up to 2 days.

DECORATING NOTE

- An easier way to decorate these Hedgehogs is to omit the pine nuts. Coat them with the chocolate glaze and, before it sets up, apply chocolate sprinkles over two thirds of each pastry. Pipe "eyes" on the uncovered portion with the royal icing.

Chocolate Tulips

Dough is pressed into fluted tins and filled with an almond paste mixture to create these delicacies. Creamy chocolate ganache tops them to make delicious multi-layered sweets. Their spectacular appearance is the result of a simple trick that transforms each dollop of ganache into a Chocolate Tulip.

DOUGH

½ recipe Miniature Tartlet Pastry (page 205)

Almond Paste Frangipane Filling

4 ounces (½ cup) almond paste

⅓ cup (65 grams) granulated sugar

1 teaspoon dark rum

1 teaspoon vanilla

1 ounce (2 tablespoons) unsalted butter, room temperature

DECORATION
Butter Ganache Cream

12 ounces semisweet chocolate, chopped

1 cup (8 ounces) heavy cream

3 ounces (6 tablespoons) unsalted butter, room temperature

½ cup (50 grams) unsifted cocoa powder, optional

1. Adjust rack to lower third of oven and preheat oven to 350 degrees. Arrange four dozen ungreased fluted tartlet tins, 1½ inches in diameter, close together on a baking sheet that measures at least 12 × 15½ × ½ inches.

2. Pinch off dough, 1 teaspoon at a time, and drop into fluted tins. One by one, roll dough pieces into balls in the palms of your hands. With index finger,

press center of each dough ball into a tin, and then press dough up the sides while rotating tin to distribute it evenly.

3. Almond Paste Frangipane Filling: Process all the filling ingredients in a food processor bowl until mixture is smooth. Fill each tartlet with about 1 teaspoon filling.

4. Bake tartlets on the baking sheet for 15 to 20 minutes, or until the filling is golden and the crust is pale golden. Place baking sheet on a wire rack until tins are cool enough to touch, about 10 minutes. Squeeze each tin gently with your thumb and forefinger, turn it upside down, and let the tartlet drop into the palm of your hand. If it's difficult to release the tartlets, they could be either underbaked or left to cool too long in the tins. In that case, return to the oven for a few minutes more.

5. Butter Ganache Cream: When the tartlets are completely cool, place the chocolate in a 3-quart mixing bowl. In a small saucepan heat the cream until it boils. Pour over chocolate pieces and whisk together until chocolate melts and mixture is shiny. Add the butter, whisking it in 1 tablespoon at a time, until completely blended. Set aside at room temperature about 30 minutes or until it develops enough body to stay in place without falling off a rubber spatula.

6. Scoop about 1 to 2 teaspoons of ganache on a small metal spatula, and apply it on top of a tartlet as illustrated. Manipulate the ganache with the spatula to a point in the center. Remove excess ganache from the spatula, and begin with another portion for the next tartlet. Repeat until all the tartlets are covered, placing them on a clean baking sheet as each is finished. Refrigerate not more than 30 minutes, or just long enough to partially firm the ganache.

7. Remove the tartlets from the refrigerator, and, if desired, gently tap cocoa through a sieve over each tartlet. Make three separate diagonal slices in each chilled ganache dome with the end of a small, flexible metal icing spatula as illustrated. Dip the spatula's blade into very hot water before each diagonal slice, and wipe the blade clean for the next cut. As you cut, press each portion of chocolate slightly outward, forming a petal effect; a small pyramid is formed in the center after you have completed the three slices.

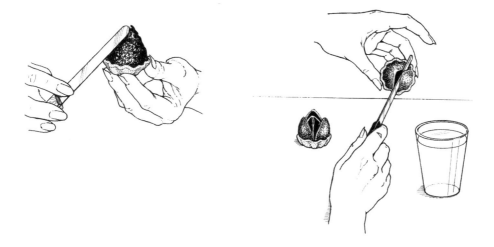

8. Stack undecorated cookies in airtight sturdy plastic containers, separating the layers with waxed paper, and freeze up to 1 month. Store decorated cookies in one layer in covered, foil-lined cardboard containers, such as cake boxes, at room temperature up to 3 days.

VARIATION NOTE

• When time is limited, try an easy alternate finish for these cookies. Pipe out mounds of the ganache cream on top of each tartlet in the shape of a "kiss." The time to pipe the ganache is when you can manipulate it as the instructions direct in the recipe above. The piped kiss shines with an ebony gloss as the ganache cream sets.

Chocolate Tulips

Tiffany Rings

Maple and milk chocolate make a dynamic duo in these cookies that get their name from the hole that's cut from the middle of each small round of thinly rolled dough. These tender cookies, sweetened with both maple sugar and maple syrup, are decorated with a shiny two-tone chocolate glaze.

DOUGH

2⅓ cups (325 grams) unsifted all-purpose flour

⅛ teaspoon salt

8 ounces (2 sticks) unsalted butter, room temperature

¼ cup (50 grams) granulated sugar

¼ cup (40 grams) granulated pure maple sugar

2 tablespoons pure maple syrup

1 teaspoon vanilla

DECORATION
Milk Chocolate Suede Glaze

¼ cup (1½ ounces) solid vegetable shortening

1 pound milk chocolate, finely chopped

2 ounces semisweet chocolate, melted

1. In a medium bowl, blend the flour and salt briefly with a wire whisk; set aside. In the large bowl of an electric mixer, cream the butter at medium-low speed until smooth, about 1 minute. Beat in the sugars at medium speed until the mixture is well combined and slightly fluffy. With a rubber spatula, scrape down the sides of the bowl. Beat in the maple syrup and vanilla until smooth and blended. Lower mixer speed, and gradually blend in the flour mixture until the mixture is thoroughly combined.

2. Divide dough in half; roll out each portion of dough between two sheets of waxed paper to form a circle 11 inches in diameter and ⅛ inch thick. Leaving

the dough between the waxed paper, transfer the circles to a baking sheet and refrigerate until firm, for at least 2 hours or up to 3 days; or freeze, well wrapped, up to 1 month.

3. Adjust rack to lower third of oven and preheat oven to 325 degrees. Line two cool baking sheets with parchment paper.

4. Remove one dough circle package at a time from the refrigerator. Peel off top waxed paper sheet, replace it loosely on top, and flip the entire package over. Peel off and discard the second sheet of waxed paper.

5. Using a 1½-inch round cutter, cut out circles in the dough. Put the circles ½ inch apart on baking sheets. Using a ½-inch plain decorating tip (such as Ateco #6) as a cutter, cut out a hole in the center of each cookie. (Dough from the centers is reusable.)

6. Bake, one sheet at a time, for 8 to 10 minutes or until the cookies are no longer shiny, are light beige, and feel slightly firm (lightly touch a few). Place baking sheet on a wire rack to cool cookies completely.

7. Milk Chocolate Suede Glaze: Combine the shortening and milk chocolate in a 3-quart mixing bowl. Place it over a saucepan filled with enough hot tap water (120 degrees) to reach the bottom of the bowl. Stir mixture occasionally until the glaze is liquid, smooth, and close to 110 degrees. If water begins to cool while melting the chocolate, maintain the 120-degree temperature over very low heat.

8. Set the cookies, spacing them 1 inch apart, on wire racks set over shallow baking pans to catch drips. Ladle about 2 tablespoons glaze over each cookie, masking it completely. After masking pastries, gently move each one slightly on the rack with a small metal spatula while the glaze is liquid, to remove chocolate drippings from its underside. This neat finish also keeps the pastries from sticking to the rack.

9. Using a small handmade paper cone with its tip snipped off, pipe thin lines of the liquid semisweet chocolate, zigzag fashion, back and forth over each glazed cookie.

10. Stack undecorated cookies in an airtight metal container and store up to 1 week. Store decorated cookies in one layer in a covered foil-lined cardboard container, such as a cake box, at room temperature up to 2 days.

BAKING NOTES

- You can find jars of pure granulated maple sugar in specialty food stores and specialty food sections in supermarkets.
- It's tricky to incorporate milk chocolate into a cookie dough and achieve a tasty result. The solution is to use it as an ingredient in a glaze as I do in these cookies.

Chocolate Coins

Chocolate, cocoa powder, and almond paste collaborate to create a delicate balance of flavors in these luxurious cookies. Dough is formed into a roll and sliced into coins. After baking, thinly rolled chocolate marzipan, the same diameter as the cookie, is used to top each one before a shiny chocolate glaze is applied. A small scalloped piece of marzipan and a jewel-like dot of jelly crown each cookie to give them a touch of drama.

DOUGH

1 cup (140 grams) unsifted all-purpose flour

⅛ teaspoon salt

2½ ounces (¼ cup) almond paste, room temperature

⅓ cup (65 grams) light brown sugar

3 ounces (6 tablespoons) unsalted butter, room temperature

1 egg yolk

¼ teaspoon vanilla

CHOCOLATE MARZIPAN FILLING

2 cups (200 grams) unsifted powdered sugar

¼ cup (25 grams) unsifted cocoa powder

½ teaspoon coffee powder

8 ounces (scant 1 cup) almond paste, room temperature

2 ounces (4 tablespoons) unsalted butter

2 tablespoons light corn syrup

⅛ teaspoon *each* vanilla and almond extract

DECORATION
European Chocolate Glaze

⅔ cup water

1 cup plus 2 tablespoons (225 grams) granulated sugar

8 ounces semisweet chocolate, finely chopped

4 ounces unsweetened chocolate, finely chopped

2 teaspoons vegetable oil

3 ounces (⅓ cup) marzipan (Odense)

2 tablespoons red currant jelly

1. In a bowl, whisk the flour and salt briefly with a wire whisk; set aside. In the large bowl of an electric mixer, break up the almond paste with mixer at low speed. Add the sugar and continue to mix until incorporated. Increase speed to medium and beat in the butter until mixture is smooth, scraping down the sides of the bowl. Add the egg yolk, then the vanilla, and beat until mixture is fluffy. Lower speed, and gradually blend in the dry ingredients, combining thoroughly.

2. Divide dough in half, and roll each portion into one 9-inch-long cylinder about 1¼ inches in diameter. Wrap in plastic and refrigerate until firm, for at least 4 hours or up to 3 days; or freeze, well wrapped, up to 1 month.

3. Adjust rack to lower third of oven and preheat oven to 325 degrees. Line two large cool baking sheets with parchment paper.

Chocolate Coins

4. Remove one cylinder of dough at a time from refrigerator. Using a sharp knife, slice the dough into rounds ⅛ inch thick, and set them about ½ inch apart on baking sheets.

5. Bake, one sheet at a time, for 8 to 10 minutes or until the cookies are no longer shiny and feel firm (lightly touch a few). Place baking sheet on a wire rack until cookies are completely cool.

6. Chocolate Marzipan Filling: In a medium bowl, blend the powdered sugar, cocoa powder, and coffee powder briefly with a wire whisk; set aside. In the large bowl of an electric mixer, break up the almond paste with the mixer at low speed. Add the butter, then the corn syrup and the vanilla and almond extracts, and mix until smooth and incorporated, scraping down the sides of the bowl. Blend in the dry ingredients just until mixture is thoroughly combined.

7. Roll out marzipan less than ⅛ inch thick on a surface lightly dusted with powdered sugar. Using a round cookie cutter the same dimension as cookies, cut out circles and set one on top of each cookie.

8. European Chocolate Glaze: In a 1-quart heavy-bottomed saucepan, heat the water with the sugar, stirring occasionally to dissolve sugar. Bring just to a boil. Off heat, stir in the chocolates and oil until smooth. If necessary, stir in additional hot tap water to adjust glaze's viscosity for coating cookies.

9. Set the cookies 1 inch apart on wire racks set over shallow baking pans to catch drips. Then, ladle about 2 tablespoons warm and liquid glaze over each cookie, to cover completely. After masking pastries, gently move each one slightly on the rack with a small metal spatula while the glaze is liquid, to remove chocolate drippings from its underside. This neat finish also keeps the pastries from sticking to the rack.

10. When glaze has set, about 1 hour, roll out the marzipan ¹⁄₁₆ inch thick on a surface lightly dusted with powdered sugar. Using a ½-inch round scalloped cutter, cut out shapes and place one in the center of each glazed cookie. Using a small paper cone with its tip snipped off, pipe a tiny dot of jelly in the center of each scalloped circle.

11. Stack undecorated cookies in an airtight metal container and store up to 1 week. Store decorated cookies in one layer in a covered, foil-lined cardboard container, such as a cake box, at room temperature up to 1 day.

DECORATING NOTE

• I make the chocolate marzipan for the filling from scratch to achieve the best flavor. However, when I need unflavored marzipan as for the Chocolate Coin decoration, I save time and buy Odense-brand marzipan.

Chocolate Starlets

These are rich with the flavor of walnuts, a hint of spice, and, of course, chocolate. Decorating them couldn't be easier, after you turn the fluted tartlets over to show off their star-like shape.

DOUGH

½ recipe Chocolate Miniature Tartlet Pastry (page 216)

FILLING

½ cup (70 grams) unsifted all-purpose flour

5 ounces (1½ cups) walnuts, finely ground

½ teaspoon ground cinnamon

4 ounces (1 stick) unsalted butter, room temperature

½ cup plus 2 tablespoons (125 grams) granulated sugar

3 egg yolks

DECORATION

½ cup (50 grams) unsifted powdered sugar

Chocolate Honey Ganache Glaze

2 tablespoons heavy cream

2 teaspoons honey

2 ounces semisweet chocolate, finely chopped

1. Adjust rack to lower third of oven and preheat oven to 350 degrees. Arrange four dozen ungreased fluted tins, 1½ inches in diameter, close together on a large baking sheet that measures at least 12 × 15½ × ½ inches.

2. Pinch off the dough, 1 teaspoon at a time, and drop into fluted tins. One by one, roll dough pieces into balls in the palms of your hands. With index finger, press center of each dough ball into a tin; then press dough up the sides of the tin while rotating the tin to distribute the dough evenly.

3. Filling: In a medium bowl, whisk the flour, nuts, and cinnamon to blend. Set aside. In the large bowl of an electric mixer at medium-low speed, cream the butter in a 1½-quart mixing bowl until soft, creamy, and smooth, about 30 seconds. Beat in the sugar until the mixture is lighter in texture and the sugar has been absorbed. Add the yolks and continue mixing until incorporated and smooth. Lower speed, and gradually add the dry ingredients until the mixture is smooth and thoroughly combined.

4. Using a 16-inch pastry bag fitted with a ⅜-inch plain decorating tip (such as Ateco #3), pipe the equivalent of ½ teaspoon of filling into each pastry-lined tin. Lift the tip slightly as each tin is filled in order to cut off the flow of filling. (Piping filling from a pastry bag is easier, more uniform, and less fattening than using a spoon since it reduces the temptation of licking your finger clean after scooping filling from the spoon.)

5. Bake for about 15 minutes, or until the top of the filling is light golden and the chocolate crust is no longer shiny but dull and feels slightly firm to the touch. Cool the tartlets, on the baking sheet, on a rack for 10 minutes, or until cool enough to touch. Remove each tartlet by pinching the tin with thumb and forefinger and turning it upside down, so that the pastry falls into your hand.

6. Place tartlets upside down on a rack so the tartlet displays its star shape. Tap the powdered sugar from a sieve to sprinkle sugar over the top of each tartlet.

7. Chocolate Honey Ganache Glaze: Combine the heavy cream and honey in a small heavy-bottomed saucepan. Heat just to boiling. Off heat, stir in the chocolate just until melted and smooth. Set aside just until it thickens to the consistency of honey, about 30 minutes. Fill a small handmade paper cone half full of the glaze, snip off the cone's tip, and pipe a small dot in the center of each tartlet.

8. Stack undecorated tartlets in an airtight metal container and store at room temperature up to 10 days or freeze up to 1 month. Store decorated tartlets in a single layer in a covered, foil-lined cardboard container, such as a cake box, at room temperature up to 2 days.

White Blossom Circles

Makes 8 dozen
1½-inch cookies

Making these chocolate shortbread cookies is a cinch. To dress them up, all you do is top each circle with a swirl of white chocolate ganache.

DOUGH

1¾ cup (245 grams) unsifted all-purpose flour

⅓ cup (35 grams) unsifted cocoa powder

¼ cup (45 grams) rice flour

7 ounces (1¾ sticks) unsalted butter, room temperature

⅔ cup (130 grams) granulated sugar

Additional granulated sugar for coating

WHITE CHOCOLATE GANACHE

⅓ cup (2½ ounces) heavy cream

5 ounces white chocolate, finely chopped

1. In a medium bowl, blend the flour, cocoa powder, and rice flour briefly with a wire whisk; set aside. In the large bowl of an electric mixer, cream the butter at medium-low speed until smooth, about 1 minute. Beat in the sugar at medium speed until well combined and slightly fluffy, scraping down the sides of the bowl. Lower speed, and gradually add the flour mixture, combining thoroughly.

2. Divide dough in quarters. Form into four cylinders 6 inches long and 1¼ inches in diameter. Roll each cylinder in granulated sugar to coat. Wrap in plastic and refrigerate until firm, for at least 4 hours or up to 3 days; or freeze, well wrapped, up to 1 month.

3. Adjust rack to lower third of oven and preheat oven to 300 degrees. Line two large cool baking sheets with parchment paper.

4. Remove one cylinder of dough at a time from refrigerator. Using a sharp knife, cut 3/16-inch-thick slices from dough and place ¾ inch apart on baking sheets.

5. Bake, one sheet at a time, for 12 to 14 minutes or until cookies are no longer shiny and feel slightly firm and set (lightly touch a few). Do not overbake, since chocolate scorches easily. Place baking sheet on a wire rack to cool. Lift cookies from parchment when cool.

6. White Chocolate Ganache: Combine the heavy cream and white chocolate in a 3-quart bowl. Place it over a saucepan filled with enough hot tap water (120 degrees) to reach the bottom of the container. Stir the mixture occasionally until it is smooth. If water begins to cool while melting the chocolate, maintain the 120-degree temperature over very low heat. Set ganache aside at room temperature about 30 minutes or until it develops enough body that when a small amount is lifted on a rubber spatula, it stays in place without falling off.

7. With a 14-inch pastry bag fitted with a swirl-shaped decorating tip (such as Ateco #5-A), pipe a flower-like form on each cookie.

8. Stack undecorated cookies in an airtight metal container and store at room temperature up to 1 week; or freeze up to 1 month. Store decorated cookies in a single layer in a covered foil-lined cardboard container, such as a cake box, at room temperature up to 2 days.

DECORATING NOTE

• An alternate decoration is to place five small white chocolate petals on each cookie to form a flower. To make the petals, place a strip of aluminum foil on a flat work surface. Melt 2 ounces finely chopped white chocolate in a small bowl set over a pan of water at 110 degrees, stirring occasionally until smooth. Remove bowl from water and, with a rubber spatula, stir chocolate occasionally to cool it a bit, about 5 minutes. While it is still smooth and liquid, dip the back side of a small table teaspoon into the chocolate, and smear it gently onto the foil, moving the spoon toward you. Repeat the procedure using about ⅛ teaspoon chocolate for each petal. Place in a cool room and allow the petals to set until firm. Slip the blade of a small metal spatula under each one to release it from the foil.

White Blossom Circles

Cocoa Cavaliers

Here's an easy technique for converting thick cylinders of dough into triangular shapes. In this case, a chocolate triangle-shaped cookie is topped with an almond paste streusel.

DOUGH

1½ cups (210 grams) unsifted all-purpose flour

¼ cup (25 grams) unsifted cocoa powder

5 ounces (1¼ sticks) unsalted butter, room temperature

⅔ cup (130 grams) granulated sugar

ALMOND PASTE STREUSEL

3 ounces (⅓ cup) almond paste, room temperature

2 tablespoons light brown sugar

1½ ounces (3 tablespoons) unsalted butter, room temperature

⅔ cup (90 grams) unsifted all-purpose flour

1. In a medium bowl, blend the flour and cocoa powder briefly with a wire whisk; set aside. In the large bowl of an electric mixer, cream the butter at medium-low speed until smooth, about 1 minute. Beat in the sugar at medium speed until well combined and slightly fluffy, scraping down the sides of the bowl. Lower speed, and gradually add the flour mixture, combining thoroughly.

2. Divide dough in thirds and roll each portion of dough into a cylinder about 8 inches long. Wrap each cylinder in plastic wrap. Working with one cylinder at a time, place a 1½-inch-wide and at least 12-inch-long ruler along *each* long side of the dough cylinder, so that both rulers are perpendicular to the work surface. Apply enough pressure to both rulers to slant them so that they meet at the top, thereby shaping the dough cylinder into a triangular-shaped log. This procedure extends the dough to about 9 inches. Twist the plastic wrap at each

end to close. Refrigerate the logs until firm, for at least 4 hours or up to 3 days; or freeze, well wrapped, up to 1 month.

3. Almond Paste Streusel: In a 3-quart bowl, mix the almond paste and sugar with your fingertips to remove any lumps in the almond paste. Add the butter until blended. Mix in the flour and, with fingertips, separate mixture into tiny crumbly pieces. Cover and set aside at room temperature.

4. Adjust rack to lower third of oven and preheat oven to 325 degrees. Line two large cool baking sheets with parchment paper.

5. Remove one triangular-shaped dough log from the refrigerator at a time. Using a sharp knife, cut ³/₁₆-inch-thick slices and space ½ inch apart on baking sheet. Using a small pastry brush, lightly brush each cookie with water, and then carefully sprinkle streusel over top (any streusel on baking sheet will burn as cookies bake). Repeat the procedure for the remaining logs of dough.

6. Bake, one sheet at a time, 10 to 12 minutes or until the cookies are no longer shiny but appear dull and feel slightly firm (lightly touch a few). Do not overbake and do not let the streusel color more than pale blond. Place baking sheet on a wire rack to cool. Lift cookies from parchment when cool.

7. Stack in an airtight metal container and store at room temperature up to 1 week; or freeze up to 1 month.

BAKING NOTES

- If the dough is not cohesive after mixing it, add 1 tablespoon water and continue to mix until thoroughly combined.
- In this recipe, use water instead of an egg wash. Water helps the streusel adhere to the cookies and becomes invisible during baking through evaporation. An egg wash would leave a film on the chocolate dough and could burn during baking.

Cocoa Cavaliers

Chocolate Mint Nuggets

Makes 6 dozen
1½-inch cookies

The natural combination of chocolate and mint is highlighted in these cookies, accented with toasted hazelnuts. Since mint tends to dominate, I've added it only as a fresh accent—a small mint leaf placed in a dollop of chocolate icing on the top of each morsel.

DOUGH

1½ cups (210 grams) unsifted all-purpose flour

¼ cup (25 grams) unsifted cocoa powder

2 ounces (⅓ cup, slightly mounded) toasted hazelnuts, finely ground

8 ounces (2 sticks) unsalted butter, room temperature

⅔ cup (130 grams) granulated sugar

1 teaspoon vanilla

DECORATION

Bittersweet Chocolate Icing

1 ounce semisweet chocolate, finely chopped

2 tablespoons (1 ounce) unsalted butter

1 tablespoon unsifted cocoa powder

Fresh mint leaves

1. Adjust rack to lower third of oven and preheat oven to 325 degrees. Line two large cool baking sheets with parchment paper.

2. In a small bowl, blend the flour, cocoa powder, and hazelnuts briefly with a wire whisk; set aside. In the large bowl of an electric mixer, cream butter at medium-low speed until smooth, about 1 minute. Increase speed to medium, add the sugar and then the vanilla, and mix until well combined and slightly fluffy. Lower speed, add the flour mixture in two additions, scraping down the sides of the bowl, and combine ingredients thoroughly.

3. With your palms, shape dough, 1 teaspoon at a time, into balls and drop 1 inch apart on the baking sheet.

4. Bake, one sheet at a time, 11 to 13 minutes or until the cookies are no longer shiny, but dull, and the bottoms are brown. Do not overbake. These cookies are especially fragile when hot. Place baking sheet on a wire rack to cool. Lift off cookies from parchment when cool.

5. Bittersweet Chocolate Icing: Combine the chocolate and butter in a small bowl. Place it over a saucepan filled with enough hot water (120 degrees) to reach the bottom of the container. Using a rubber spatula, stir occasionally until melted. Add the cocoa powder, and continue stirring over the hot water until mixture blends together smoothly.

6. While the icing is liquid, using a small handmade paper cone with its tip snipped off, pipe a tiny dot of icing in the center of each cookie. Set a small mint leaf slightly off center in the icing dot to anchor it.

7. Stack undecorated cookies in airtight metal containers and store at room temperature up to 1 week; or freeze up to 1 month. Store decorated cookies in a single layer in covered foil-lined cardboard containers, such as cake boxes, in a cool room up to 2 days.

Chocolate Mint Nuggets

Chocolate Pistachio Cigarettes

Makes 3½ dozen
1½-inch-long
cigarettes

To decorate these intensely flavored chocolate cookies, dip both ends in melted chocolate, then in blanched, roasted finely ground pistachio nuts.

BATTER

⅓ cup (45 grams) unsifted all-purpose flour

2 tablespoons unsifted cocoa powder

2 ounces (½ stick) unsalted butter, room temperature

½ cup (100 grams) granulated sugar

¼ cup (about 2 large) egg whites, room temperature

1 teaspoon vanilla

DECORATION

2 ounces semisweet chocolate, finely chopped

2 ounces pistachios, blanched, roasted, and finely ground

1. Adjust rack to lower third of oven and preheat oven to 375 degrees. Unwrap an end of a chilled stick of unsalted butter and rub it over two large cool Teflon-coated baking sheets to apply a very thin film of fat.

2. In a small bowl, briefly blend the flour and the cocoa powder with a wire whisk or rubber spatula; set aside. In the large bowl of an electric mixer, cream the butter at medium speed until smooth, about 2 minutes. Beat in the sugar until mixture is light and fluffy. Gradually add the egg whites, then the vanilla. Don't worry if the mixture appears curdled at this point. Lower mixer speed and blend in dry ingredients until mixture is smooth and thoroughly combined.

3. Drop four ½ teaspoonsful of batter on each baking sheet. Using a small offset metal spatula, spread into paper-thin squares approximately 1½ × 1½ inches.

4. Bake, one sheet at a time, for 5 to 7 minutes or until wafers no longer appear glossy, but are dull. Do not overbake or cookies will scorch. Place baking sheet on a wire rack.

5. While cookies are warm and pliable, roll one at a time, baked-bottom side in, around a wooden dowel ³/₈ inch in diameter and 6 inches long. After shaping a cookie, gently slip it off the dowel to a wire rack until cool. Repeat baking and rolling procedure with remaining batter.

6. Melt the chocolate in a small bowl set over a saucepan of hot water at 120 degrees. Dip just the tips of the cigarette cookies in the chocolate, then in the pistachio nuts. Set cookies on aluminum foil until chocolate sets.

7. Stack cigarettes in an airtight metal container and store at room temperature up to 3 days. (See the information on nontoxic blue crystals on page 12.)

BAKING NOTE

• When baking these cookies, it won't take too long to complete the batch if you set up a system similar to a production line. When I remove one baking sheet from the oven, I replace it with another, then I shape the just-baked cigarettes while they are still warm, then I form batter into squares on another sheet to exchange with the one that is baking. This keeps a constant flow of baking and shaping.

Chocolate Pistachio Cigarettes

195

Chocolate Shadows

When I want a simple but elegant cookie for entertaining, I bake these butter cookies topped with a swirl of chocolate dough. Orange sorbet and orange sections served in stem glasses with these fine-textured Chocolate Shadows make a grand dessert.

BUTTER DOUGH

- 6 ounces (1½ sticks) unsalted butter, room temperature
- ¼ cup (50 grams) granulated sugar
- ½ cup (50 grams) unsifted powdered sugar
- 1 egg yolk
- 1 teaspoon vanilla
- 1½ cups (210 grams) unsifted all-purpose flour

CHOCOLATE DOUGH

- 2 cups (280 grams) unsifted all-purpose flour
- ⅛ teaspoon salt
- 8 ounces (2 sticks) unsalted butter, room temperature
- ¾ cup (150 grams) granulated sugar
- ½ cup (50 grams) unsifted cocoa powder
- 3 large eggs, room temperature
- 2 teaspoons finely grated orange zest

DECORATION

- ½ cup strained apricot or cherry jam

Chocolate Butter

- 1 ounce (2 tablespoons) unsalted butter
- 3 ounces semisweet chocolate, finely chopped

1. Butter Dough: In the large bowl of an electric mixer, cream the butter at medium-low speed until smooth, about 1 minute. Beat in the sugars at medium speed until creamy. Add the egg yolk, and then the vanilla, beating just until fluffy, and scraping down the sides of the bowl. Lower mixer speed, gradually add the flour, and mix just until thoroughly combined.

2. Divide dough in half; roll one portion at a time between two sheets of waxed paper to form a circle about 11 inches in diameter and ⅛ inch thick. Leaving the dough between the waxed paper, transfer the circles to a baking sheet and refrigerate until firm, for at least 2 hours or up to 3 days; or freeze, well wrapped, up to 1 month.

3. Chocolate Dough: In a mixing bowl, blend the flour and salt briefly with a wire whisk; set aside. In the large bowl of an electric mixer, cream the butter at medium-low speed until fluffy. Add the sugar and continue to mix until well combined and fluffy, scraping down the sides of the bowl. Add the cocoa powder, beating until incorporated. Then beat in the eggs, one at a time, until mixture is fluffy. Add the orange zest. Lower speed, and gradually blend in the flour mixture, combining thoroughly. Set aside.

4. Adjust rack to lower third of oven and preheat oven to 325 degrees. Line two large cool baking sheets with parchment paper.

5. Remove one butter dough package from the refrigerator at a time. Peel off top waxed paper sheet, replace it loosely on top, and flip the entire package over. Peel off and discard the second sheet of waxed paper.

6. Using a 1½-inch round scalloped cookie cutter, cut out shapes in the dough. Place the cutouts about ½ inch apart on baking sheets.

7. Fill a 16-inch pastry bag fitted with an open star decorating tip (such as Ateco #2) with half the chocolate dough. Pipe a rosette of chocolate dough the equivalent of 1 teaspoon on top of each unbaked butter cookie. Refill bag with remaining dough when needed.

8. Bake, one sheet at a time, 10 minutes or until the cookies' scalloped edges and bottoms are faintly colored. Do not overbake. Place baking sheet on a wire rack for 10 minutes. Lift cookies from parchment to a rack to cool completely.

9. Heat the jam just to warm and liquefy it. Using a small pastry brush, coat the chocolate rosettes with the jam.

10. Chocolate Butter: Melt the butter and chocolate in a small bowl set over a saucepan of water at 120 degrees. Using a small handmade paper cone with its tip snipped off, pipe a small dot of chocolate on top of each cookie.

11. Stack undecorated cookies in an airtight metal container, using strips of aluminum foil between layers to pad the cookies and prevent abrasions that might disturb the cookies' shapes, and store at room temperature up to 1 week; or freeze, well wrapped, up to 1 month. (Aluminum foil does not absorb the butter from the cookies.) Store decorated cookies in one layer in covered foil-lined cardboard containers, such as cake boxes, at room temperature up to 3 days.

TECHNIQUE NOTE

- Use only half the chocolate dough in the pastry bag at a time. Filling it too full makes the pastry bag too difficult to manipulate.

Part III

Miniature Pastries

*J*ust as miniature cookie doughs with an abundance of butter owe their short tender texture to the fact that the flour is completely coated by the butter, miniature pastry doughs can be flaky, tender, crisp, and/or short according to how you blend the butter with the flour.

Mixing Miniature Pastry Doughs

The ratio of butter to flour, the butter's temperature—chilled or room temperature—and the type of liquid added, such as sour cream, egg, or water, all contribute to the texture of miniature pastries. However, the key to making miniature pastries successfully is the proper blending of fat and flour.

In the Sour Cream Pastry recipe on page 239, it's the incomplete blending of chilled butter into the flour that gives it a flaky texture. In the Cream Cheese Pastry recipe on page 255, the chilled butter is blended more intimately into the flour to make it a more tender pastry rather than a flaky or crisp one. And in the Miniature Tartlet Pastry recipe on page 205, it's the complete blending of the butter into the sugar and flour that yields it a short, crisp, and tender crust.

In the Heavy Cream Flaky Pastry recipe on page 262, chilled butter is blended into the flour until the particles are the size of small peas before the dough is rolled and folded to produce a flaky and tender pastry that lifts slightly during baking. The Blitz Puff Pastry recipe on page 272 has a crisp flaky texture similar to traditional puff pastry. Though the Blitz may not rise as high, it's quicker and easier to make. Blitz Puff Pastry begins like a flaky pie dough before the rolling and folding procedure.

Though each pastry recipe specifies proper blending procedures for successful results, you may choose to make the pastry either by hand or machine.

Pastries, especially small quantities, made by hand are flakiest since there's less chance of overmanipulating. Hands, even using a metal pastry blender, move more slowly than a machine, giving you more control when blending the butter into the flour.

But that is not to say that very fine pastries cannot be made in a heavy-duty mixer or a food processor. When using a mixer, use the paddle attachment and blend the butter into the flour on low speed. When using a food processor, remember that its power makes things happen very fast.

Rolling Miniature Pastry Doughs

A cool, smooth-surfaced work area at about hip level provides the best leverage for rolling the dough.

To roll a rectangular or square shape, begin with an oblong or square piece of chilled dough. Set it on a lightly floured work surface. Flatten dough lightly. Roll from the center away from you, then lift rolling pin and return it to the center and roll toward you, each time stopping short of the edges. For uniform thickness, use even strokes. Lift dough often to make sure it does not stick. Redust the work surface with just enough flour to keep the dough sliding as it extends without sticking. If the rolling pin sticks to the dough, lightly dust it with flour.

To lift a large piece of dough without tearing or stretching it, roll pastry loosely onto rolling pin, and transfer it to a baking sheet or wherever the recipe specifies.

Never turn the dough over and roll on the other side. If the dough sticks to the work surface, carefully slide a metal spatula under the stuck portion, and then lift dough and dust surface with a little flour. Rub off any pieces of dough adhering to the rolling pin; they could puncture the dough.

To roll a circular shape, begin with a round disk of chilled dough. Beginning in the center of the disk, push the rolling pin outward in one stroke, using enough pressure to extend the dough gradually. Avoid rolling over the edges; this helps avoid cracking or creating too thin an edge. Lift and rotate the dough a one-eighth turn clockwise (one-eighth turns keep the dough circular, one-quarter turns make it square). Follow procedures described for the rectangular or square shape, except always roll dough from the center outward.

Tartlet Miniatures

Miniature Tartlet Pastry
205

Caramel Carmenitas
207

Garnet Tartlets
210

Chocolate Cherry Chaps
212

Rose Tartlets
214

Double Chocolate Tartlets
216

Mazarine Tartlets
218

Lemon Meringue Tartlets
220

Scheherazade Tartlets
222

Pumpkin Tartlets
224

Jade Buttercups
226

Poirettes
228

Lemon Drops
230

Raspberry Lemon Tartlets
232

Swiss Bettinas
234

Midas Cups
235

Miniature Tartlet Pastry

This favorite not-too-sweet cookie recipe is my first choice for miniature tartlet shells. The butter-rich, not overly sweet, egg-enriched dough with fat intimately mixed into the sugar and flour yields a short, crisp, and tender crust after baking and a well-balanced taste to complement any filling.

These characteristics make it perfect for lining tartlet tins and pans for bar cookies. Therefore, I think it's more appropriate to classify it as a sweetened short pastry than as a cookie. This dough is a joy to handle because the sugar curtails gluten development, reducing the risk of shrinkage or toughness. You can press it into tartlet tins, roll it, or even reroll it.

Makes 8 dozen round fluted miniature tartlet shells, 1½ inches in diameter

DOUGH

2½ cups (350 grams) unsifted all-purpose flour	8 ounces (2 sticks) unsalted butter, chilled and cut into ¼-inch slices
⅛ teaspoon salt	1 large egg
⅓ cup (65 grams) granulated sugar	1 teaspoon vanilla

1. Put the flour, salt, and sugar in a food processor bowl. Process just to blend ingredients. Scatter all the butter slices over the flour mixture, and process with on/off bursts until the mixture has the consistency of cornmeal.

2. Whisk the egg and vanilla together in a small bowl. With the motor on, pour egg mixture down the feed tube. Process until the ingredients form a ball. Remove the dough to work surface, and with the heel of your hand press the dough together until it is smooth and cohesive.

3. Adjust rack to lower third of oven and preheat oven to 350 degrees. Arrange four dozen ungreased 1½-inch fluted tartlet tins close together on a 12- × 15½- × ½-inch baking sheet.

4. Pinch off 1 teaspoon of dough and drop it into a tin. Repeat until all the tins contain dough. One by one, roll each piece of dough into a ball in the palm

of your hands. This step aids in shaping the tartlet shells more evenly. To press dough into tins, with index finger, press center of dough ball into the tin, then press dough up the sides while rotating the tin to distribute the dough evenly. The object is to use just enough dough to line the tartlet tin without creating a thick shell. (Notice that I recommend completing one task before beginning another: Fill baking sheet with tins, pinch off a teaspoon of dough for each tin, roll dough between your palms to form a smooth ball, and last press the balls evenly into the tins. Handling one movement at a time is easier and faster. You discover your own rhythm from the repetition.)

5. Bake tartlet shells in oven for 12 to 15 minutes, or until light golden. Remove baking sheet from oven to rack to cool. When the tins are cool enough to touch, squeeze each tin gently with your thumb and forefinger, turn it upside down, and let the miniature tartlet shell drop into the palm of your hand.

6. Repeat the filling and baking procedure with remaining dough.

7. Stack cooled unfilled shells in an airtight metal container and store at room temperature up to 1 week.

STORING NOTE

- Refrigerate the dough, well wrapped, up to 1 week; or freeze up to 1 month. Bring dough to room temperature before working with it.

VARIATION NOTE

- To make whole-wheat tartlets, substitute unbleached whole-wheat flour for half the all-purpose flour.

Miniature Tartlet Pastry

Caramel Carmenitas

The genuine taste of the popular pecan is a treasure when added to a silky smooth creamy caramel filling.

DOUGH

1 recipe Miniature Tartlet Pastry
(page 205)

CARAMEL PECAN BUTTERCREAM

½ cup (100 grams) granulated
sugar

1 ounce (2 tablespoons) unsalted
butter

⅓ cup heavy cream, room
temperature

4 ounces (1 stick) unsalted
butter, room temperature

2 ounces (½ cup) pecans,
toasted, finely ground

DECORATION

4 ounces (1 cup) pecans, finely
chopped

1. To make these tartlets, you may form individual balls of dough and press them into 1½-inch fluted tins as the Miniature Tartlet Pastry recipe specifies. For variety, however, this recipe uses barquette (boat-shaped) tartlet tins, 2½ inches long, 1 inch wide on top, with ½-inch-deep sloping sides. I've discovered that rolling a thinly rolled portion of room-temperature dough up on a rolling pin and unrolling it over a quantity of tins is the quickest, easiest, and most efficient way to fill a lot of them all at once.

2. Adjust rack to lower third of oven and preheat oven to 350 degrees. Lay moist towels on work surface, and group barquette molds on top of the towels to ready them for filling with rolled-out dough.

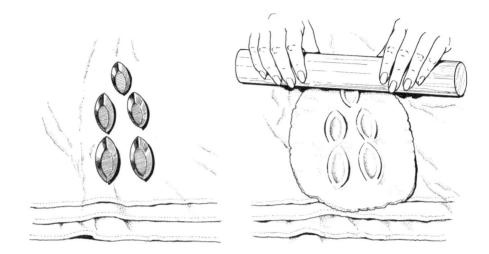

3. Set room-temperature dough on the work surface. Then, with the heel of your hand, smear a small amount of the dough, about the size of an egg, on your work surface by pushing it away from you. Repeat with small amounts of the remaining dough. When you've worked all the dough in this manner, give it a few more strokes to bring it together. This kneading action is called *fraisage* and aids in developing just enough structure to make rolling and working with the dough more manageable. It reduces the dough's tendency to tear or crack while being rolled and lifted.

4. Divide dough in fourths. Roll out one portion at a time on a lightly floured surface until it is no more than ⅛ inch thick. Rearrange the tins, close together, in the approximate shape of the dough. Roll up dough on rolling pin and unroll over barquettes. Dust the dough lightly with flour and, with a small ball of dough, ease the dough into the molds. Roll rolling pin over molds to trim edges and remove excess dough.

5. Arrange the dough-filled tins on a baking sheet. Bake 12 to 15 minutes or until light golden. Remove baking sheet with the tins to a wire rack to cool. When tins are cool enough to handle, turn each one upside down and let the tartlet fall into the palm of your other hand. Repeat the rolling and baking process with the remaining dough.

6. Caramel Pecan Buttercream: Heat the sugar in a 1½-quart heavy-bottomed saucepan or an unlined copper sugar pot over low heat. Stir occasionally with a small wooden spoon until the sugar dissolves. Increase the heat to medium-high and cook until the melted sugar becomes amber in color, about 7 minutes. Off heat, add the 2 tablespoons butter, then the cream. Be careful—the mixture bubbles madly. With the spoon, stir until the ingredients blend together smoothly. Pour into a bowl and refrigerate until cold.

Using an electric mixer at medium speed, whip the 4 ounces of butter in a medium mixing bowl until light and fluffy, about 2 minutes. Gradually add the caramel cream, a couple of tablespoons at a time. When the mixture is airy and the ingredients are fully incorporated, stir in the ground pecans.

7. Scoop the equivalent of 1 to 2 teaspoons of the buttercream onto a small metal spatula, and put it in a shell. With the spatula, manipulate the buttercream into a mound in the center. Slope the sides with the spatula to crest at the top. Remove excess buttercream from the spatula, and begin with another portion for the next barquette.

8. Dip each tartlet into the pecans, tipping it so that only one side of the buttercream is coated.

9. Stack unfilled tartlet shells in an airtight metal container and store at room temperature up to 1 week. Store filled tartlets in one layer in a covered foil-lined cardboard container, such as a cake box, at room temperature up to 1 day.

TECHNIQUE NOTE

• Filling a quantity of tins all at once works well with any shape tin—round, square, rectangle, or even barquette. The only requirement is that the tins have sharp edges in order to enable you to cut off excess dough neatly after lining.

Caramel
Carmenitas

Garnet Tartlets

The combination of cream cheese and hazelnuts, glazed with red currants, produces a tart reminiscent of a nutty cheesecake.

DOUGH

½ recipe Miniature Tartlet Pastry
(page 205)

CREAMY HAZELNUT FILLING

8 ounces cream cheese

1½ ounces (scant ⅓ cup) hazelnuts, toasted and finely ground

½ cup (100 grams) granulated sugar

1 large egg

1 tablespoon sour cream

1 teaspoon finely grated lemon zest

DECORATION

1 cup red currant jelly

3 tablespoons cassis liqueur

1. To make these tartlets, you may form individual balls of dough and press them into 1½-inch fluted tins as the Miniature Tartlet Pastry recipe specifies. For variety, however, this recipe uses tins that measure 1½ inches in diameter with ¾-inch-deep sloping sides or 1¾ inches in diameter with ½-inch-deep sloping sides. I've discovered that filling these tins when the dough is chilled and firm is the quickest, easiest, and most efficient way.

2. Divide dough in half. Roll out each portion between two sheets of waxed paper to a circle slightly less than ⅛ inch thick and 10 inches in diameter. Leaving the dough between the waxed paper, transfer to a baking sheet and refrigerate until firm, for at least 2 hours or up to 3 days; or freeze, well wrapped, up to 1 month.

3. Adjust rack to lower third of oven and preheat oven to 350 degrees. Arrange four dozen ungreased tins, 1½ inches in diameter with ¾-inch-deep sloping sides or 1¾ inches in diameter with ½-inch-deep sloping sides, close together on large baking sheet.

4. Remove one dough circle at a time from the refrigerator, peel off the top waxed paper sheet, replace it loosely on top, and flip the entire package over. Peel off the second sheet of waxed paper.

5. Using a 2¼-inch round cutter, cut out circles in the dough. Place a dough circle on each tin. Using your index finger or a tin the same shape, press dough into tins.

6. Creamy Hazelnut Filling: Process all the ingredients in food processor bowl until mixture is smooth, about 30 seconds. Spoon or pipe, with a 14-inch pastry bag fitted with a ¼-in plain decorating tip (such as Ateco #2), about 1 teaspoon filling into each tartlet.

7. Bake for 12 to 15 minutes or until the crust is light golden. Place baking sheet on a wire rack for 10 minutes, or until tins are cool enough to touch. Squeeze each tin between your thumb and forefinger, turn upside down, and let the miniature tartlet fall into the palm of your other hand. Place on a rack to cool completely.

8. Heat jelly just to warm and liquefy it. Off the heat, stir in the cassis. With a pastry brush, coat each tartlet.

9. Stack undecorated tartlets in an airtight sturdy plastic container, separating layers with waxed paper, and freeze up to 1 month. Store decorated tartlets in one layer in a covered foil-lined cardboard container, such as a cake box, at room temperature up to 1 day.

Garnet Tartlets

Chocolate Cherry Chaps

Makes 4 dozen
1½-inch round
fluted tartlets

A single chocolate-covered cherry in a sour cherry–glazed tender tartlet is similar to a piece of candy in its own edible paper case. After eating the sweet juicy fruit dressed in semisweet chocolate, you'll agree: Chocolate never had it so good.

DOUGH

4 dozen (½ recipe) baked
Miniature Tartlet Pastry shells
(page 205)

FILLING

1 cup sour cherry jelly

Dark Chocolate Fruit Glaze

4 ounces (1 stick) unsalted butter

5 ounces semisweet chocolate,
finely chopped

1 ounce unsweetened chocolate,
finely chopped

4 dozen (1 pound) fresh bing
cherries with stems, room
temperature

1. Arrange the baked tartlet shells on a large tray or baking sheet.

2. Filling: Heat the jelly in a small saucepan just to warm and liquefy it. Using a pastry brush, coat each shell with a thin glaze of jelly.

3. Dark Chocolate Fruit Glaze: Place the butter and chocolates in a 1-quart bowl that fits snugly over a saucepan half filled with 120- to 130-degree water, to melt ingredients. Stir occasionally until smooth. If necessary, maintain the water's temperature over very low heat.

Chocolate Cherry Chaps

4. Dip cherries, one at a time, into liquid chocolate glaze, and then set each cherry in a tartlet shell. With scissors, trim each cherry stem, leaving a stem between ½ inch and ¾ inch.

5. Store tartlets in one layer in a covered foil-lined cardboard container, such as a cake box, at room temperature up to 1 day.

TECHNIQUE NOTE

• Clipping the cherry stems decorates each tartlet uniformly *and* reminds the person eating it that the cherry contains a pit.

Chocolate Cherry
Chaps

Rose Tartlets

These rich dark chocolate–glazed tartlets, filled with whipped cream delicately scented with almond liqueur and thin strips of red rose petals, capture the essence of romance in taste, presentation, and aroma.

DOUGH

½ recipe Miniature Tartlet Pastry
(page 205)

FILLING

Chocolate Butter Glaze

3 ounces unsalted butter

4 ounces semisweet chocolate, finely chopped

2 ounces unsweetened chocolate, finely chopped

Whipped Cream Filling

1 cup (8 ounces) heavy cream

2 tablespoons granulated sugar

1 tablespoon Amaretto liqueur

⅓ cup fragrant edible red rose petals, cut in chiffonade (thin strips)

DECORATION

2 tablespoons fragrant edible red rose petals, minced

1. To make these tartlets, you may form individual balls of dough and press them into the 1½-inch fluted tins as the Miniature Tartlet Pastry recipe specifies. For variety, however, this recipe uses oval-shaped tartlet tins, 2 inches long, 1¼ inches wide, with slightly sloping sides. I've discovered that when I use an unusual-shaped tin, the quickest, easiest, and most efficient way to fill the tins is to trace a stencil of the dough shape needed since a standard cutter is not available in a similar form.

2. To make a stencil of the tartlet's dimensions, press a small piece of waxed paper into the tartlet tin to make an impression. Cut out the tartlet's shape from the waxed paper, then trace these dimensions onto a piece of sturdy cardboard. Cut out the shape with a utility knife to finish the template.

3. Adjust rack to lower third of oven and preheat oven to 350 degrees. Set oval tartlet tins close together on large baking sheets.

4. Roll room-temperature dough on a lightly floured work surface until close to $\frac{1}{16}$ inch thick. Using the template, trace shapes in dough with a small paring knife. Set the cutouts on the tins. Dip a tin with the same dimensions and shape into flour, then press the dough cutouts into the tins.

5. Bake for 12 to 15 minutes or until the crust is light golden. Place baking sheet on a wire rack until the tins are cool enough to handle, about 10 minutes. Then turn each upside down, and let it drop into the palm of your hand. Set the pastries on a rack to cool completely. Transfer to a large tray or baking sheet.

6. Chocolate Butter Glaze: Place the butter and chocolates in a 1-quart bowl that fits snugly over a saucepan half filled with 120- to 130-degree water, to melt ingredients. Stir occasionally until smooth. If necessary, maintain the water's temperature over very low heat. Using a pastry brush, lightly coat each tartlet with melted chocolate butter. Set aside in a cool room until chocolate sets.

7. Whip the heavy cream with the sugar and liqueur until soft peaks form; fold in the rose fragments. Using a pastry bag fitted with an open star tip (such as Ateco #2), pipe decorative swirls into chocolate-coated shells.

8. Sprinkle rose pieces over the whipped cream filling and refrigerate until serving.

9. These are at their best if served within 2 hours of filling and decorating.

Rose Tartlets

Double Chocolate Tartlets

Makes 8 dozen
1½-inch round
fluted tartlets

Although figs are my favorite fresh fruit with this combination of tender chocolate short pastry and almond-chocolate filling, after tasting these tartlets, you'll find that variations with plums, pears, or peaches work well too.

CHOCOLATE MINIATURE TARTLET PASTRY

- 2 cups plus 1 tablespoon (297 grams) unsifted all-purpose flour
- ½ cup (100 grams) granulated sugar
- ⅓ cup (35 grams) unsifted cocoa powder
- 8 ounces (2 sticks) unsalted butter, chilled and cut into ¼-inch slices
- 1 large egg
- 1 teaspoon vanilla

CHOCOLATE FRANGIPANE FILLING

- 4 ounces (1 stick) unsalted butter
- ½ cup (100 grams) granulated sugar
- 2 large eggs
- 1 teaspoon vanilla
- 4 ounces (¾ cup) blanched almonds, finely ground
- 1 ounce unsweetened chocolate, finely ground

DECORATION

- 6 fresh figs, thinly sliced

1. Put the flour, sugar, and cocoa powder in a food processor bowl. Process just to blend ingredients. Scatter all the butter slices over the flour mixture, and process with on/off bursts until the mixture has the consistency of cornmeal.

2. Whisk the egg and vanilla together in a small bowl. With the motor on, pour egg mixture down the feed tube. Process until the ingredients form a ball.

Remove the dough to work surface, and with heel of your hand press the dough together until it is smooth and cohesive.

3. Adjust rack to lower third of oven and preheat oven to 350 degrees. Arrange four dozen ungreased 1½-inch round fluted tins close together on a 12- × 15½- × ½-inch baking sheet.

4. Pinch off 1 teaspoon of dough and drop it into a tin. Repeat until all the tins contain dough. One by one, roll each piece of dough into a ball in the palms of your hands. (This step aids in shaping the tartlets more evenly.) With index finger, press center of dough ball into the tin, then press dough up the sides while rotating the tin to distribute the dough evenly.

5. Chocolate Frangipane Filling: Process all the filling ingredients in a food processor bowl until the mixture is smooth and free of lumps. Spoon about 1 teaspoon of it into each shell.

6. Bake for 15 to 17 minutes, or until the crusts' edges appear dry and slightly firm to the touch. Place the baking sheet with tartlets on a wire rack for about 10 minutes, or until tins are cool enough to touch. Squeeze each tin between your thumb and forefinger, turn it upside down, and let the miniature tartlet drop into the palm of your hand. Place on rack to cool completely.

7. Repeat the filling and baking procedure with remaining dough.

8. Just before serving, place a thin fig slice on top of each tartlet.

9. Stack undecorated tartlets in an airtight sturdy plastic container and freeze up to 10 days. Store decorated tartlets in one layer in a covered foil-lined cardboard container, such as a cake box, at room temperature up to 3 hours.

NOTE

- When you're searching for a food gift, give just the baked tartlet shells neatly stacked in a decorative metal container with the recipe tucked inside.

Double Chocolate Tartlets

Mazarine Tartlets

Wherever I travel, I always see versions of this tartlet. I think these are the best mini–fruit tarts you'll find. They're made with buttery pastry, sweet jam, nutty filling freshened with lemon, and a sparkling crown of assorted fresh fruits. Choose whatever is best: Small blueberries, stemmed red currants, champagne grapes, or tiny strawberries work especially well.

DOUGH

½ recipe Miniature Tartlet Pastry
(page 205)

FILLING

¼ cup strawberry jam

Almond Filling

¼ cup (2 ounces) almond paste

1 ounce (2 tablespoons) unsalted butter

⅓ cup (30 grams) unsifted powdered sugar

1 egg yolk

1 teaspoon vanilla

1 teaspoon kirsch

½ teaspoon finely grated lemon zest

DECORATION

1¼ cups assorted fresh fruit

⅓ cup red currant jelly

1. Arrange four dozen ungreased fluted 1½-inch tins close together on a 12- × 15½- × ½-inch baking sheet.

2. Pinch off 1 teaspoon of dough and drop it into a tin. Repeat until all the tins contain dough. One by one, roll each piece of dough into a ball in the palms of your hands. With index finger, press center of dough ball into the tin, then press dough up the sides while rotating the tin to distribute the dough evenly.

3. Adjust rack to lower third of oven and preheat oven to 350 degrees.

4. Filling: Spoon, or pipe from a small handmade paper cone, a small dot of jam in the bottom of each tartlet.

5. Almond Filling: Process all the ingredients in a food processor bowl until mixture is smooth, about 30 seconds. Spoon, or pipe with another handmade paper cone, about 1 teaspoon filling into each tartlet to cover the jam.

6. Bake for 15 to 20 minutes, or until the crusts' edges are light golden. Remove baking sheet from the oven, and place on a rack to cool for 10 minutes.

7. Squeeze each tin between your thumb and forefinger, turn it upside down, and let the tartlet drop into the palm of your hand. If it cannot be removed easily, it is either still too warm from the oven or underbaked. Return a few tartlets to the oven to bake 5 minutes more. Cool and remove. If these tartlets can be removed, then bake those remaining.

8. Put room-temperature fruit in a 3-quart mixing bowl. Heat the jelly just to warm and liquefy it, then pour it down the side of the bowl. Slide a rubber spatula under the fruit, and fold to lightly coat with the jelly. With fingertips, place fruit to top each tartlet.

9. Stack undecorated tartlets in an airtight sturdy plastic container and freeze up to 10 days. Store decorated tartlets in one layer in a covered foil-lined cardboard container, such as a cake box, at room temperature up to 12 hours.

Mazarine
Tartlets

Lemon Meringue Tartlets

Makes 8 dozen 1½-inch round fluted tartlets

If your weakness is lemon meringue pie, these baby versions will break your willpower. The tangy creamy lemon, balanced by the sweet airy meringue, packs a great deal of flavor and texture in one small pastry package.

PASTRY

8 dozen (1 recipe) baked Miniature Tartlet Pastry shells (page 205)

LEMON CURD

1 egg

2 egg yolks

½ cup (100 grams) granulated sugar

6 tablespoons (2 lemons) fresh lemon juice

2 teaspoons finely grated lemon zest

FLUFFY MERINGUE

½ cup (about 4 large) egg whites

1 cup (200 grams) granulated sugar

1. Arrange the baked tartlet shells on two large baking sheets.

2. Lemon Curd: Combine the egg, yolks, and sugar in a 1½-quart heavy-bottomed saucepan. Stir in the juice and zest. Cook over medium-low heat, stirring occasionally, for 2 to 3 minutes or until the mixture thickens to a hollandaise consistency. Pour into a bowl, cover the surface of the lemon curd with plastic, and refrigerate until chilled, or up to 3 days.

Spoon or pipe from a 14-inch pastry bag fitted with a ¼-inch plain decorating tip (such as Ateco #2) the equivalent of ½ teaspoon lemon curd into each shell.

3. Adjust rack to lower third of oven and preheat oven to 375 degrees.

4. Fluffy Meringue: In a large mixing bowl, blend the egg whites with the sugar. Place the bowl over another bowl of hot tap water and stir until the mixture is body temperature. Using an electric mixer, preferably with a whisk attachment, whip until the mixture has peaks that are thick and shiny, about 10 to 15 minutes.

5. Using another 14-inch pastry bag fitted with a ¼-inch open star decorating tip (such as Ateco #2), pipe a tall swirl on top of each tartlet. Bake for 3 to 4 minutes or until the meringue is light golden. Place baking sheet on a wire rack until tartlets are cool. It's natural for the meringue to puff in the oven and deflate slightly during cooling. Piping tall swirls of meringue on each tartlet before baking maintains a dramatic appearance even with the meringue's adjusted height after baking.

6. Serve the same day the tartlets are filled and decorated.

VARIATION NOTE

Red Currant Meringue Tartlets

Look for fresh red currants in the produce department in June or July and substitute the fruit for the lemon cream filling. Then top the tartlets with the fluffy meringue.

Scheherazade Tartlets

A romantic name seems apropos for these tartlets filled with cranberries, America's rubies of the fruit world, and pomegranate seeds, famous as the fruit of love since ancient days.

PASTRY

8 dozen (1 recipe) baked Miniature Tartlet Pastry shells (page 205)

FILLING
Chocolate Butter Glaze

3 ounces (¾ stick) unsalted butter

4 ounces semisweet chocolate, finely chopped

2 ounces unsweetened chocolate, finely chopped

Candied Cranberries

5 ounces water

1 cup plus 2 tablespoons (225 grams) granulated sugar

2 cups cranberries

⅓ cup fresh pomegranate seeds

1. Arrange the baked tartlet shells on two large trays or baking sheets.

2. Chocolate Butter Glaze: Place the butter and chocolates in a 1-quart bowl that fits snugly over a saucepan half filled with 120- to 130-degree water, to melt ingredients. Stir occasionally until smooth. If necessary, maintain the water's temperature over very low heat. Using a pastry brush, apply a thin coating of glaze in each tartlet. Set aside in a cool room until the chocolate sets.

3. Candied Cranberries: In a heavy 2½-quart saucepan over medium heat, combine the water and sugar. Stir occasionally, washing down any sugar crystals clinging to the sides of the pan with a brush dipped in cold water, until the sugar dissolves. Increase the heat to medium high and cook, without stirring, until the sugar syrup reaches 220 degrees on a mercury candy thermometer. Remove from heat. Stir in the cranberries. When the mixture has cooled to 115 degrees, pour through a large medium-mesh sieve to separate the cranberries from the syrup. Discard syrup.

4. In a 3-quart bowl, gently toss the cranberries and pomegranate seeds together with a rubber spatula. Any syrup clinging to the cranberries will coat the pomegranate seeds to give the fruit a glazed appearance.

5. With your fingertips, gently lift the glazed fruit to fill each tartlet generously. For best flavor and appearance, serve the same day they are filled.

BAKING NOTE

- Look for pomegranates in the produce department throughout the winter, beginning in late August, September, and peaking in October. To remove the crunchy seeds filled with tangy juice from the fruit, cut out the blossom end and score the skin in several places. Then, with your fingertips, break into the fruit in these places to release the seeds. Avoid cutting pomegranates, or you'll pierce the seeds and release their juice.

*Scheherazade
Tartlets*

Pumpkin Tartlets

Makes 4 dozen
1½-inch round
fluted tartlets

These light, refreshing pumpkin tartlets, richly flavored with brown sugar and a touch of orange and cinnamon, are ideal to serve with mulled cider to family and friends.

PASTRY

4 dozen (½ recipe) baked Miniature Tartlet Pastry shells (page 205)

FILLING

½ cup orange marmalade

Pumpkin Filling

2 cups pumpkin puree, fresh or canned

1 cup (200 grams) light brown sugar

2 teaspoons finely grated orange zest

½ teaspoon ground cinnamon

⅔ cup (5 ounces) heavy cream

1. Arrange the baked tartlet shells on a large tray or baking sheet.

2. Filling: In a small saucepan, heat the marmalade just to warm and liquefy it. Using a pastry brush, apply a light coating inside the shells. Allow to air dry at room temperature for 30 minutes.

3. Pumpkin Filling: Drain liquid from the pumpkin puree through a sieve for 30 minutes before making the filling. In a medium bowl, blend the puree with the brown sugar, zest, and cinnamon until smooth.

4. In a 1½-quart deep mixing bowl, whip the cream until stiff peaks form. Remove 1 tablespoon whipped cream to a small bowl for decorating the tartlets.

Fold the remaining cream into the puree. Using a 14-inch pastry bag fitted with a ½-inch plain decorating tip (such as Ateco #6), pipe swirls of filling in each shell.

5. Using the tip of a small paring knife, deposit a dot from reserved whipped cream on top of piped swirl.

6. These are at their best if served within two hours of filling.

BAKING NOTE

- When I use a fresh vegetable puree for these tartlets, I prefer banana squash to pumpkin. I prefer the flavor of banana squash, and fresh pumpkin puree contains too much liquid and makes tartlets in this recipe become too soggy.

  To make Banana Squash Puree: Place a 1½-pound portion of cut-up squash on baking sheet. Bake in a preheated 350-degree oven for about 40 minutes, or until the flesh is tender when pierced with a fork. Remove from oven, and cool.

  Remove the skin by slipping a paring knife between skin and meat. Cut the meat into small pieces, and place them in a food processor bowl. Process with on-off bursts until smooth, about 30 seconds. Or grind the squash, a few pieces at a time, in a food mill for a finer, smoother-textured puree. Cover and refrigerate for up to 2 days. Makes about 2 cups.

Pumpkin Tartlets

Jade Buttercups

The freshness of kiwi and lemon, matched with the richness of buttercream, gives this fruit tartlet distinction. Fill a small pastry shell with creamy lemon buttercream, put a slice of kiwi over the top, and brush with lemon gelee to produce a shimmering finish.

PASTRY

4 dozen (½ recipe) baked
Miniature Tartlet Pastry shells
(page 205)

LEMON CURD BUTTERCREAM

1 egg

2 egg yolks

½ cup (100 grams) granulated
   sugar

6 tablespoons (2 lemons) fresh
   lemon juice

2 teaspoons finely grated lemon
   zest

6 ounces (1½ sticks) unsalted
   butter, room temperature

DECORATION
Lemon Gelee

⅓ cup water

1 teaspoon gelatin

1 tablespoon sugar

1 tablespoon fresh lemon juice,
   strained

5 kiwifruit

1. Arrange the baked tartlets shells on a large baking sheet.

2. Lemon Curd Buttercream: Combine the egg, yolks, and sugar in a 1½-quart heavy-bottomed saucepan. Stir in the juice and zest. Stir constantly over medium-low heat for 2 to 3 minutes, or until the mixture thickens to a hollandaise

consistency. Pour lemon curd into a bowl, cover its surface with plastic, and refrigerate until chilled, or up to 3 days.

In a 1½-quart mixing bowl, cream the butter with an electric mixer until light and fluffy. Add ½ cup of the lemon curd, 1 tablespoon at a time, beating until the mixture is airy and fully incorporated. Return remaining lemon curd to the refrigerator for another use.

3. Spoon or pipe, using a 14-inch pastry bag fitted with a ¼-inch plain decorating tip (such as Ateco #2), about ½ teaspoon of the filling into each shell.

4. Lemon Gelee: Pour the water into a liquid-measure measuring cup. Sprinkle the gelatin over surface, and set aside until softened. Pour into a small saucepan, add the sugar, and heat over low heat just to dissolve the gelatin and sugar. Remove from heat, add lemon juice, and pour into a 2-quart bowl; chill just until the mixture thickens to the consistency of egg whites, about 30 minutes.

5. Using a serrated knife, cut the unpeeled kiwifruit into thin slices about ¹⁄₁₆ inch thick. With a 1½-inch round cutter, cut a circle from each kiwi slice. Place a kiwi slice on top of each tartlet.

6. Brush the lemon gelee on top of each kiwi slice, and place baking sheet in the refrigerator just to set the gelatin mixture.

7. These are best served within 2 hours of filling and decorating.

VARIATION NOTE

• You may substitute a white wine such as Gewürztraminer for the water and lemon juice in the lemon gelee.

Jade Buttercups

Poirettes

Tender tartlets bake with tiny pear pieces in an almond paste filling. The simple apricot and chocolate topping completes a sublime combination. When I want more chocolate flavor, I make the tartlets from the Chocolate Miniature Tartlet Pastry on page 216.

DOUGH

½ recipe Miniature Tartlet Pastry
    (page 205)

FILLING

1 poached pear, diced into
    ¼-inch cubes

Almond Paste Frangipane

4 ounces (⅓ cup plus 1 tablespoon) almond paste

⅓ cup (65 grams) granulated sugar

1 teaspoon rum

1 teaspoon vanilla

1 ounce (2 tablespoons) unsalted butter, room temperature

1 teaspoon finely grated lemon zest

2 large eggs

DECORATION

½ cup strained apricot jam

4 ounces semisweet chocolate

1. Arrange four dozen ungreased 1½-inch tins close together on a 12- × 15½- × ½-inch baking sheet.

2. Pinch off 1 teaspoon dough and drop it into a tin. Repeat until all the tins contain dough. One by one, roll each piece of dough into a ball in the palms of your hands. (This step aids in shaping the tartlets more evenly.) With index

finger, press center of dough ball in the tin, then gradually press dough up the sides while rotating the tin to distribute the dough evenly.

3. Adjust rack to lower third of oven and preheat oven to 350 degrees.

4. Drop one pear piece into each tartlet shell.

5. Almond Paste Frangipane: Process all the ingredients in a food processor bowl until the mixture is smooth. Spoon about 1 teaspoon of the filling into each shell to cover the pear.

6. Bake for 15 to 17 minutes, or until the crusts' edges are light golden. Place baking sheet with tartlets on a wire rack for about 10 minutes, or until tins are cool enough to touch. Squeeze each tin between your thumb and forefinger, turn upside down, and let the miniature tartlet drop into the palm of your hand. Place on rack to cool completely.

7. Heat the jam just to warm and liquefy it. Then brush over each tartlet. After glazing the pastries, place them on a rack.

8. Using a 2-inch paring knife, scrape the tip of the blade firmly but gently across the bar of chocolate to make fine flakes: Hold the chocolate bar close to the glazed pastries, so the fine shavings are sprinkled over each tartlet and stick to the glaze. You can shave the chocolate ahead: Freeze the shavings in an airtight container, then pick them up in a teaspoon, and sprinkle over each tartlet. Using a teaspoon keeps the chocolate from melting from the heat in your fingers.

9. Stack undecorated tartlets in an airtight sturdy plastic container and freeze up to 10 days. Store decorated tartlets in one layer in a covered foil-lined cardboard container, such as a cake box, at room temperature up to 1 day.

BAKING NOTE

- Sometimes I use 1 teaspoon grated fresh ginger in the filling to replace the rum and vanilla. For a more subtle ginger flavor, use 1 teaspoon fresh ginger juice. Rub a peeled portion of ginger along a stainless steel box grater, put the grated ginger in a cloth towel, and twist to extract juice.

Poirettes

Lemon Drops

Makes 4 dozen
1½-inch round
fluted tartlets

I adore the combination of tangy lemon and velvety caramel. These little pastries are glazed with rich caramel cream before filling with a lemon curd lightened with whipped cream.

PASTRY

4 dozen (½ recipe) baked Miniature Tartlet Pastry shells (page 205)

FILLING
Lemon Curd

1 egg

2 egg yolks

½ cup (100 grams) granulated sugar

6 tablespoons (2 lemons) fresh lemon juice

2 teaspoons finely grated lemon zest

Caramel Cream

½ cup (100 grams) granulated sugar

1 ounce (2 tablespoons) unsalted butter

⅓ cup (2½ ounces) heavy cream, room temperature

½ cup (4 ounces) heavy cream, whipped to soft peaks

DECORATION

4 dozen candied lilacs

1. Arrange the baked tartlet shells on a large baking sheet.

2. Lemon Curd: Combine the egg, yolks, and sugar in a 1½-quart heavy-bottomed saucepan. Stir in the juice and zest. Stir constantly over medium-low heat for 2 to 3 minutes, or until the mixture thickens to a hollandaise consistency.

Pour the lemon curd into a bowl, cover its surface with plastic, and refrigerate until chilled, or up to 3 days.

3. Caramel Cream: Put the sugar in a 1½-quart heavy-bottomed saucepan or an unlined copper sugar pot over low heat. Stir occasionally with a small wooden spoon until the sugar dissolves. Increase the heat to medium-high and cook, without stirring, until the melted sugar becomes amber in color, about 7 minutes. Off heat, add the butter, then the room-temperature cream. Be careful—the mixture bubbles madly. With the spoon, stir until the ingredients blend together smoothly.

4. Using a pastry brush, apply a thin coating of caramel cream to the shells. Dry at room temperature for 30 minutes or up to 1 day.

5. Fold the whipped cream into ½ cup of chilled lemon curd. Refrigerate remaining lemon curd for another use. Using a 14-inch pastry bag fitted with a ¼-inch plain decorating tip (such as Ateco #2), pipe the filling decoratively into the caramel cream–glazed shells.

6. Top each tartlet with a candied lilac.

7. Store glazed shells in one layer in covered foil-lined cardboard containers, such as cake boxes, at room temperature up to 1 day. These are best served within 2 hours after filling.

VARIATION NOTES

- It's easy to mix lemon curd with other ingredients. These Lemon Drops combine lemon curd with whipped cream, the Jade Buttercups (page 226) combine lemon curd with butter to make buttercream, and the Lemon Meringue Tartlets (page 220) combine the sharp lemon filling with a fluffy meringue.
- The caramel cream is as versatile as the lemon curd. It is combined with butter and ground nuts for a buttercream in Caramel Carmenitas (page 207) or just mixed with nuts and a bit of honey in Swiss Bettinas (page 234). Caramel cream and chocolate taste divine in Midas Cups (page 235) or it can even glaze tartlet shells, as in this recipe.

Lemon Drops

Raspberry Lemon Tartlets

Makes 4 dozen
1½-inch round
fluted tartlets

This is one of the easiest tartlets in the miniature repertoire, but this ease of preparation certainly is not evident in the finished product. Fill tartlets with a simple lemon custard, and, after baking, decorate with a sweet red raspberry and mint leaf for a colorful and tasty garnish.

DOUGH

½ recipe Miniature Tartlet Pastry
(page 205)

LEMON CUSTARD FILLING

2 egg yolks

3 tablespoons unsalted butter, melted and cooled to lukewarm

½ cup (50 grams) unsifted powdered sugar

1 tablespoon granulated sugar

2 tablespoons lemon juice

2 teaspoons finely grated lemon zest

DECORATION

4 dozen fresh mint leaves

1 pint fresh raspberries

1. Adjust rack to lower third of oven and preheat oven to 350 degrees. Arrange four dozen ungreased round fluted tartlet tins close together on a large baking sheet.

2. Pinch off dough, 1 teaspoon at a time, and drop into tins. One by one, roll dough pieces into balls in the palms of your hands. With index finger, press center of dough ball into the tin, then press dough up the sides while rotating the tin to distribute the dough evenly.

3. Lemon Custard Filling: In a small bowl, lightly whisk together all the filling ingredients just until blended. Spoon about ½ teaspoonful into each tartlet.

4. Bake for about 10 minutes or until crust is light golden. Place baking sheet on a wire rack to cool. When the tins are cool enough to touch, squeeze each tin gently with your thumb and forefinger, turn it upside down, and let the miniature tartlet drop into the palm of your hand.

5. Set a fresh mint leaf on top of each tartlet, then place a raspberry on each leaf, letting the leaf peek from under the berry.

6. Freeze undecorated tartlets in airtight sturdy plastic containers up to 10 days. Serve decorated tartlets the same day.

Raspberry
Lemon Tartlets

Swiss Bettinas

The crunchy toasted walnuts, smothered in a rich creamy caramel, that fill each tender tartlet shell remind me of a luscious version of these tartlets I sampled in a charming pastry shop in Zurich, Switzerland.

DOUGH

4 dozen (½ recipe) baked Miniature Tartlet Pastry shells (page 205)

ENGADINER CREAM

½ cup (100 grams) granulated sugar

1 ounce (2 tablespoons) unsalted butter

⅓ cup heavy cream, room temperature

½ cup walnuts, toasted and chopped

2 teaspoons honey

DECORATION

48 chocolate coffee bean candies

1. Arrange the baked tartlet shells on a large tray or baking sheet.

2. Engadiner Cream: Put the sugar in a 1½-quart heavy-bottomed saucepan or an unlined copper sugar pot over low heat. Stir occasionally with a small wooden spoon until the sugar dissolves. Increase the heat to medium high and cook, without stirring, until the melted sugar reaches an amber color, about 7 minutes. Off heat, add the butter, then the cream. Be careful—the mixture bubbles madly. With the spoon, stir until the ingredients blend together smoothly. Stir the walnuts and honey into caramel cream while hot. Cool 30 minutes, and then spoon 1 teaspoonful of filling into each baked shell.

3. Top each tartlet with a coffee bean candy.

4. Store in one layer in a covered foil-lined cardboard container, such as a cake box, at room temperature up to 2 days.

Midas Cups

A flake of gold leaf sparkling on top of an extravagant chocolate-caramel tart signals the eye that this sweet is truly special. The silky chocolate caramel cream is a perfect balance of flavors from the toasty caramelized sugar, heavy cream, and semisweet chocolate. Sheets of edible 24-karat gold leaf are available at artists' supply stores or commercial sign companies.

Makes 4 dozen 1½-inch round fluted tartlets

PASTRY

4 dozen (½ recipe) baked
  Miniature Tartlet Pastry shells
  (page 208)

CHOCOLATE CARAMEL CREAM

3 ounces semisweet chocolate,
  chopped

½ cup (100 grams) granulated
  sugar

1 ounce (2 tablespoons) unsalted
  butter

⅓ cup heavy cream, room
  temperature

DECORATION

24-karat gold leaf

1. Arrange the baked tartlet shells on a large tray or baking sheet.

2. Chocolate Caramel Cream: Place the chopped chocolate in a medium bowl. Put the sugar in a 1½-quart heavy-bottomed saucepan or an unlined copper sugar pot over low heat. Stir occasionally with a small wooden spoon until the sugar dissolves. Increase the heat to medium high and cook, without stirring, until the melted sugar reaches an amber color, about 7 minutes. Off heat, add the butter, then the cream. Be careful—the mixture bubbles madly. With the spoon, stir until the ingredients blend together smoothly. When the caramel cream's bubbling subsides, pour it into bowl with the chocolate. Stir until the chocolate has melted and the mixture is smooth and shiny. Cool 30 minutes, and then spoon 1 teaspoonful of filling into each shell. Put aside until chocolate filling is set, about an hour.

3. With tweezers, pluck off a tiny piece of gold leaf, the size of an oatmeal flake, and deposit it on top of the glossy chocolate filling for decoration. With fingertip, press the gold lightly to anchor it to the filling and to capture the gold's sparkle.

4. Store in one layer in a covered foil-lined cardboard container, such as a cake box, at room temperature up to 2 days.

Midas Cups

Flaky Miniatures

Sour Cream Pastry
239

Sweet Cheese Puffs
240

Pumpkin Pastries
242

Eccles Tarts
244

Heartovers
246

Shreveshire Tarts
248

Eva Deutsch's Almond Slices
250

Four-Star Rugelach
252

Cinnamon Twists
254

Cream Cheese Pastry
255

Sweet Ravioli
256

California Rolls
258

Dried Fruit Pastry Strips
260

Heavy Cream Flaky Pastry
262

Sour Cream Pastry

Utopia for a baker is a foolproof pastry, one that never gets tough no matter how much you handle it. Look no further than this page: Sour Cream Pastry is a dream to work with and heaven to eat. The star ingredient in the pastry is a thick liquid—sour cream. Its acid tenderizes, its fat contributes flakiness. You can make it easily in a food processor, but I prefer making it by hand for a flakier pastry.

DOUGH

2 cups (280 grams) unsifted all-purpose flour

⅛ teaspoon salt

8 ounces (2 sticks) unsalted butter, chilled and cut into ¼-inch slices

½ cup (5 ounces) sour cream

1. Put the flour and salt in a 3-quart bowl; stir to blend. Scatter the butter slices over the flour, and cut in with a pastry blender until the mixture consists of particles that vary in size from small peas to bread crumbs.

2. Stir in the sour cream with a fork. The pastry will appear dry because the sour cream is thick and doesn't disperse easily. With your hands, manipulate the dough into a ball.

3. Divide in half, or as recipe directs. Wrap in plastic, and refrigerate until cold and firm, at least 4 hours, and up to 3 days; or freeze, well wrapped, up to 1 month.

BAKING NOTE

- I love to experiment in baking. This "What if?" makes it possible for me never to stop learning. A good example was when I substituted another thick liquid, unflavored lowfat yogurt, for the sour cream in this recipe. It led to Yogurt Pastry, which is just as flaky and delicious as the Sour Cream Pastry. The difference in taste is subtle: The Yogurt Pastry is not as tangy as the Sour Cream Pastry.

Sour Cream Pastry

Sweet Cheese Puffs

If I were to become famous for any of my creations, I hope it would be for the Sweet Cheese Puffs. A dollop of lemon-and-vanilla-flavored cream cheese is encased in Sour Cream Pastry and pinched at the top, much like a "beggar's purse"; during baking the pastries blossom open. The taste is equally as wonderful as the look, like cheesecake wrapped in rich flaky pastry.

DOUGH

1 recipe Sour Cream Pastry
   (page 239)

CREAM CHEESE FILLING

8 ounces cream cheese

1 large egg

½ cup (100 grams) granulated
   sugar

1 teaspoon vanilla

1 teaspoon finely grated lemon
   zest

DECORATION

½ cup (50 grams) unsifted
   powdered sugar

1. Divide the pastry into three equal pieces. Shape each into a 5-inch square about ⅝ inch thick. Wrap in plastic, and refrigerate until cold and firm, at least 4 hours.

2. Cream Cheese Filling: Process all the filling ingredients in a food processor bowl until mixture is smooth.

3. Remove one pastry square from refrigerator. Set aside for 10 minutes before rolling it. On a floured surface, roll the pastry into a rectangle slightly less than ⅛ inch thick. With a ruler and a pastry wheel, trim the ragged edges; then measure and cut the pastry into 3-inch squares.

4. Lay the pastry squares across the top of ungreased 12-cup miniature muffin pans, each cup measuring 1½ inches across and ¾ inch deep, centering each square over one cup. Spoon 1 heaping teaspoon of filling on each square; then bring opposite corners to the center, and press lightly to seal. This process will also ease the pastry into each cup. Refrigerate for at least 30 minutes. Roll and shape the remaining pastry squares in the same fashion.

5. Adjust rack to lower third of oven; preheat oven to 375 degrees.

6. Bake two to three pans at a time for about 20 to 25 minutes, or until pastries are light brown. Remove pan from oven to a wire rack for about 10 minutes. Remove pastries from pan to a wire rack to cool completely.

7. Sprinkle with powdered sugar before serving at room temperature.

8. If not serving the same day baked, stack undecorated pastries in airtight sturdy plastic containers and freeze up to 2 weeks. To serve, reheat to freshen in a 325-degree preheated oven for about 7 to 12 minutes or until warm; cool slightly, then sprinkle with powdered sugar.

VARIATION NOTE

- If you feel like embellishing the cheese filling a bit, it's nice to add a ½ cup diced poached apple or pear pieces. In the fall, I suggest you look for quinces in the produce section of the supermarket. Add a ½ cup of poached and diced quince to the cream cheese filling. Though it is a richly flavored fruit, it is not as popular as the apple or pear. In my opinion, seeing the quince's golden peach color, inhaling its distinct scent, and tasting its concentrated perfume is culinary magnificence.

Sweet Cheese Puffs

241

$\mathscr{P}umpkin\ \mathscr{P}astries$

Makes 2½ to
3 dozen 1½-inch
pastries

Pair a flaky, buttery pastry with a filling similar to pumpkin cheesecake, and even people who swear the flavor of pumpkin will never make it on their hit parade list will convert.

DOUGH

1 recipe Sour Cream Pastry
(page 239)

PUMPKIN CREAM CHEESE FILLING

6 ounces cream cheese

¼ cup pumpkin puree, fresh or canned

1 large egg

½ cup (100 grams) brown sugar, packed

½ teaspoon finely grated orange zest

DECORATION

½ cup (50 grams) unsifted powdered sugar

½ teaspoon ground cinnamon

1. Divide the pastry into three 5-inch squares about ⅝ inch thick. Wrap in plastic, and refrigerate until cold and firm, at least 4 hours.

2. Pumpkin Cream Cheese Filling: Process all the filling ingredients in a food processor bowl until mixture is smooth and well blended.

3. Remove one pastry square from refrigerator. Set aside for 10 minutes before rolling it. On a floured work surface, roll the pastry into a rectangle until less than ⅛ inch thick. With a ruler and a pastry wheel, trim the ragged edges; then measure and cut the pastry into 3-inch squares.

4. Lay the pastry squares across the top of ungreased 12-cup miniature muffin pans, each cup measuring 1½ inches across and ¾ inch deep, centering each square over one cup. Spoon 1 heaping teaspoon of filling on each square;

then bring opposite corners to the center, and press lightly to seal. This process will also ease the pastry into each cup. Refrigerate for at least 30 minutes. Roll and shape the remaining pastry squares in the same fashion.

5. Adjust rack to lower third of oven; preheat oven to 375 degrees.

6. Bake two to three pans at a time for about 20 to 25 minutes, or until pastries are light brown. Remove pan from oven to a wire rack for about 10 minutes. Remove pastries from pan to a wire rack to cool completely.

7. Sift powdered sugar and cinnamon together; sprinkle pastries before serving at room temperature.

8. If not serving the same day baked, stack undecorated pastries in airtight sturdy plastic containers and freeze up to 2 weeks. To serve, reheat to freshen in a 325-degree preheated oven for about 7 to 12 minutes or until warm; cool slightly, then sprinkle with powdered sugar and cinnamon.

Pumpkin
Pastries

Eccles Tarts

Makes 3½ dozen

1- × 2-inch

pastries

Sample these lemon-scented flaky pastries with a freshly brewed cup of your favorite tea. These pastries were inspired by the traditional English tarts of the same name.

DOUGH

1 recipe Sour Cream Pastry
   (page 239)

DRIED FRUIT FILLING

1 tablespoon unsalted butter, melted

1 tablespoon granulated sugar

1 teaspoon finely grated lemon zest

¼ cup fresh bread crumbs (about 1 thin slice bread, crusts removed)

1 ounce (scant 3 tablespoons) dried currants

1 ounce (2 tablespoons) golden raisins

1 ounce (2 tablespoons) glacé citron, finely chopped

1 ounce (¼ cup) walnuts, toasted and coarsely chopped

EGG WASH

1 large egg

DECORATION

½ cup (100 grams) granulated sugar

1. Divide the pastry into three equal pieces. Shape each into a 4-inch square about ½ inch thick. Wrap in plastic and refrigerate until firm, at least 4 hours.

2. Dried Fruit Filling: In a 1½-quart bowl, toss all the filling ingredients to blend together. On a cutting board, coarsely chop them. The additional chopping

makes this group of ingredients more uniform in size. Transfer ingredients back into a bowl, tossing with fingertips to mix the ingredients and break up any large clumps of fruit sticking together.

3. Adjust rack to lower third of oven and preheat oven to 375 degrees. Line two large cool baking sheets with parchment paper.

4. Remove one pastry square from refrigerator. Set aside for about 10 minutes before rolling. In a small bowl, whisk the egg until smooth.

5. Roll out the pastry on a lightly floured surface until it is $\frac{1}{16}$ inch thick. Using a 2¾-inch round cutter, cut out shapes in the dough. Using a small pastry brush, lightly coat each circle with the egg wash. Spoon about ¾ teaspoonful of filling in the center of each pastry circle. Lift one half of the pastry over the filling as though you were forming a turnover. Press the edges together to seal. With fingertips, hold this half circle pastry at the seam, perpendicular to the work surface, with the folded edge touching the work surface.  Still using your fingertips, press down to flatten the pastry and manipulate into an oval shape. Turn pastry over with its seam side down. This technique sounds more difficult than it really is. Lightly coat pastries with egg wash and sprinkle with sugar. With the tip of a small sharp paring knife, cut an X in the pastry as a vent and decoration. Roll and shape the remaining pastry squares in the same fashion.

6. Bake, one sheet at a time, for 12 to 15 minutes or until golden. Using a metal spatula, lift pastries off the parchment to a wire rack to cool.

7. These are best eaten at room temperature the same day baked. Or stack in an airtight sturdy plastic container and freeze up to 2 weeks. To serve, reheat to freshen in a 325-degree preheated oven for about 5 minutes or until warm; serve at room temperature.

Eccles Tarts

245

Heartovers

Makes 6 dozen
1½-inch pastries
(or 3 dozen pairs)

These pastries begin as heart-shaped cutouts. Then, one side of the pastry is folded over to enclose the filling and form a turnover. Generally, a turnover starts as a circle before it becomes a semicircle. But in this case, the cutout is a heart that transforms into a half heart—thus the name Heartovers. For a novel presentation, match one Heartover next to another to form a pair—or a heart.

For these Heartovers, it's nice to use two fillings—one half of a pair, apricot-pistachio; the other half, apple (page 256).

DOUGH

½ recipe Sour Cream Pastry
  (page 239)

APRICOT-PISTACHIO FILLING

3 ounces dried apricots

⅓ cup fresh orange juice

1 tablespoon light brown sugar

1 tablespoon unsalted butter

½ ounce (2 tablespoons) pistachios, toasted and finely chopped

EGG WASH

1 large egg

DECORATION

½ cup fresh egg-bread crumbs (about 2 thin slices, crusts removed)

Heartovers

246

1. Form half the pastry into two 4-inch squares, each ½ inch thick. Wrap in plastic and refrigerate until firm, at least 4 hours.

2. Apricot-Pistachio Filling: In a 1-quart saucepan, bring the apricots, juice, and sugar to a boil. Reduce the heat to medium low, and simmer until almost all

the liquid is evaporated, about 7 minutes. Stir in the butter; pour on a heatproof plate to cool. When cool, chop coarsely; stir in the pistachios.

3. Adjust rack to lower third of oven and preheat oven to 375 degrees. Line a large cool baking sheet with parchment paper.

4. Remove one pastry square from refrigerator. Set aside for 10 minutes before rolling it. In a small bowl, whisk the egg until smooth.

5. Roll out dough on a lightly floured surface until it is $1/16$ inch thick. Using a 2-inch heart cutter, cut out shapes in dough. Using a small pastry brush, apply a light coating of egg wash over each heart cutout. Pipe or spoon $1/2$ teaspoon filling in the center of each pastry. Lift one half of the pastry over the filling. Using the tines of a fork, press the edges together to seal. Space 1 inch apart on the baking sheet and refrigerate about 15 minutes to firm the pastries and make it easier to handle them to decorate them.

6. Remove pastries from the refrigerator on the baking sheet and apply a thin coat of egg wash on top of each pastry. Dip one at a time in the bread crumbs. Bake for 10 to 13 minutes or until light golden brown. Using a metal spatula, lift them off the parchment to a wire rack to cool.

7. These are best eaten at room temperature the same day baked. Or stack in an airtight sturdy plastic container and freeze up to 2 weeks. To serve, reheat to freshen in a 325-degree preheated oven for about 5 minutes or until warm; serve at room temperature.

Shreveshire Tarts

If you like pastry with a little spirit, try these tarts. A flaky pastry surrounds a filling flavored with fresh mint and orange zest. These tarts remind me of a pastry I ate on a recent visit to London, thus the English name.

DOUGH

1 recipe Sour Cream Pastry (page 239)

DRIED CURRANT FILLING

1 tablespoon unsalted butter, melted

1 tablespoon granulated sugar

1 teaspoon honey

1 teaspoon finely grated orange zest

1 tablespoon fresh mint, finely minced

2½ ounces (½ cup) dried currants

EGG WASH

1 large egg

DECORATION

½ cup (100 grams) granulated sugar

1. Divide the pastry into three equal pieces. Shape each into a 4-inch round about ½ inch thick. Wrap in plastic and refrigerate until firm, at least 4 hours.

2. Dried Currant Filling: In a 1½-quart bowl, toss all the filling ingredients to blend together. On a cutting board, coarsely chop them; return ingredients to bowl.

3. Adjust rack to lower third of oven and preheat oven to 375 degrees. Line two large cool baking sheets with parchment paper.

4. Remove one pastry disk from refrigerator. Set aside for about 10 minutes before rolling. In a small bowl, whisk the egg until smooth.

5. Roll out the pastry on a lightly floured surface to a $1/16$-inch-thick circle, about 14 inches in diameter. Using a $2^3/4$-inch round cutter, cut out shapes in the dough. Using a small pastry brush, lightly coat each circle with the egg wash. Spoon about $3/4$ teaspoonsful of filling in the center of each pastry circle. Lift one half of the pastry over the filling as though you were forming a turnover. Press the edges together to seal. With fingertips, hold this half-circle pastry at the seam, perpendicular to the work surface, with the folded portion touching the work surface. Still using your fingertips, press down to flatten the pastry and manipulate into an oval shape. Turn pastry over with its seam side down. This technique sounds more difficult than it really is. Lightly coat pastries with egg wash and sprinkle with the sugar. With the tip of a small sharp paring knife, cut two slits diagonally in the pastry, both as a vent and as decoration. Roll and shape the remaining pastry squares in the same fashion.

6. Bake, one sheet at a time, for about 12 to 15 minutes or until golden. Using a metal spatula, lift pastries off the parchment to a wire rack to cool.

7. These are best eaten at room temperature the same day baked. Or stack in an airtight sturdy plastic container and freeze up to 2 weeks. To serve, reheat to freshen in a 325-degree preheated oven for about 5 minutes or until warm; serve at room temperature.

Shreveshire Tarts

Eva Deutsch's Almond Slices

Seattle's Eva Deutsch, mother of one of my best friends, is probably the best cookie maker I know, something you'll discover when you try her rich Almond Slices. Tender, flaky Sour Cream Pastry is rolled around a filling of almond paste, hazelnuts, and lemon zest, before being baked and sliced. The not-too-sweet pastries are absolutely delicious.

DOUGH

½ recipe Sour Cream Pastry
  (page 239)

ALMOND-HAZELNUT FILLING

8 ounces (1 scant cup) almond paste, room temperature

1 ounce (3 tablespoons) hazelnuts, toasted and ground to yield ⅓ cup

2 tablespoons (25 grams) granulated sugar

2 tablespoons (25 grams) light brown sugar, packed

2 teaspoons finely grated lemon zest

⅛ teaspoon ground cinnamon

1 large egg

EGG WASH

1 large egg

DECORATION

1½ ounces (¼ cup) unblanched almonds, split in half at seam

½ cup (100 grams) granulated sugar

1. Form the pastry into two 4-inch squares each about ½ inch thick. Wrap in plastic and refrigerate until firm, at least 4 hours.

2. Almond Hazelnut Filling: Put all the ingredients in a food processor bowl and process until the mixture comes together in a smooth mass.

3. Divide the filling into four equal portions, each about ¼ cup. Roll each portion back and forth on a floured surface with the lightly floured fingertips of both hands into a rope about 13 inches long. Set aside while you roll out the pastry.

4. Adjust rack to lower third of oven and preheat oven to 375 degrees. Line a large cool baking sheet with parchment paper.

5. Remove one portion of dough from the refrigerator. Set aside for 10 minutes before rolling it. In a small bowl, whisk the egg until smooth.

6. On a lightly floured surface, roll the dough into a 6½- × 15-inch rectangle ¹⁄₁₆ inch thick. With a ruler and pastry wheel, trim the edges to measure approximately 6 inches wide and 14½ inches long. Lightly brush the pastry with the egg wash.

7. With a ruler and pastry wheel, cut the pastry strip in half to create two strips, each about 2¾ × 14½ inches.

8. Center a rope of filling on one pastry strip. Flatten it with your fingertips, then lift one side of the pastry to the center of the filling; lift the other side of pastry to overlap the other side and cover the filling. Press with fingertips again to seal the pastry layers together and to flatten the roll to ⅜ inch thick and 1½ inches wide. Place seam side up on the cool baking sheet. Repeat with the other pastry strip, and space the pastry rolls 1½ inches apart on the baking sheet.

9. Repeat procedure with the other portion of pastry and place the assembled pastry rolls parallel to the others on the baking sheet. Lightly brush each roll with the egg wash, then press the almond halves 1 inch apart along the seams. Sprinkle lightly with the sugar. Bake for 12 to 15 minutes, or until pastries are light golden brown and flaky. Using a metal spatula, lift them off the parchment to a wire rack to cool.

10. When the pastries are cool, cut them, between the almonds, into 1-inch slices with a sharp knife.

Eva Deutsch's Almond Slices

11. These are best eaten at room temperature the same day baked. Or stack in airtight sturdy plastic containers and freeze up to 2 weeks. To serve, reheat to freshen in a 325-degree preheated oven for about 7 minutes or until warm; serve at room temperature.

Four-Star Rugelach

Makes 5 dozen
1½-inch crescents

These popular croissant-shaped cookies are made from an easy-to-handle cottage cheese dough. Rugelach (roog-uh-luh) are flaky and rich, but not overly sweet. The cottage cheese adds its distinctive tangy flavor to this pastry.

COTTAGE CHEESE DOUGH

- 1 pint small curd cottage cheese (4% milkfat)
- 2 cups (280 grams) unsifted all-purpose flour
- ⅛ teaspoon salt
- 8 ounces (2 sticks) unsalted butter, chilled and cut into ¼-inch slices

FILLING

- ½ cup (100 grams) granulated sugar
- 1 teaspoon ground cinnamon
- 4 tablespoons strained apricot jam
- 1 cup (4 ounces) finely chopped walnuts
- 2½ ounces (½ cup) dried currants, optional

1. Spoon cottage cheese into a sieve over a bowl and allow it to drain for at least 2 hours. Using a rubber spatula, toss the cottage cheese occasionally. Remove 1 cup of the drained cottage cheese for the dough. Reserve remaining cheese for another use.

2. Process the flour and salt in a food processor just to combine. Scatter all the butter pieces over the flour mixture and process with on/off pulses until the butter appears to disappear into the flour mixture. Scatter the 1 cup cottage cheese over the mixture and process with on/off pulses just until mixture comes together into a cohesive ball.

3. Divide dough into quarters; shape each into a flat disk. Wrap in plastic and refrigerate until firm, at least 4 hours; or freeze, well wrapped, up to 1 month.

4. Adjust rack to the lower third of the oven and preheat oven to 350 degrees. Line a large baking sheet with aluminum foil. In a small bowl combine the sugar and cinnamon.

5. Remove one dough package at a time from the refrigerator. Set aside for 10 minutes before rolling it. On a lightly floured surface, roll the dough into a 10- to 11-inch circle, $1/8$ inch thick. With a small metal spatula, spread only 1 tablespoon jam very thinly over dough. Sprinkle with 2 tablespoons cinnamon-sugar, then with $1/4$ cup nuts and 2 tablespoons currants. With rolling pin, lightly roll to press filling ingredients into the dough.

6. Using a sharp knife, cut the circle into 16 pie-shaped wedges; roll each one up, beginning at the wide end. Place rolls 1 inch apart, point down, on foil-lined baking sheet. Bake 15 to 20 minutes, or until golden brown. Toward the end of baking, if the pastries are browning too much on the bottom from some of the jam oozing out, move them off the jam to a clean spot on the baking sheet. Continue to bake until done. Remove pan to a rack to cool 5 minutes. Then, with a metal spatula, transfer rugelach to a wire rack to cool. Repeat shaping and baking procedure with remaining dough and filling.

Four-Star
Rugelach

Cinnamon Twists

Long, slender pastry straws, flavored with cinnamon sugar, are handsome on a plate of fresh fruit or assorted ice creams.

DOUGH

1 recipe Cottage Cheese Dough
(page 252)

CINNAMON SUGAR

½ cup unsifted powdered sugar

½ teaspoon ground cinnamon

1. Prepare dough and divide it into quarters. Wrap individually in plastic and refrigerate until firm. (These Cinnamon Twists use just two of the dough packages; reserve the remaining for another recipe.)

2. Adjust rack to lower third of oven and preheat oven to 350 degrees. Center an 8-inch-wide strip of aluminum foil on a baking sheet, leaving at least an inch of the sheet uncovered on either side of the foil.

3. In a small bowl, stir to combine sugar and cinnamon. Sprinkle ¼ cup of the cinnamon sugar on a work surface, and roll out one quarter of the dough on it into an 11- × 12-inch rectangle, about ⅛ inch thick. As you roll, turn dough over and continue to roll it out so that both sides are coated with the sugar.

4. Cut ½-inch-wide strips, each about 11 inches long. To twist strip, hold each end between thumb and forefinger. Turn one end toward you and the other one away until twisted 3 or 4 times. (It's best to twist strip loosely rather than too tight.) Place strips, 1 inch apart, across the aluminum foil strip on the baking sheet. Press the ends of the strips that extend beyond the foil onto the sheet to anchor them.

Cinnamon Twists

5. Bake for 15 minutes, or until light golden brown. Cool in pan on a rack. Trim ends and cut into 2-inch-long pieces. Repeat shaping and baking procedure with remaining dough and cinnamon.

6. Store in an airtight tin at room temperature up to 1 week.

Cream Cheese Pastry

Here is another rich flaky pastry, a bit sweeter and somewhat less flaky than the Sour Cream Pastry (page 239). Both the Sour Cream Pastry and the Cream Cheese Pastry are foolproof and provide only the most delicious results.

Makes 1½ pounds

DOUGH

2¼ cups (315 grams) unsifted all-purpose flour

2 tablespoons granulated sugar

1 teaspoon finely grated lemon zest

⅛ teaspoon salt

8 ounces (2 sticks) unsalted butter, chilled and cut into ¼-inch slices

6 ounces cream cheese, cut into small cubes

1. Process the flour, sugar, lemon zest, and salt in the food processor bowl a few seconds just to mix ingredients. Scatter the butter slices over the flour mixture, and process with on/off bursts until the mixture has the consistency of cornmeal. Scatter the cheese cubes over mixture and process just until ingredients come together in a ball.

2. Divide dough in half. Shape into two 5-inch squares, each about ¾ inch thick. Wrap in plastic and refrigerate until firm, for at least 4 hours or up to 3 days; or freeze, well wrapped, up to 2 weeks.

Sweet Ravioli

These look like Italian ravioli and taste like mini apple pies. The "pasta" is made from tender Cream Cheese Pastry and the filling from an intensely flavored apple mixture with a hint of Cheddar cheese.

DOUGH

1 recipe Cream Cheese Pastry (page 255)

APPLE FILLING

1 ounce (2 tablespoons) unsalted butter

1 pound (about 3) Gravenstein or Golden Delicious apples, peeled, cored, and quartered

¼ cup (50 grams) granulated sugar

½ teaspoon finely grated lemon zest

1 ounce finely grated sharp Cheddar cheese, optional

EGG WASH

1 large egg

DECORATION

½ cup (100 grams) granulated sugar

1. Apple Filling: In a 2½-quart heavy saucepan, melt the butter. Add apple pieces, sprinkle with the sugar, and cook over medium heat for about 20 minutes, or until the apples are soft, and the liquid is thick and caramelized. With a wooden spoon, stir occasionally, and mash the apples during cooking, to form a mixture similar to caramelized applesauce. Remove from the heat and stir in the lemon

zest. Spread the mixture on a heatproof plate to cool quickly. When completely cool, add the cheese, if desired.

2. Adjust rack to lower third of oven and preheat oven to 375 degrees. Line a large cool baking sheet with parchment paper.

3. Remove dough squares from refrigerator. Set aside for 10 minutes before rolling them out. In a small bowl, whisk the egg until smooth.

4. Roll out one portion of pastry on a lightly floured surface until it is $1/8$ inch thick. With the edge of a ruler, mark faint indentations $1\frac{1}{2}$ inches apart in the dough. With a pastry brush, apply a light coating of egg wash to the dough. Spoon or pipe out, using a pastry bag fitted with a $1/2$-inch plain decorating tip (such as Ateco #6), small mounds of filling equivalent to $3/4$ teaspoon on the indentations marked in the dough.

5. Roll out the remaining portion of dough to the same dimensions as the first. Cover the filled sheet of pastry with the dough and press the sheets of pastry together firmly around each mound of filling. Cut the ravioli into $1\frac{1}{2}$-inch squares with a fluted pastry wheel. Check that each square's edges are sealed.

6. Transfer the ravioli to the baking sheet. Lightly coat with egg wash, sprinkle with the sugar, and cut a small vent in the center of each square. Bake for 12 to 15 minutes or until puffed and light golden brown. Using a metal spatula, lift them off the parchment to a wire rack to cool.

7. These taste best served at room temperature the same day baked. Or stack in an airtight sturdy plastic container and freeze up to 2 weeks. To serve, reheat to freshen in a 325-degree preheated oven for about 5 minutes or until warm; serve at room temperature.

TECHNIQUE NOTE

- Making these sweet ravioli employs a time-saving technique for forming many small pastries quickly.

Sweet Ravioli

Fresh Plum Filling

Cut fresh French or Italian pitted plums in quarters, dip into flour, and substitute for the apple filling recipe.

Fresh Quince Filling

Substitute ½ pound quince for half of the apples in the apple filling recipe.

California Rolls

Makes 3 dozen
1¼-inch rolls

Though these are similar to rugelach, the shape and filling are different. You can substitute dried cherries or dried cranberries for the apricots and golden raisins—and even brown sugar for the granulated sugar.

DOUGH

1 recipe Cottage Cheese Dough
(page 252)

FILLING

¼ cup granulated sugar

½ teaspoon ground cinnamon

2 tablespoons strained apricot jam

¼ cup golden raisins, finely chopped

¼ cup dried apricots, finely chopped

¼ cup pistachios, finely chopped

California Rolls

258

1. Prepare dough and divide it into quarters. Wrap individually in plastic and refrigerate until firm. (California Rolls use two of the dough packages; reserve the remaining for another recipe.)

2. Adjust rack to the lower third of the oven and preheat oven to 350 degrees. Line baking sheet with aluminum foil.

3. Filling: Combine the sugar and cinnamon in a small bowl.

4. Remove one dough package from the refrigerator 10 minutes before rolling it. On a lightly floured surface, roll the dough into an 11- × 12-inch rectangle, 1/8 inch thick. Using a small metal spatula, spread only 1 tablespoon jam very thinly over dough. Sprinkle with 2 tablespoons cinnamon sugar, then with 2 tablespoons *each* raisins, apricots, and pistachios. With rolling pin, lightly roll to press filling ingredients into the dough.

5. Using a sharp knife, cut the rectangle in half so that each strip measures 5½ × 12 inches. Roll up each one lengthwise. With a sharp knife, cut 1¼-inch-wide slices from each long roll. Place small rolls 1 inch apart, flap down, on the foil-lined baking sheet. Bake 15 to 20 minutes, or until golden brown. Toward the end of baking, if the pastries are browning too much on the bottom from some of the jam oozing out, move them off the jam to a clean spot on the baking sheet. Continue to bake them until done. Remove pan to a rack to cool 5 minutes. Then, with a metal spatula, transfer rolls to a wire rack. Repeat shaping and baking procedure with remaining dough and filling.

California Rolls

Dried Fruit Pastry Strips

Makes 3 dozen
1- × 2-inch slices

To create this pastry, fold rich cream cheese pastry around a dried fruit mixture and bake. Then cut into strips to reveal filling and layers of pastry. The combination of tangy dried fruit and flaky pastry is irresistible. When I need several dozen assorted cookies to feed a crowd, this recipe is perfect since Dried Fruit Pastry Strips are easy to assemble.

DOUGH

½ recipe Cream Cheese Pastry
  (page 255)

EGG WASH

1 large egg

DRIED CURRANT FILLING

2 tablespoons unsalted butter, melted

2 tablespoons granulated sugar

2 teaspoons honey

2 teaspoons finely grated orange zest

2 tablespoons fresh mint leaves, finely minced

5 ounces (1 cup) dried currants

DECORATION

3 tablespoons granulated sugar

1. Adjust rack to lower third of oven and preheat oven to 375 degrees. Line a large cool baking sheet with parchment paper.

2. Remove the pastry from the refrigerator. Set aside for 10 minutes before rolling it. In a small bowl, whisk the egg until smooth.

3. Dried Currant Filling: In a 1½-quart bowl, toss all the filling ingredients to blend together. On a cutting board, coarsely chop ingredients; return to bowl.

4. On a lightly floured surface roll the dough into a 14½- × 11½-inch rectangle. Using a ruler and pastry wheel, trim the edges to measure approximately 14 inches long × 11 inches wide. Lightly brush the pastry with the egg wash.

5. With a ruler and pastry wheel, cut the pastry into thirds to create three strips about 4½ inches wide and 11 inches long. Spoon about ½ cup of the filling lengthwise down two thirds of each dough strip. Spread the filling to within about ½ inch of the shorter edges. Fold the unfilled third over half the filling, then lift this portion and fold it over so the edges meet. Press the edges on the short sides and along the seam to seal.

6. Transfer pastry strip, seam side down, onto baking sheet. With fingertips, flatten the pastry slightly to evenly distribute the filling in the pastry and realign the rectangular shape. Repeat the procedure with the remaining strips of dough. Set them on the baking sheet parallel to each other and 2 inches apart. Brush rolls with egg wash, and, using the tines of a fork or the tip of a paring knife, score the pastry surface to decorate it. Sprinkle pastry lightly with the granulated sugar.

7. Bake for 12 minutes, then reduce oven temperature to 350 and bake about 5 to 6 minutes more or until golden brown. Lift strips on the parchment paper to a wire rack until cool. Using a sharp knife, cut diagonally into 1-inch slices.

8. These taste best at room temperature the same day baked. Or store, unsliced, well-wrapped in aluminum foil, at room temperature up to 2 days. Slice as needed.

VARIATION NOTE

• Substitute other fillings such as the Apricot-Pistachio Filling (page 246) and the Dried Fruit Filling (page 244), even the Fig Filling (page 270), for the

Dried Fruit
Pastry Strips

dried currant filling. If you've never baked with dried tart red cherries, this recipe offers the perfect opportunity. Substitute them in place of the dried currants in the filling above.

Heavy Cream Flaky Pastry

Makes 1⅓ pounds This easy-to-make pastry puffs in the oven much like puff pastry, but it is more delicate and tender. Making the pastry by hand rather than with a machine gives flakier results. Applying a simple rolling and folding technique to the dough makes a cohesive, layered dough. It's these layers that lift the pastry magically and evenly while baking.

DOUGH

2 cups (280 grams) unsifted all-purpose flour

¼ teaspoon salt

8 ounces (2 sticks) unsalted butter, chilled and diced into small cubes

½ cup (4 ounces) heavy cream, chilled

1. Put the flour and salt in a 3-quart mixing bowl; stir to blend. With a pastry blender, cut in the butter until particles are the size of small peas. With a fork, gradually stir in the heavy cream until the mixture comes together into a cohesive dough. If it seems to dry to come together, you need not add more heavy cream. Just use your hands to press it against the sides of the bowl to form a cohesive mass.

2. On a lightly floured board, roll the dough to form a 9- × 7-inch rectangle; fold in half to form a 4½- × 7-inch rectangle. Rotate the dough 90 degrees and roll out again to 9- × 7-inch rectangle, and again fold in half to form a 4½- × 7-inch rectangle. Wrap in plastic and refrigerate until firm and cold, for at least 3 hours or up to 2 days; or freeze, well wrapped, up to 1 week.

Flaky Windmills

When I need a cookie with an unusual twist for an interesting assortment on a petits fours tray, I make these high-tech windmill designs from leftover pastry scraps that I patch together. Shape scraps into a disk, wrap in plastic wrap, and refrigerate to firm butter and relax dough before rerolling.

Makes 2 dozen
1½-inch pastries

DOUGH

10 ounces Heavy Cream Flaky
   Pastry scraps (page 262)

ROYAL ICING

1 cup (100 grams) unsifted
   powdered sugar

2 tablespoons (1 large) egg white

⅛ teaspoon cream of tartar

1. Adjust rack to lower third of oven and preheat oven to 375 degrees. Line a large cool baking sheet with parchment.

2. Royal Icing: Whip ingredients in a deep mixing bowl with an electric mixer at medium speed until the mixture has a creamy, marshmallow-like consistency, about 5 minutes.

3. Remove the pastry from the refrigerator and roll it on a lightly floured surface until it is ³/₁₆ inch thick. Trim to a rectangle approximately 8 × 12 inches. With a small metal spatula, spread a very thin layer of royal icing over the pastry. With a ruler and pastry wheel, trim the ragged edges; then measure and cut the pastry into 2-inch squares. Space the pastry squares 1 inch apart on the cool baking sheet. With a small paring knife, cut 1-inch slashes at each corner toward the center. Fold alternate corners into the center in pinwheel fashion; press gently in the center. Using a small handmade paper cone, pipe a tiny dot of the royal icing in the center of each pastry.

Flaky
Windmills

263

4. Bake for 10 minutes, reduce temperature to 350, and bake 4 minutes longer or until light golden brown. Place the baking sheet on a wire rack for 5 minutes, then lift pastries off parchment to a rack to cool.

5. These are best eaten at room temperature the same day baked. Store in one layer in a covered foil-lined cardboard container, such as a cake box, in a dry room at room temperature up to 1 day; or stack in an airtight sturdy plastic container and freeze up to 2 weeks. To serve, reheat to freshen in a 325-degree preheated oven for about 5 minutes or until warm; serve cool.

Pecan Strudel

I can't say enough about this pastry, one of my all-time favorite taste treats. It's a straightforward combination of flaky pastry wrapped around a luscious not-too-sweet pecan filling. It's rolled strudel-fashion and sliced into individual servings. To dress up the small slices, I often use a tiny stencil and paint a design with Glossy Chocolate Ganache Glaze (page 170) on each piece.

Makes 4 dozen
½-inch slices

DOUGH

½ recipe Heavy Cream Flaky
    Pastry (page 262)

PECAN FILLING

3 ounces (¾ stick) unsalted
   butter, room temperature

½ cup (100 grams) granulated
   sugar

1 large egg

8 ounces (2 cups) pecans, finely
   chopped to yield 2 cups (see
   Baking Note)

3 tablespoons unsifted all-purpose
   flour

EGG WASH

1 large egg

1. Pecan Filling: Beat the butter and sugar together in an electric mixer until creamy. Add the egg and beat until creamy and smooth. Stir in the pecans and flour.

2. Adjust rack to lower third of oven and preheat oven to 375 degrees. Line a large cool baking sheet with parchment paper.

3. Remove dough from refrigerator. Divide it in half, refrigerate one portion, and set aside the other for 10 minutes before rolling it. In a small bowl, whisk the egg until smooth.

4. On a lightly floured surface roll the dough into a 12- × 6- × $\frac{1}{16}$-inch-thick rectangle. Using a ruler and pastry wheel, trim the edges to measure approximately 12 inches long × $5\frac{3}{4}$ inches wide. Lightly brush with the egg wash.

5. Spoon half the filling lengthwise down the center of the pastry to within $\frac{1}{2}$ inch of the edges on the short ends. With fingertips pat the filling to shape it to resemble a sausage. Lift one long side of the dough lengthwise over the filling. Lift the other portion so the pastry overlaps, and press to seal. Press the ends together to seal.

6. Gently transfer the pastry to the baking sheet, sealed-seam side down. With fingers, reshape pastry into a rectangular log, about 12 inches long, 2 inches wide, and $\frac{3}{4}$ inch high. Brush the entire surface with egg wash. With the tines of a fork or the tip of a paring knife, lightly score the pastry with intersecting lines, or shapes such as leaves, for decoration. Repeat the procedure for the remaining dough and filling. Set this pastry parallel to the first one, about 3 inches apart. Bake for 25 to 30 minutes or until golden brown. Lift the pastries, on the parchment paper, from the baking sheet to a wire rack to cool.

7. Transfer the pastry rolls to a cutting board. Using a sharp knife, cut them diagonally into $\frac{1}{2}$-inch slices.

8. These are best eaten at room temperature the same day baked; or freeze unsliced and undecorated, well wrapped in aluminum foil, up to 1 week. To serve, reheat to freshen in a 325-degree preheated oven for about 10 minutes or until warm; cool before slicing and decorating.

Pecan Strudel

- Thanks to Californian Joan Chamberlain for giving me this luscious nut filling recipe for my Heavy Cream Flaky Pastry.
- Because the nuts provide structure as well as flavor in this filling recipe, it is important to measure the chopped nut pieces as accurately as possible. With a food processor, through variations of brand, speed, blade, timing, and force, you can grind a given weight of nuts into widely varying volumes of chopped nuts. A nut mill grinds nuts into the same volume every time, so for this recipe use a nut mill to chop the nuts to yield 2 cups.

Pecan Strudel

Miniature Caramel Cream Vol-au-Vents

Makes 3½ dozen 1½-inch miniature vol-au-vents

Small circles of Heavy Cream Flaky Pastry, each with a tiny circular cut in the center, bake into a flaky pastry container to fill with the ultimate caramel filling. If you don't want to make the pastry, the filling is fabulous drizzled over ice cream or poached fruit, such as peaches or pears.

DOUGH

1 recipe Heavy Cream Flaky Pastry (page 262)

CARAMEL SYRUP FILLING

⅓ cup light corn syrup

⅔ cup (130 grams) granulated sugar

½ cup (4 ounces) heavy cream, room temperature

DECORATION

42 candied lilacs

1. Caramel Syrup Filling: In a 1½-quart heavy-bottomed saucepan, heat the corn syrup and sugar over low heat until the sugar is dissolved. Then, increase the heat to medium high and boil the mixture until the caramel is light amber-colored, about 10 minutes. Remove from the heat, and pour in the heavy cream all at once. The mixture will foam. Carefully stir the mixture with a wooden spoon to distribute the heat and blend the ingredients together. Pour into a small bowl to thicken and cool thoroughly before filling pastries, about 2 hours.

2. Adjust rack to lower third of oven and preheat oven to 375 degrees. Line a large cool baking sheet with parchment paper.

3. Divide dough in half, refrigerate one half, and roll out the other on a lightly floured surface to form a rectangle 12 inches long, 8 inches wide, and ⅛ inch thick. Using a 1¾-inch scalloped round cutter, cut shapes from the dough. With a ¾-inch round cutter, stamp each pastry center, without cutting all the way through the dough. Space the circles 1 inch apart on the baking sheet. Bake for 12 to 13 minutes or until light golden brown. Transfer baking sheet to a wire rack to cool 5 minutes. Using the tip of a paring knife, carefully remove the small pastry circle marked in the center. (Some pastry should remain under each small circle.) Allow the shells to cool completely before filling.

4. Repeat this procedure with the other portion of dough. Shape scraps into a disk, wrap in plastic wrap, and refrigerate to firm butter and relax dough before rerolling for another recipe. (See Flaky Windmills, page 263.)

5. Spoon caramel syrup filling, a teaspoon at a time, into each pastry shell. Sprinkle finely chopped candied lilacs over pastries.

6. These are best eaten at room temperature the same day baked and filled; or store in one layer in a covered foil-lined cardboard container, such as a cake box, in a dry room at room temperature up to 1 day. Stack unfilled pastries in an airtight sturdy plastic container and freeze up to 2 weeks. To serve, reheat to freshen in a 325-degree preheated oven for about 5 minutes or until warm; add caramel filling and lilacs, and serve at room temperature.

TECHNIQUE NOTE

- If the caramel forms lumps when you add the heavy cream, put the saucepan back over a very low flame and slowly stir until smooth.

Miniature Caramel Cream Vol-au-Vents

Fig Pastry Rolls

Dried figs have never tasted better. Here's my contemporary version of that old favorite, fig bars.

DOUGH

½ recipe Heavy Cream Flaky
  Pastry (page 262)

FIG FILLING

1 cup (6 ounces) dried figs,
  stems removed, chopped

3 tablespoons granulated sugar

½ cup water

1 ounce (2 tablespoons) unsalted
  butter

1 tablespoon fresh lemon juice

1 teaspoon vanilla

EGG WASH

1 large egg

1. Fig Filling: In a 1½-quart heavy-bottomed saucepan, combine the figs, sugar, and water. Simmer over medium heat, stirring constantly, just until thick. Remove from heat, and stir in the butter. Cool to room temperature. Add the lemon juice and vanilla. Place in bowl of food processor and pulse just until the mixture forms a puree.

2. Adjust rack to lower third of oven and preheat oven to 375 degrees. Line a large cool baking sheet with parchment paper.

3. Remove pastry from the refrigerator. Divide it in half, refrigerate one portion, and set aside the other for 10 minutes before rolling it. In a small bowl, whisk the egg until smooth.

4. On a lightly floured surface, roll the dough into a 12- × 6- × $\frac{1}{16}$-inch-thick rectangle. Using a ruler and pastry wheel, trim the edges to measure approximately 12 inches long × $5\frac{3}{4}$ inches wide. Lightly brush with the egg wash.

5. Spoon half the filling lengthwise down the center of the pastry, to within $\frac{1}{2}$ inch of the edges on the short ends. With fingertips pat the filling to shape it to resemble a sausage. Lift one long side of the dough over the filling. Lift the other portion, allowing the pastry to overlap, and press to seal. Press the ends together to seal.

6. Gently transfer the pastry to the baking sheet, sealed-seam side down. With fingers, reshape pastry into a rectangular log, about 12 inches long, 2 inches wide, and $\frac{3}{4}$ inch high. Brush the entire surface lightly with egg wash. Using the tines of a fork or the tip of a paring knife, decorate pastry surface with lines or shapes. Repeat the procedure for the remaining dough and filling. Set this pastry parallel to the first one, about 3 inches apart. Bake for 25 to 30 minutes or until golden brown. Lift the pastries, on the parchment paper, from the baking sheet to a wire rack to cool.

7. Transfer the pastry rolls to a cutting board. Using a sharp knife, cut them diagonally into $\frac{1}{2}$-inch slices.

8. These are best at room temperature the same day baked; or freeze unsliced, well wrapped in aluminum foil, up to 1 week. To serve, reheat to freshen in a 325-degree preheated oven for about 10 minutes or until warm; cool before slicing.

Fig Pastry Rolls

Blitz Puff Pastry

A blitz puff pastry recipe, written with careful details to guarantee successful results, resembles a pie crust recipe. Both recipes call for a lot of fat and require attention when working with it to achieve a proper flaky texture.

Though the blitz variety is easier and quicker to make than classic puff pastry, it's important that the butter be well chilled after cutting it into ½-inch-thick slices. Chilled butter withstands the rolling of the dough a few times to create layers. If the butter is too soft, the dough absorbs the butter, while too firm butter breaks through the dough and prevents any layer formation.

DOUGH

- 1 pound (4 sticks) unsalted butter, chilled
- 1 pound (3¼ cups) unsifted all-purpose flour
- 1 cup ice water
- ¾ teaspoon salt

1. Cut the sticks of butter into ½-inch-thick slices; then cut each slice in half lengthwise to give you 12 to 16 oblong chunks per stick of butter. Since it takes time to cut the butter into pieces, place them on a baking sheet and refrigerate them for at least 10 minutes to rechill and firm after handling.

2. Scatter the butter pieces over the flour in the bowl of a heavy-duty mixer; with a rubber spatula, toss them briefly to coat with the flour.

3. Add the salt to the ice water in a liquid-measure measuring cup; stir to dissolve it.

4. With the paddle attachment, mix the butter and flour on the lowest speed just long enough for the flour to coat the butter pieces lightly, about 10 seconds (or as long as it takes to say "perfect puff pastry" five times). The majority of chunks should remain the size of walnuts.

5. Resume the mixer's lowest speed while pouring the ice water on the flour mixture in a steady stream, not too slowly or too quickly. As soon as all the water

has been added, stop the mixer. Most of the butter chunks should look almost the way they did when you began the blending process. The mixture will appear messy and uncohesive and there will still be loose flour particles in the bottom of the bowl.

6. Using your fingertips, scoop up a large portion of the dry flour particles from the bottom of the bowl and place them on the messy uncohesive mass; press them together in an attempt to form a dough. Don't be concerned if some dry particles remain.

7. Cover the dough with plastic wrap; press the wrap down onto the surface of the dough to prevent its drying. Refrigerate for 15 minutes, allowing the butter chunks to rechill and the dough to relax and mellow.

8. Dust work surface lightly with flour. To layer the dough, pat it into a 10- × 6-inch rectangle 1 inch thick. If it resembles potato salad, you're doing just fine.

9. Roll the dough into a rectangle close to 16 × 8 inches and $\frac{1}{2}$ inch thick, dusting with flour if necessary. At this point a short end of the dough is closest to you, though it won't be completely cohesive. Brush off any excess flour with a brush. Now fold the bottom third up over the center; next, fold the top third down over the bottom until it resembles a business letter. This is a single fold, and the dough still isn't smooth.

10. Rotate the dough 90 degrees to the right so its top flap opens like a page in a book. Again lightly flour the work surface and the pastry, and roll into a rectangle measuring 16 × 8 inches and $\frac{1}{2}$ inch thick. Brush off any excess flour; then, with the short end closest to you, fold it into the center of the rectangle. Fold the other short end so that the two short ends meet in the center. Fold the dough in half again, forming a double fold consisting of four layers. Now the mixture is beginning to look like a dough.

11. Wrap in foil; refrigerate for 20 minutes. You have just completed one single fold and one double fold in a short time, so remember the resting period is approximate. If at any time the dough resists rolling or the butter becomes too soft, a longer refrigeration period may be needed.

12. Lightly dust the work surface and dough with flour, and place the refrigerated dough so that the last fold is at a right angle to you and the flap on top opens like a book. Roll again into a 16- × 8-inch rectangle. Brush off any excess flour; then, fold the short end closest to you into the center of the rectangle. Fold the other short end so that the two short ends meet in the center. Now fold the dough in half again, forming another double fold. You'll notice the pastry is beginning to take form. Rewrap in the foil, and return to the refrigerator for 20 minutes more. Remember this is the third turn.

13. Position the dough so that the last fold is at a right angle to you and the top flap opens like a book. Repeat the rolling and folding as directed for the third turn in Step 12. This is the fourth and final turn. Rewrap in the foil, and refrigerate for at least 1 hour before shaping for use.

14. After the puff pastry has rested, roll it into a more manageable shape, a 13- × 8-inch rectangle.

15. Refrigerate it for up to 2 days; or freeze, well wrapped, up to 2 months.

BAKING NOTES

- It's easy to make Blitz Puff Pastry with whole wheat pastry flour: Substitute 2 cups unsifted whole wheat pastry flour for 2 cups (280 grams) of unsifted all-purpose flour.
- Whole wheat pastry flour is available in most health food stores.

Blitz Puff
Pastry

Florentine Pastry Strips

Puff pastry is baked until flaky and golden, then a syrupy almond, honey, and butter mixture is spread on top and the pastry is returned to the oven briefly before it is cut into rectangles. Every bite is as seductive as a sticky bun.

DOUGH

½ pound (about ¼ recipe) Blitz
   Puff Pastry (page 272)

DECORATIVE TOPPING

⅓ cup (65 grams) granulated
   sugar

2 tablespoons heavy cream

1 tablespoon light corn syrup

1 tablespoon honey

1½ ounces (3 tablespoons)
   unsalted butter

3 ounces (1 cup) sliced almonds

1. Roll the dough into a ⅛-inch-thick 14-inch square; transfer to a large baking sheet such as one 17 × 14 × ½ inches. Cover completely with plastic wrap, pressing the plastic directly onto the dough. Refrigerate for at least 30 minutes before baking.

2. Adjust rack to lower third of oven and preheat oven to 425 degrees. Line a large cool baking sheet with parchment paper. Transfer the chilled dough from the refrigerator to the baking sheet; prick entire surface with fork tines. Trim off ¹⁄₁₆ inch from all edges to encourage an even, uninhibited rise in the pastry while baking.

3. Bake 10 minutes, then reduce temperature to 375 degrees, and bake for 10 minutes longer. After the initial 10 to 15 minutes of baking, check occasionally to see if the puff pastry is lifting evenly. Prick any uneven area with a skewer to release trapped air before the outer portion of pastry sets.

Florentine
Pastry Strips

4. A high lift is not important, so if almost the entire pastry sheet has lifted, place a baking sheet on top to weight it. Bake for 1 minute; then remove the baking sheet from the top of the pastry.

5. Reduce the oven temperature to 325 degrees, and bake for 12 to 17 minutes longer, or until the pastry is golden brown and sounds and feels crisp when pierced with a skewer or toothpick in four or five places. Place the baking sheet on a wire rack to cool completely.

6. Combine the sugar, cream, corn syrup, honey, and butter in a 1-quart heavy-bottomed saucepan. Place over low heat, and stir often until sugar dissolves and butter melts, about 3 minutes. Bring mixture to a boil, and remove from heat. Add the almonds, and stir to blend. Set aside for 5 to 10 minutes to cool and thicken slightly.

7. Adjust the rack 7 to 8 inches from the broiling element; preheat broiler.

8. Pour the slightly cooled topping onto the pastry, spreading evenly with a rubber spatula until surface is covered. Place under broiler for about 30 to 60 seconds, or until the top is bubbly and the nuts are golden. Place the baking sheet on a wire rack to cool slightly.

9. With a ruler and a sharp knife, cut about thirteen 1-inch-wide strips about 13 inches long. Cut each strip into rectangles about 2 inches long.

10. These are best eaten the same day they are baked. Or stack in airtight sturdy plastic containers and freeze up to 2 weeks. To serve, reheat to freshen in a 325-degree preheated oven for about 7 minutes or until warm; serve at room temperature.

BAKING NOTE

• Puff pastry scraps work beautifully for this recipe.

Florentine
Pastry Strips

Streusel Pastry Strips

Cover puff pastry with a streusel to create these crisp, sweet, flaky puff pastry strips. It's a perfect accompaniment to scrambled eggs for a special breakfast, or with a serving of morning fruit, such as grapefruit.

Makes 6 dozen
1- × 2-inch
strips

DOUGH

½ pound (about ¼ recipe) Blitz Puff Pastry (page 272)

STREUSEL

½ cup (50 grams) unsifted powdered sugar

¼ cup (50 grams) granulated sugar

1 cup plus 2 tablespoons (160 grams) unsifted all-purpose flour

4 ounces (1 stick) unsalted butter, room temperature, cut into 8 pieces

DECORATION

½ cup (50 grams) unsifted powdered sugar

1. Roll the dough into a ⅛-inch-thick 14-inch square; transfer to a large baking sheet, such as one 17 × 14 × ½ inches. Cover completely with plastic wrap, pressing the plastic directly on the dough. Refrigerate for at least 30 minutes before baking.

2. Streusel: Combine the sugars and flour in a 1½-quart bowl with a pastry blender. Scatter the butter pieces over the dry ingredients, and work the butter in with your fingertips until the mixture resembles coarse crumbs.

Streusel Pastry Strips

277

3. Adjust rack to lower third of oven and preheat oven to 425 degrees. Line a large cool baking sheet with parchment paper. Transfer the chilled dough to the baking sheet; prick entire surface with fork tines. Trim off $\frac{1}{16}$ inch from all edges to encourage an even, uninhibited rise in the pastry while baking. Brush a thin film of water over the pastry. Sprinkle the streusel over the pastry, and gently press it so it will stick.

4. Bake for 10 minutes, then reduce temperature to 375 degrees, and bake for 10 minutes longer. After the initial 10 to 15 minutes of baking, check occasionally to see if the puff pastry is baking evenly. Prick any uneven area with a skewer to release trapped air.

5. A high lift is not important, so if almost the entire pastry sheet has lifted, place a baking sheet on top to weight it. Bake for 1 minute; then remove the baking sheet from the top of the pastry.

6. Reduce temperature to 325 degrees, and bake for 12 to 17 minutes longer, or until the pastry is golden brown and sounds and feels crisp when pierced with a skewer or toothpick in four or five places. Place baking sheet on a wire rack to cool completely.

7. Lightly dust entire surface with the powdered sugar. With a ruler and a sharp knife or pastry wheel, cut about thirteen 1-inch-wide strips about 13 inches long. Cut each strip into rectangles about 2 inches long.

8. These are best eaten the same day they are baked. Or stack in airtight sturdy plastic containers and freeze up to 2 weeks. To serve, reheat to freshen in a 325-degree preheated oven for about 7 minutes or until warm; serve at room temperature.

BAKING NOTE

• Puff pastry scraps work beautifully for this recipe.

Streusel Pastry Strips

Phyllo Accordions

Bring these easy-to-prepare flaky pastries to a party and I guarantee your dance card will be full all evening. Actually, invite a friend to make these with you since four hands are always better than two when working with phyllo. Four hands speed up the process of forming the pastries and assist in keeping the phyllo under wraps to ensure it does not dry in the air.

PASTRY

4 ounces (1 cup) walnuts, finely chopped

4 ounces (1 cup) pecans, finely chopped

1/4 cup *each* sesame seeds and granulated sugar

12 sheets (1/2 pound) phyllo dough, approximately 16 × 12 inches, room temperature

8 ounces (2 sticks) unsalted butter, melted and cooled to tepid

HONEY BUTTER GLAZE

1/2 cup water

1 cup (200 grams) granulated sugar

1/4 cup honey

1 ounce (2 tablespoons) unsalted butter

1 tablespoon finely grated lemon zest

1 tablespoon fresh lemon juice

1. Adjust rack to lower third of oven; preheat oven to 325 degrees. Line two cool large baking sheets with parchment paper.

2. Mix the nuts, sesame seeds, and sugar in a small bowl; set aside.

3. Place the phyllo sheets on the work surface. Using a sharp knife or scissors, cut sheets in half to make them 12 × 8 inches; cut again to make them 6 × 8 inches. Stack quarter sheets together, cover with a strip of plastic wrap, then with a damp towel.

4. Remove two sheets at a time; brush top sheet lightly with melted butter. Sprinkle with 1 tablespoon nut mixture.

5. Roll the sheets lengthwise, beginning loosely, around a long wooden spoon handle or 14-inch wooden dowel, ½ inch in diameter. Brush phyllo pastry lightly with melted butter again. With fingertips, gently push in both ends of pastry to wrinkle and condense it from 8 inches to 3½ or 4 inches. Then, holding the pastry at one end with fingertips, carefully pull the wooden stick out. Place seam side down on baking sheet. Cover with plastic wrap.

6. Repeat procedure with remaining phyllo sheets, spacing pastries 1 inch apart.

7. Remove plastic and bake until crisp and golden, about 20 minutes. Using a metal spatula, lift pastries off the parchment to a wire rack to cool. Cut rolls crosswise in half or thirds.

8. Honey Butter Glaze: Combine all the ingredients except the lemon juice in a 1½-quart saucepan. Heat over low heat just until sugar is dissolved. Raise heat and cook 5 minutes. Remove from heat, and stir in the lemon juice. Cool 10 minutes. Then, brush over pastries just to glaze them.

9. Stack unglazed pastries in an airtight metal container at room temperature up to 3 days. Serve glazed pastries at room temperature the same day baked.

TECHNIQUE NOTE

- San Franciscan Loni Kuhn, the well-known cooking professional and a dear friend, has a great tip. If possible, work with phyllo dough when the weather is humid. This way, there's less risk that the phyllo will dry out so quickly.

BAKING NOTE

- If you have the time, clarify the butter to ensure that the pastries bake evenly without burning. Clarifying removes the milk solids, the liquid in butter that can make phyllo dough soggy, and leaves an oil with a nutty sweet butterfat flavor.

  The clarifying process is simple: In a 1-quart heavy-bottomed saucepan, melt the butter over very low heat. Off heat, skim off the foamy particles on top. Slowly pour the oil into a glass jar; be careful to leave the milky solids behind in the saucepan. Cover the jar and refrigerate until needed.

Flaky Cheesecake Turnovers

Here's a favorite filling I've used many times for my miniature tartlets. Using up leftovers can lead the way to a delicious treat. In this case, the filling and phyllo dough combine to make flaky, crunchy pastries on the outside with a creamy smooth almond paste cheesecake inside.

Makes 3½ dozen 1½-inch triangles

FILLING

4 ounces (⅓ cup plus 1 tablespoon) almond paste

¼ cup granulated sugar

8 ounces cream cheese, room temperature

1 large egg

1 teaspoon finely grated lemon zest

PASTRY

16 sheets (¾ pound) phyllo dough, approximately 16 × 12 inches

8 ounces (2 sticks) unsalted butter, melted and cooled to tepid

1. Adjust rack to lower third of oven and preheat oven to 350 degrees. Line two baking sheets with parchment paper.

2. Filling: In a medium bowl, mix together the almond paste and sugar. Beat in the cream cheese, then the egg and lemon zest until creamy and smooth.

3. Place stacked sheets of the phyllo on work surface. Cut the rectangular sheets into five equal strips about 3 inches wide by 12 inches long. Take two strips from a stack, leaving one on top of the other, and brush just the top portion

with melted butter. While working, keep the rest of the phyllo strips covered with plastic wrap.

4. Spoon 1 rounded teaspoon cheesecake filling in center of one narrow end of a double-thickness strip, an inch from edge of dough. Starting from lower right, fold the right bottom corner over the filling on an angle, to form a triangle. Fold over on line created by the top edge, and continue folding back and forth to the end of the strip to make one multilayered triangle. (Fold each strip as you would a flag.) Set pastry seam side down on baking sheet and brush with melted butter. Keep triangles covered with plastic wrap until baking. Prepare remaining strips in same way.

5. Remove plastic wrap and bake for 15 minutes or until golden. Using a metal spatula, lift triangles off the parchment to a wire rack to cool.

6. To assemble ahead, set pastries on parchment-lined baking sheets, and place in freezer, uncovered, just 30 minutes to solidify the butter coating. Remove from the freezer just to cover the sheets with plastic; overwrap with aluminum foil. Return to freezer. Bake pastries while frozen, but first transfer the pastries, on the parchment, to another parchment-lined baking sheet to prevent the pan from buckling in the preheated oven. Bake the frozen pastries a few minutes longer than unfrozen ones.

TECHNIQUE NOTES

- My good friend and fellow cookbook author Louise Fiszer has great advice about phyllo dough: Only work with phyllo when it has reached room temperature—then it will behave as though it were silk, easy to maneuver and not brittle. Remove the unwrapped box of phyllo from the refrigerator about 1 hour before you intend to use it.
- There is a reason for forming the triangular pastries with a double thickness of phyllo. It makes them extra flaky.

Flaky Cheesecake Turnovers

282

Part IV

Miniature Cakes

$\mathcal{T}$he Genoise Sheet Cake (page 289), the Almond Cake (page 316), the Chocolate Almond Cake (page 304), and the Butter Cake (page 307) provide versatile foundations from which to create stunning miniature cakes. These simple yet flavorful cakes are not too rich that they can't be enhanced by buttercreams or chocolate, or just simply glazed with apricot jam.

Mixing Miniature Cakes

The Genoise Sheet Cake begins as a thick foamy foundation of whipped eggs and sugar before a small amount of flour and a minimum of melted butter are folded in. It is light yet firm enough to cut into individual shapes for Pistachio Petits Fours (page 289) and Parisers (page 295), and at the same time thin and flexible enough for rolling Calypso Minirolls (page 298) and Sweet Sushi Swirls (page 300).

The other cakes are denser in texture, not as light or spongy as the genoise, because they contain an abundance of butter and flour. Their solid foundations make them easy to cut without crumbling. They're perfectly suited to dipping or glazing, as for Polka Dot Minicakes (page 316), Chocolate Galaxy Petitcakes (page 304) and Dominoes (page 307), since they don't leave behind a number of crumbs each time a piece is dipped or glazed.

Cutting Miniature Cakes

Large cakes such as the Genoise Sheet Cake (page 289) and the Butter Cake (page 307) are ideal for providing many portions without spending a lot of time baking and decorating.

You can glaze and decorate each portion individually as you do when making the Parisers (page 295) or Honey Bee Minicakes (page 292), or you can decorate the entire cake as demonstrated in the Pistachio Petits Fours (page 289) and cut it into daintier portions later.

Another simple procedure is to mark portions on the cake, decorate each one identically, as for Polka Dot Minicakes (page 316), and later cut the cake where marked.

It's possible to cut any shape or design to create a variety of miniature cakes. Straight edges are easier to cut and less wasteful of cake than rounded edges. Round cutters, such as circles and flower shapes, usually aren't as sharp as a knife that cuts straight-edged portions.

I've designed the miniature cake recipes so that you can conveniently and easily make an assorted variety from only one cake. For example, from one Genoise Sheet Cake (page 289), you can fashion Honey Bee Minicakes (page 292), Sweet Sushi Swirls (page 300), and Grape Cake Triangles (page 302). I've also provided a recipe for Punsch Cakelets (page 319) which is ideal for using those trimmings left over from the Almond Cake (page 316), Butter Cake (page 307), Genoise Sheet Cake (page 289), and Chocolate Almond Cake (page 304). To accumulate the necessary amount of trimmings for these cakelets, keep the leftovers, well covered, in a sturdy plastic container in the freezer.

Follow these tips for cutting precision shapes and sizes and you'll find it's simpler and easier to achieve uniform results for daintier, more finished-looking miniature cakes.

- Partially freezing the cake, about 30 minutes, makes cutting easier.
- When cutting genoise cake, use a serrated knife. Cut with a sawing motion. Sometimes scissors are quicker than a knife for cutting and do the job even better, as in Sweet Sushi Swirls (page 300).
- When cutting cakes with a closer texture such as the Butter Cake (page 307) and Almond Cake (page 316), use a sharp paring knife.
- If using a cookie cutter, select one with a sharp edge. Press into cake and wiggle slightly to right and left. Don't force straight through the cake or the sides will be ragged and crumbly.

Cake Miniatures

Pistachio Petits Fours

I adore pistachios, and when used in this miniature I love them all the more. A sandwich of spongy genoise and silken, nutty buttercream is frozen after assembling to make cutting into small triangles easy.

Makes 6 dozen 1½-inch triangles

GENOISE SHEET CAKE BATTER

- ½ cup plus 1 tablespoon (56 grams) sifted cake flour
- 1 tablespoon granulated sugar
- ⅛ teaspoon salt
- 3 large eggs
- 2 egg yolks
- ½ cup (100 grams) granulated sugar
- 1 teaspoon vanilla

PISTACHIO SILK BUTTERCREAM

- 4 egg yolks
- ¼ cup water
- ½ cup (100 grams) granulated sugar
- 8 ounces (2 sticks) unsalted butter, room temperature
- 2 ounces (½ cup) sliced almonds, toasted and chopped
- 4 ounces (¾ cup) pistachios, blanched, toasted, and chopped to yield 1 cup
- ½ teaspoon almond extract
- Green liquid food coloring

DECORATION

- ½ cup (50 grams) unsifted powdered sugar
- 1 ounce (3 tablespoons) blanched pistachios, split

1. Adjust rack to lower third of oven and preheat oven to 450 degrees. Line a 12- × 15½- × ½-inch baking sheet with aluminum foil, leaving a 2-inch overhang on short ends. Fold overhangs under the ends of the pan. Grease and flour aluminum foil; tap out excess flour.

Pistachio Petits Fours

289

2. Sift the flour, 1 tablespoon sugar, and salt on a sheet of waxed paper; set aside. In a large mixing bowl, using a whisk, stir the eggs, egg yolks, and the ½ cup sugar over a shallow pan of hot water until the mixture is body temperature. Remove the bowl from hot water, and, using an electric mixer, preferably with a whisk attachment, whip the egg mixture at medium speed until it has cooled and increased considerably in volume. Add the vanilla during the final moments of whipping. When mixture is thick enough that when whisk is lifted, some of the mixture falls from the whisk into the bowl in ribbons and remains on the surface, fold in the dry ingredients with a rubber spatula.

3. Gently pour the batter down the center of the pan, spreading as evenly as possible, using the pan's sides as a guide: The batter should be level with the sides of the pan. Bake until the cake springs back when lightly touched near its center and has a light golden color, about 5 minutes.

4. Remove pan from the oven, and place it on a wire rack. Using a knife, gently release any portion of the cake sticking to the sides of pan. Cover the cake with another baking sheet, and invert. Remove the original baking sheet, and peel off the foil carefully to avoid tearing the cake; then turn foil over so that the sticky side faces up, and reposition it back on the cake. Cover with a large wire rack, and invert right side up. Cool completely.

5. Using your fingertips or a small paring knife, carefully peel off the soft, brown, paper-thin crust from the cake's surface. Now the cake is more flexible when rolling, more porous when moistened with flavored syrups, and more attractive when sliced since the cake layer and its filling form a pattern.

6. Cut cake in half to make two 12- × 7½-inch pieces. Lift one portion of cake onto a clean baking sheet.

7. Pistachio Silk Buttercream: In the large bowl of an electric mixer, whip the egg yolks until light and fluffy, about 4 minutes. Remove bowl from mixer stand. Combine the water and sugar in a 1-quart heavy saucepan over low heat. Stir occasionally, washing down any sugar crystals clinging to the sides of the pan with a brush dipped in cold water, until the sugar is dissolved. Increase the heat and cook the syrup, without stirring, until it registers 238 degrees on a mercury candy thermometer. Pour into the center of the yolks and quickly whisk vigorously to combine. Return bowl to electric mixer, and whip at medium speed until the mixture thickens and cools to body temperature, about 5 minutes. Maintaining medium speed, add the butter to the cooled egg yolk mixture, 2 tablespoons at a time. Continue mixing until all the butter has been incorporated and the butter-cream is smooth and homogeneous.

8. When buttercream is soft and smooth, stir in the nuts, almond extract, and 2 drops green food coloring until thoroughly combined. Reserve 3 tablespoons buttercream for finishing.

9. Spread the buttercream evenly over cake on baking sheet. Gently press other half of cake on top to sandwich the buttercream. Spread the reserved buttercream over the top of the cake to provide a thin coating. Cover the cake's surface with plastic wrap and freeze until buttercream has firmed, or up to 2 weeks.

10. One hour before serving, remove cake from freezer. Using a sharp knife, trim edges evenly. With the aid of a ruler, measure and cut five 1½-inch-wide strips, each 12 inches long. Cut each strip into eight 1½-inch squares. Then, while still frozen and firm, cut each square in half to form triangles. Dip the knife in hot water and wipe it before each cut to make cutting easier and neater.

11. Transfer frozen pastries to a jelly roll pan or a covered foil-lined card-board container, such as a cake box. Sprinkle with the powdered sugar and center a pistachio half on top of each triangle before serving at room temperature.

TECHNIQUE NOTE

- Freezing the cake with its filling firms the cake and buttercream so it's easier to cut neat portions carefully. The precise pattern of the cake and butter-cream when sliced is important.

Pistachio Petits Fours

Honey Bee Minicakes

Luscious sticks of spongy genoise and silken honey buttercream are glazed with dark chocolate before crowning with a cheery buttercream bee.

CAKE

⅓ Genoise Sheet Cake, 12 x 5 inches (page 289)

DECORATION

Honey Silk Buttercream

4 egg yolks

¼ cup water

½ cup (100 grams) granulated sugar

8 ounces (2 sticks) unsalted butter, room temperature

2 tablespoons honey

Dark Chocolate Satin Glaze

¼ cup (1½ ounces) solid vegetable shortening

1 pound semisweet chocolate, chopped

1 ounce (¼ cup) sliced almonds

1. Transfer the cake to a large baking sheet.

2. Honey Silk Buttercream: In the large bowl of an electric mixer, whip the egg yolks until light and fluffy, about 4 minutes. Remove bowl from mixer stand. Combine the water and sugar in a 1-quart heavy saucepan over low heat. Stir occasionally, washing down any sugar crystals clinging to the sides of the pan with a brush dipped in cold water, until sugar is dissolved. Increase the heat and cook the syrup, without stirring, until it registers 238 degrees on a mercury candy thermometer. Pour into the center of the yolks and quickly whisk vigorously to combine. Return bowl to electric mixer, and whip at medium speed until the egg yolk mixture thickens and cools to body temperature, about 5 minutes. Maintain-

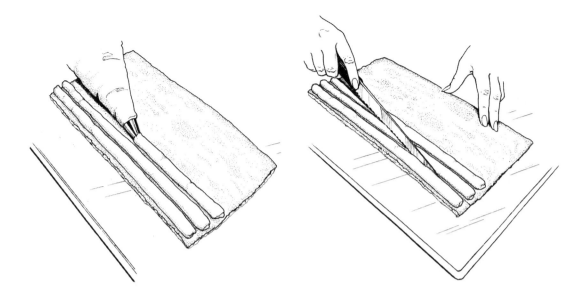

ing medium speed, add the butter to the cooled egg yolk mixture, 2 tablespoons at a time. Continue mixing until all the butter has been incorporated and the buttercream is smooth and homogeneous. Whip in the honey.

3. Using a flexible metal icing spatula, spread only 2 tablespoons buttercream evenly over top of cake to give it a smooth finish.

4. Using a pastry bag fitted with a ¹/₂-inch plain decorating tip (such as Ateco #6), pipe ¹/₂-inch-thick strings of buttercream lengthwise on the cake in parallel lines about ¹/₈ inch apart. Place in the freezer, uncovered, for about an hour to partially freeze the pastry to facilitate cutting easily into individual sticks.

5. Dark Chocolate Satin Glaze: Combine the shortening and chocolate in a 3-quart bowl. Place it over a saucepan filled with enough hot water (120 to 130 degrees) to reach the bottom of the bowl. Stir mixture occasionally until the glaze is liquid and smooth and registers 110 degrees on a mercury candy thermometer. If water cools while melting the chocolate, maintain the 120-degree temperature over very low heat. Set aside.

6. To make buttercream bees: Slip a ¹/₄-inch plain decorating tip (such as Ateco #2) *over* the ¹/₂-inch plain decorating tip. Hold the tip in place with one

Honey Bee Minicakes

293

hand, and with the other hand squeeze the bag and pipe out thirty-six ¾-inch-long ovals on a sheet of aluminum foil. Stick a sliced almond on each side of a buttercream oval to serve as wings for the bees. Using a small handmade paper cone, pipe stripes of chocolate glaze over the bee bodies. Place bees, on the foil, in the freezer.

7. Remove cake from freezer. With a sharp knife, cut between the strings of buttercream. Then cut each strip into 2-inch-long pieces. Transfer the small cake strips to wire racks, spacing them 1 inch apart. Place racks over a jelly roll pan to catch drips when glazing.

8. Ladle about 2 tablespoons of glaze over each pastry, masking it completely. When no glaze remains in the bowl, pour glaze from the jelly roll pan back into the bowl, set over hot water, and reheat. It's useful to pour the glaze through a sieve before reheating, since some cake crumbs may have fallen into it during the masking.

9. After coating all the pastries, move each pastry gently from its base with a small metal spatula so that any drips are cut from its underside while the glaze is liquid. This neat finish also keeps the pastries from sticking to the rack.

10. The warm glaze sets up rather quickly after touching the cold, firm buttercream, leaving a gorgeous sheen. When the coating firms, it will not stick to your fingers as you lift the pastries.

11. Remove bees from the freezer; lift one at a time off the foil to place on top of each chocolate-coated honey stick.

12. Carefully lift pastries, one by one, with a small metal spatula, and transfer them to a foil-lined cardboard container, such as a cake box. Store, uncovered, in a cool room up to 1 day.

Honey Bee
Minicakes

294

Parisers

A Pariser looks like a bonbon, but it is actually a coin of genoise mounded with a decadent chocolate buttercream and encased in a satiny, dark chocolate glaze. To make it look as appealing as it tastes, I pipe a pale yellow buttercream flower and a pair of pale green buttercream leaves on top.

Makes 2 dozen 1¼-inch round cakes

CAKE

½ Genoise Sheet Cake, 12 x 7½ inches (page 289)

DECORATION

Chocolate Silk Buttercream

4 egg yolks

¼ cup water

½ cup (100 grams) granulated sugar

8 ounces (2 sticks) unsalted butter, room temperature

2 ounces unsweetened chocolate, melted

Dark Chocolate Satin Glaze

¼ cup (1½ ounces) solid shortening

1 pound semisweet chocolate, chopped

Decorative Icing

1 cup (100 grams) unsifted powdered sugar

3½ ounces (7 tablespoons) unsalted butter, room temperature

⅛ teaspoon salt

½ teaspoon almond extract

½ teaspoon vanilla

Green and yellow liquid food coloring

1. Put the cake on a cutting board, and, using the wide end of a ½-inch plain decorating tip (such as Ateco #6) as a cutter, cut out 1¼-inch circles.

(Partially freezing the cake before cutting it facilitates neater shapes.) Transfer the cake circles to a clean baking sheet.

2. Chocolate Silk Buttercream: In the large bowl of an electric mixer, whip the egg yolks until light and fluffy, about 4 minutes. Remove the bowl from the mixer stand. Combine the water and sugar in a 1-quart heavy saucepan over low heat. Stir occasionally, washing down any sugar crystals clinging to the sides of the pan with a brush dipped in cold water, until the sugar is dissolved. Increase heat and cook the syrup, without stirring, until it registers 238 degrees on a mercury candy thermometer. Pour into the center of the yolks and quickly whisk vigorously to combine. Return bowl to electric mixer, and whip at medium speed until the egg yolk mixture thickens and cools to body temperature, about 5 minutes. Maintaining medium speed, add the butter to the cooled egg yolk mixture, 2 tablespoons at a time. Continue mixing until all the butter has been incorporated and the buttercream is smooth and homogeneous.

3. Spoon 1½ cups buttercream into a large bowl and stir until soft and smooth. (Save remaining buttercream for another miniature.) Stir about ½ cup of the buttercream into the 2 ounces melted chocolate until well blended; add to the bowl of buttercream, stirring until smooth.

4. Using a pastry bag fitted with a ½-inch plain decorating tip (such as Ateco #6), pipe out a bulb of buttercream on top of each cake circle. Refrigerate to firm the buttercream, about 1 to 2 hours.

5. Place the chilled pastries on wire racks, spacing them 1 inch apart. Glaze one rack at a time, keeping remaining pastries on racks in refrigerator. When ready to glaze, place rack over a jelly roll pan to catch drips.

6. Dark Chocolate Satin Glaze: Combine the shortening and chocolate in a 3-quart bowl. Place it over a saucepan filled with enough hot water (120 to 130 degrees) to reach the bottom of the bowl. Stir mixture occasionally until the glaze is liquid and smooth and registers 110 degrees on a mercury candy thermometer. If water cools while melting the chocolate, maintain the 120-degree temperature over very low heat.

Parisers

7. Ladle about 2 tablespoons of the chocolate glaze over each pastry, masking it completely. Repeat with remaining racks of pastries. When no glaze remains in the bowl, pour glaze from the jelly roll pan back into the bowl, set over hot water, and reheat. It's useful to pour the glaze through a sieve before reheating, since some cake crumbs may have fallen into it during the masking.

8. After all pastries have been coated, move each pastry gently from its base with a small metal spatula so that any drips are cut from its underside while the coating is liquid. This neat finish also keeps the pastries from sticking to the rack when they are removed. The warm coating sets up rather quickly after touching the cold, firm buttercream, leaving a gorgeous sheen. When the coating firms, it will not stick to your fingers as you lift the pastries.

9. Decorative Icing: Sift the powdered sugar onto a sheet of waxed paper. In a medium mixing bowl, mix the butter, salt and about one-half the powdered sugar until smooth and creamy. Gradually add the remaining sugar, then the flavorings, beating until smooth and creamy.

10. When the glaze has set, color small portions of the decorative icing in shades of pastel yellow and green with the food coloring. Using two small hand-made paper cones, pipe yellow flower-like shapes on each pastry and two green leaves on opposite sides of each flower.

11. Carefully lift pastries, one by one, with a small metal spatula, and transfer them to a foil-lined cardboard container, such as a cake box. Store, covered, in a cool room up to 1 day.

VARIATION NOTE

- For shaping flowers and leaves, you can substitute butter royal icing for the decorative icing. Beat $1\frac{1}{3}$ cups powdered sugar with 1 egg white and 1 tablespoon soft unsalted butter until smooth and glossy. If too thin to pipe, beat until stiffer or add more powdered sugar; if too thick, add water, drop by drop.

Parisers

Calypso Minirolls

Makes 3 dozen
2-inch-long
minirolls

The toasty quality of caramel is accented by the sweet tang of fresh orange in these bite-sized jelly rolls. Small strips of genoise, flavored with orange juice and a buttery caramel filling, are rolled to create cakes that are ideal for an afternoon tea or with coffee after a meal.

CAKE

1 Genoise Sheet Cake (page 289)

FILLING

¼ cup fresh orange juice

Caramel Filling

¼ cup water

½ cup (100 grams) granulated
   sugar

2 ounces (4 tablespoons)
   unsalted butter

¼ cup heavy cream

DECORATION

¼ cup (25 grams) powdered
   sugar

36 candied lilacs

1. Trim the cake of any crisp edges. Roll a rolling pin over cake to compress it. Brush the orange juice over the cake with a pastry brush.

2. Caramel Filling: Combine the water, sugar, and butter in a 1-quart heavy-bottomed saucepan. Over medium high heat, bring to a boil and cook, stirring occasionally, until light tan in color, about 7 minutes. Off heat, add the heavy

Calypso
Minirolls

298

cream, stirring until blended. Cool no longer than 30 to 40 minutes, to thicken. Using a metal icing spatula, spread the filling thinly over the cake.

3. Using a ruler and sharp serrated knife, cut six 2-inch-wide strips, each about 12 inches long. Cut each strip into three 2½-inch pieces.

4. With fingertips, roll up each cake portion and place the minirolls seam side down on a clean baking sheet. Cover the minirolls with plastic wrap.

5. Sprinkle lightly with the powdered sugar and stick a candied lilac on top of each roll before serving.

6. Store in a covered foil-lined cardboard container, such as a cake box, at room temperature up to 1 day.

VARIATION NOTE

Swiss Tea Cakes

For a shape variation, spread the cake with the caramel filling as the recipe specifies, then cut cake into 2-inch squares. Fold each square in half, almost corner to corner, but slightly off center, short of corners meeting and just short of forming a perfect triangle. Stick a candied lilac in the apex of each pastry's imperfect triangle for decoration.

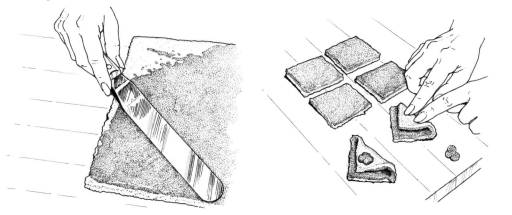

Sweet Sushi Swirls

Makes about

2 dozen

½-inch slices

I created this whimsical recipe for a magazine, after my first trip to Japan. These cake rolls look like sushi but taste like a wonderful apricot-chocolate genoise with a subtle hint of sesame. The cake is rolled around dried apricots and it's all coated with a thin layer of dark chocolate plastic that resembles the seaweed that encases the rice in sushi.

CAKE

½ Genoise Sheet Cake,
  5½ × 15 inches (page 289)

FILLING
Sesame Gianduja

1 ounce (¼ cup) sesame seeds, toasted

¼ cup (25 grams) unsifted powdered sugar

6 to 8 dried apricots

4 ounces semisweet chocolate, melted

DARK CHOCOLATE PLASTIC

4 ounces semisweet chocolate, melted

3 level tablespoons light corn syrup

1. Sesame Gianduja: In a food processor bowl, process the sesame seeds with the sugar until pasty. Add the chocolate and process until smooth and thoroughly blended.

2. Spread a thin layer (about ½ cup) of the sesame gianduja over the cake. Cut the cake in half to make two rectangles about 5½ × 7½ inches. Place each cake rectangle on a sheet of parchment paper about 10 inches wide × 15 inches long.

3. With the 7½-inch edge of cake facing you, lay 3 to 4 apricots, rolled up tightly, along the edge. Using your fingertips, roll the cake over the apricots and continue to roll jelly roll fashion.

4. Position the cake roll across the bottom third of the parchment paper. Bring the top edge of the paper toward you and drape it over the cake, allowing at least a 2-inch overhang. Place the edge of a rimless baking sheet at a 45-degree angle to the roll and the work surface. Press against the cake, trapping the paper overhang, and push while simultaneously pulling the bottom portion of the paper toward you. This push-pull motion creates a resistance that results in compressing the spongy cake roll. Wrap the excess parchment paper around the roll and slip one or two thin rubber bands over it. Repeat procedure with second roll. Let the rolls stand for at least 30 minutes to maintain their shape.

5. Dark Chocolate Plastic: Combine the melted chocolate with the corn syrup. Stir until the mixture is smooth and elastic. Wrap in plastic, and set aside in a cool room until the mixture is firm, yet pliable enough to roll with a rolling pin, about 30 to 45 minutes.

6. Lightly sprinkle a clean work surface with cornstarch. Using a rolling pin, roll half the dark chocolate plastic into a 7½-inch square. Brush off any excess cornstarch. With a ruler and a pastry wheel, trim any uneven edges. Dab the surface of the rolled chocolate with 1 teaspoon of the sesame gianduja.

7. Remove the parchment paper from one cinched cake roll and lay the roll over the lower third of the dark chocolate square. Lift the dark chocolate square up and wrap it around the roll, pressing where the seams meet. To make slicing the roll easier, wrap in plastic and refrigerate for just 30 minutes. Repeat the procedure for the remaining cake roll.

8. Using a serrated knife, cut rolls into ½-inch-wide slices.

9. Transfer slices to a foil-lined cardboard container, such as a cake box, covering cakes' surface with a strip of plastic wrap, and store in a cool room. Serve them the same day they are decorated.

Sweet Sushi Swirls

Grape Cake Triangles

Makes 3 dozen
1½-inch triangles

These pastries are easy to produce, but the look is dramatic and the taste is rich and sweet. Spread orange-flavored red currant jelly thinly over a sheet of genoise, top with a grape-colored layer of marzipan, and cut into triangles. A simple technique transforms each triangle so that it resembles a cluster of grapes.

CAKE

½ Genoise Sheet Cake, 12 x 7½ inches (page 289)

GLAZE

3 tablespoons red currant jelly   1 tablespoon fresh orange juice

DECORATION

Red and blue liquid food coloring   Candied angelica

6 ounces (⅔ cup) marzipan

Powdered sugar

1. Heat the jelly just to warm and liquefy it. Off heat, stir in the orange juice. Using a metal icing spatula, spread a thin layer over cake's surface.

2. In a small bowl, mix 4 drops red and 2 drops blue liquid food coloring together to make purple coloring. Add this coloring into center of marzipan. Knead on a work surface lightly sprinkled with powdered sugar to distribute the color evenly into the marzipan until it is a pale shade of purple.

3. With a rolling pin, roll out the marzipan paper-thin, about ¹⁄₁₆ inch thick, on a work surface lightly sprinkled with powdered sugar. Drape it over the rolling pin and place on the cake. With fingertips, gently push the marzipan to extend it to completely cover the cake. The jam underneath makes it easy to slide the marzipan over the cake. Be gentle, or the marzipan tears.

4. Using a ruler and small serrated knife, cut the marzipan-topped cake into five strips, 1½ inches wide and 12 inches long. Then cut across each strip diagonally in alternate directions to form 1½-inch triangular shapes.

5. Using the tip of a plastic straw as a cutter, pierce, without cutting completely through, the marzipan to form tiny rounds, about fifteen on each cake triangle, to resemble a cluster of grapes.

6. Cut small pieces from the candied angelica. Put one on each cake triangle as a stem for the grape cluster.

DECORATION NOTE

• Look for angelica, the candied stalk of a biennial herb plant, in specialty food stores and well-stocked supermarkets—especially around holiday time. Angelica is green for the grape stem.

Grape Cake
Triangles

Chocolate Galaxy Petitcakes

Makes 1 dozen
1¾-inch
petitcakes

A galaxy of rich flavor awaits in these star-shaped chocolate almond cakes. Each cake is topped with white chocolate butter glaze and studded with shiny silver beads (dragées). The cake tastes particularly good with the addition of fresh cranberries or raspberries in the batter.

CHOCOLATE ALMOND CAKE

- ¼ cup (25 grams) unsifted cocoa powder
- ¼ cup (25 grams) sifted cake flour
- ⅛ teaspoon salt
- 8 ounces (scant 1 cup) almond paste, room temperature

- ½ cup (100 grams) granulated sugar
- 6 ounces (1½ sticks) unsalted butter, room temperature
- 3 large eggs, room temperature
- 1 tablespoon kirsch

DECORATION
White Chocolate Butter Glaze

- 4 ounces (1 stick) unsalted butter, cut into cubes
- 1 tablespoon solid vegetable shortening

- 8 ounces white chocolate, finely chopped
- ½ cup tiny silver dragées

1. Adjust rack to lower third of oven and preheat oven to 350 degrees. Grease and flour a straight-sided 8-inch round cake pan; place an 8-inch parchment paper liner or waxed paper round in the pan.

2. In a small bowl, blend the cocoa powder, flour, and salt briefly with a whisk.

3. In the large bowl of an electric mixer, break up the almond paste with the mixer on low speed. Slowly add the sugar; beat until incorporated and mixture is smooth with no lumps.

4. On medium-low speed, gradually add the butter and beat until the mixture is smooth and fluffy, about 2 to 3 minutes. Add the eggs, one at a time, and beat until mixture is smooth and creamy. Scrape the sides of the bowl whenever necessary. Add the kirsch. On low speed, add the flour mixture just until incorporated.

5. Spread the batter evenly in the pan. Bake for 20 to 25 minutes, or until the top springs back when lightly touched. Cool the cake in the pan on a rack for about 10 minutes. Remove from the pan and place on the rack to cool completely.

6. With a star cutter (about 1¾ inches across), cut out star shapes in the cake. To facilitate cutting the shapes, freeze the cake just 15 minutes.

7. Transfer the stars to a wire rack, spacing them 1 inch apart, and set rack over a jelly roll pan to catch drips when glazing.

8. White Chocolate Butter Glaze: Melt the butter, vegetable shortening, and chocolate in a 1-quart mixing bowl that fits snugly over a pan of 120-degree water. Stir the mixture often with a dry rubber spatula to ensure that the white chocolate melts evenly.

9. When the glaze is smooth and liquid, ladle about 2 tablespoons of it over each star-shaped cake, masking it completely. If necessary, coax the glaze over the tops and down the sides with a thin metal icing spatula or lift and tilt the wire rack.

10. When no glaze remains in bowl, pour glaze from the jelly roll pan back into the bowl, and reheat over hot water. It's useful to pour glaze through a sieve before reheating, since some crumbs may have fallen into it during the masking.

11. After all cakes have been coated, move each one gently from its base with a small metal spatula so that any drips are cut from its underside while the coating is liquid. This neat finish also keeps the cakes from sticking to the rack.

12. Allow the glaze to set before completely covering the tops of the cakes with the tiny silver dragées.

13. Carefully lift pastries, one by one, with a small metal spatula, and transfer them to a foil-lined cardboard container, such as a cake box. Store in a cool room up to 1 day.

VARIATION NOTE

- It's easy to add seasonal flavor to the Chocolate Almond Cake: In winter, fold ½ cup cranberries into the batter; in summer, fold in 1 cup fresh raspberries. These variations remind me of the popular dessert old-fashioned summer pudding.

BAKING NOTE

- The small amount of solid vegetable shortening in the white chocolate butter glaze ensures a smooth, shiny finish.

Chocolate Galaxy Petitcakes

 Dominoes

These butter cake petits fours with thin layers of apricot, marzipan, and chocolate, are playful recreations of the domino tiles. They are easy to make for a crowd.

Makes 6 dozen
1- × 2-inch
cakes

BUTTER CAKE BATTER

- 2 cups (200 grams) sifted cake flour
- 1 teaspoon baking powder
- 1/4 teaspoon salt
- 9 ounces (2 1/4 sticks) unsalted butter, room temperature

- 1 1/2 cups (300 grams) granulated sugar
- 4 large eggs, room temperature
- 1 tablespoon finely grated orange zest

DECORATION

- 1/3 cup strained apricot jam

- 12 ounces marzipan

  Powdered sugar

Dark Chocolate Satin Glaze

- 1/4 cup (1 1/2 ounces) solid vegetable shortening

- 1 pound semisweet chocolate, chopped

Royal Icing

- 1/2 cup (50 grams) unsifted powdered sugar

- 2 teaspoons egg white

1. Adjust rack to lower third of oven and preheat oven to 375 degrees. Grease and flour a 10- × 15- × 1-inch baking pan.

2. Sift the flour, baking powder, and salt on a sheet of waxed paper; set aside. In the large bowl of an electric mixer, cream the butter at medium speed until it is creamy, smooth, and lighter in color, about 45 seconds. Beat in the sugar until creamy. Add the eggs, one at a time, beating until light and fluffy.

With a rubber spatula, scrape the mixture clinging to the sides into the center of the bowl when necessary. Add the orange zest, then lower mixer speed and blend in flour mixture in three additions. Mix just until smooth and thoroughly combined.

3. Spread the batter evenly over the baking pan. Bake 20 to 22 minutes or until the cake springs back when lightly touched near the center and has a light golden color. Remove to a wire rack until cool.

4. Heat the apricot jam just to warm and liquefy it. Spread thinly over the cake.

5. With a rolling pin, roll out the marzipan to about $1/16$ inch thick on a surface lightly sprinkled with powdered sugar. Drape over rolling pin and place on the cake. With fingertips, gently push the marzipan to extend it to completely cover the cake. The jam underneath makes it easy to slide the marzipan over the cake. Be gentle, or the marzipan tears.

6. Using a ruler as a guide, cut the cake into five 2-inch-wide strips, each 15 inches long. Cut each strip into fifteen 1-inch rectangles.

7. Dark Chocolate Satin Glaze: Combine the shortening and chocolate in a 3-quart bowl. Place it over a saucepan filled with enough hot water (120 to 130 degrees) to reach the bottom of the bowl. Stir occasionally until the glaze is liquid and smooth and registers close to 110 degrees on a mercury candy thermometer. If water cools while melting the chocolate, maintain the 120-degree temperature over very low heat.

8. Transfer the pastries to wire racks, spacing them 1 inch apart. Place racks over a jelly roll pan to catch drips when glazing. Ladle about 2 tablespoons of the glaze over each pastry, masking it completely.

9. When no more glaze remains in the bowl, pour glaze from the jelly roll pan into the double boiler, and reheat. It's useful to pour the glaze through a sieve before reheating, since some cake crumbs may have fallen into it during the masking of the pastries.

10. After masking all the pastries, move each pastry gently from its base with a small metal spatula to remove any chocolate drips from its underside while the glaze is liquid. This neat finish also keeps the pastries from sticking to the rack.

11. Royal Icing: Combine the sugar and egg white in a small bowl. Mix together until icing is creamy, thick, and forms a string when poured from a spoon.

12. When the glaze has set, using a small handmade paper cone, pipe a domino pattern with royal icing on each pastry. (The glaze has set when it does not stick to your fingers as you lift the pastries.)

13. Carefully lift pastries, one by one, with a small metal spatula, and transfer them to a foil-lined cardboard container, such as a cake box. Store, covered, in a cool room up to 1 day. When ready to serve, place the pastries in small paper cases, if you prefer.

Dominoes

Jewel Fruit Prisms

As the name implies, these small butter cakes sparkle like jewels. The effect is achieved by making a wine jelly from orange muscat wine and cutting it into tiny squares, then scattering them over the cake. The results are moist and refreshing. Eating a game aspic garnish with a chilled duck terrine gave me the idea for the fruity wine jelly. It flavors and decorates these little cakes beautifully.

CAKE

½ Butter Cake, 10 × 7½ inches
   (page 307)

WINE JELLY

⅔ cup Essencia (Quady California Orange Muscat)

2 teaspoons gelatin

2 tablespoons sugar

1. Place the cake on a large clean baking sheet.

2. Wine Jelly: Pour the wine into a liquid-measure measuring cup. Sprinkle the gelatin over the surface, and set aside until softened. Then pour into a small saucepan, add the sugar, and heat over low heat just to dissolve the gelatin and sugar. Remove from heat and pour into a shallow Pyrex baking dish, about 9 x 13 inches. The wine mixture should be ⅛ inch deep. Refrigerate to gel.

3. Remove the jelly from the refrigerator, and, with the tip of a paring knife, cut lines close to ⅛ inch apart in both directions (the pattern looks like graph paper) to form wine jewels.

4. With a spatula, lift the jelly from the pan to break the cut pieces apart. With a serving spoon, arrange over the cake. Refrigerate 30 minutes.

5. With a ruler and a sharp knife, cut cake into 1-inch squares. To cut neat and precise squares, cut straight down with the knife; don't pull the blade through the cake each time you cut. Wipe the knife clean after each cut.

6. Cover cake with aluminum foil, taking care that the foil does not rest directly on the topping, and return the cake on its tray to the refrigerator until an hour before serving.

VARIATION NOTES

- For variety, substitute an extra-dry champagne, dessert Sauterne, or even fresh orange juice for the wine in the jelly.
- Fold 1 cup fresh room-temperature blueberries into the butter cake batter to add a fruity flavor to this simply luscious cake.

Jewel Fruit Prisms

Miniature Fruit Meringues

Makes 3 dozen
1-inch cakes

This is my interpretation of the classic Baked Alaska, without the ice cream, so it's easy to serve. The rich taste of butter cake, the freshness from a medley of fruits, and a fluffy meringue topping really shine.

CAKE

½ Butter Cake, 10 × 7½ inches
(page 307)

DECORATION

2 cups assorted small fresh fruits,
such as raspberries, blueberries,
and strawberries

Fluffy Meringue

½ cup (about 4 large) egg
whites

1 cup (200 grams) granulated
sugar

1. Place cake on a large clean baking sheet. In a large bowl, toss the fruit to mix.

2. Adjust the oven rack 6 to 7 inches from the broiler, and preheat it.

3. Fluffy Meringue: In a large mixing bowl, blend the egg whites with the sugar. Place it over another bowl of hot tap water and stir until the mixture is body temperature. Remove from water, and using an electric mixer, preferably with a whisk attachment, whip until the mixture has peaks that are thick and shiny, about 10 to 15 minutes.

4. Spread about ½ cup of the meringue evenly over cake to cover. Sprinkle the fruit over meringue. With fingertips, press fruit into meringue to anchor in place. With a metal icing spatula, spread the remaining meringue over the fruit to cover.

5. Place the baking sheet under the broiler just until the meringue's surface is light golden in color. Place baking sheet on a wire rack to cool.

6. With a ruler and a sharp knife, cut the cake into 1-inch squares. To cut neat and precise squares, cut straight down with the knife; don't pull the blade through the cake each time you cut. Wipe the knife clean after each cut.

7. Serve these at room temperature the same day they are baked.

BAKING NOTE

- Egg whites freshly separated from eggs, rather than leftover egg whites, are best for this meringue so it will cut easily and neatly without sticking to the knife blade.

Tiny Raspberry Cheesecakes

Makes 2 dozen
1¾-inch
minicakes

Creamy raspberry-studded cheesecake is baked into individual bite-sized desserts that are small in size but not in flavor. All the flavor and texture of a slice of cheesecake is contained in one of these miniatures. Short baking in a water bath ensures even baking and a satin smooth result. These promise to be seductive—every time.

BROWNIE SHEET

2 ounces unsweetened chocolate, coarsely chopped

4 ounces (1 stick) unsalted butter

1 cup (200 grams) granulated sugar

2 large eggs, room temperature

1 teaspoon vanilla

6 tablespoons unsifted all-purpose flour

RASPBERRY CHEESECAKE

1 pound cream cheese, room temperature

⅔ cup (130 grams) granulated sugar

2 large eggs, room temperature

1 teaspoon vanilla

1 cup fresh raspberries, room temperature

1. Adjust rack to lower third of oven and preheat oven to 375 degrees. Grease and flour a 10- × 15- × 1-inch jelly roll pan, shaking out excess flour.

2. In a small heavy-bottomed saucepan, melt the chocolate and butter over very low heat. Transfer mixture to a medium bowl, stir in sugar until blended; and set aside 5 minutes to cool. Add the eggs, one at a time, then add the vanilla. Stir in the flour until thoroughly combined.

3. Spoon into pan and spread evenly. Bake in preheated oven 11 to 13 minutes or until no longer shiny on top. Don't overbake. Check cake after baking

6 to 7 minutes. If it puffs up, poke the raised areas with a metal skewer to release steam.

4. Remove the pan to a wire rack to cool.

5. Crumble one third of the brownie sheet into small pieces. Place in food processor bowl and process until fine crumbs. Wrap the remaining brownie sheet cake with plastic wrap until ready to serve.

6. Adjust rack to lower third of oven and preheat oven to 325 degrees. Grease two 12-cup mini muffin pans, each cup measuring 1½ inches across and ¾ inch deep. Spoon about 2 teaspoons brownie crumbs into each cup. Shake or press crumbs to coat each cup. Tilt pans to tap out excess. Don't worry if the crumbs do not completely coat each cup, but leave the equivalent of ½ teaspoon crumbs in the bottom of each cup.

7. Raspberry Cheesecake: In the large bowl of an electric mixer, cream the cheese at medium-low speed until it is smooth. Add the sugar and continue to cream the mixture until it is creamy. Add the eggs, one at a time, and continue mixing until mixture is slightly runny, about 5 minutes. Add the vanilla. Gently fold in the raspberries. Spoon 1 rounded tablespoon into each mini cup. Tap muffin pans lightly on work surface.

8. Set the two muffin pans on a jelly roll pan and place in the oven. Carefully pour 4 to 5 cups hot water into the jelly roll pan. Bake 30 minutes, turn oven off, and leave cheesecakes in oven for 25 minutes more. Using a bulb baster, remove the hot water from the jelly roll pan. Then remove the jelly roll pan with the muffin pans to a wire rack to cool for 15 to 20 minutes. One by one, run a small metal spatula around each cheesecake to loosen it and tap it out into the palm of your hand. Transfer to a foil-covered plate. Cover plate of mini cheesecakes with plastic wrap and refrigerate until serving or up to 2 days.

9. Using a 1½-inch heart-shaped cutter, cut out hearts from the remaining brownie sheet cake. Place on top of each cheesecake as decoration.

Tiny Raspberry Cheesecakes

Polka Dot Minicakes

The elegant appearance of these minicakes belies their easy decoration. Cover little rounds of almond cake with a creamy white chocolate glaze, then apply several tiny dark chocolate polka dots on top before the glaze sets.

ALMOND CAKE BATTER

8 ounces (1 scant cup) almond paste, room temperature

¼ cup (50 grams) granulated sugar

3 large eggs, room temperature

1 teaspoon lemon zest

⅓ cup plus 1 tablespoon (36 grams) sifted cake flour

DECORATION

White Chocolate Glaze

4 ounces (1 stick) unsalted butter, diced

1 tablespoon vegetable shortening

8 ounces white chocolate, finely chopped

1 ounce semisweet chocolate, finely chopped

1. Adjust rack to lower third of oven and preheat oven to 350 degrees. Grease and flour a 7-inch square baking pan. (Check the bottom measurement of your 8-inch square pans—most pans measure only 7 inches square on the bottom.)

2. In the large bowl of an electric mixer, beat the almond paste at low speed just to break it up, about 30 seconds. Add the sugar in a steady stream, and beat until incorporated. Add the eggs, one at a time, and continue beating until the mixture is light and fluffy. Add the zest. Using a rubber spatula, scrape the mixture from the sides into the center of the bowl when necessary. Lower speed,

and blend in the flour until mixture is smooth and thoroughly combined. Spread evenly into pan.

3. Bake for 25 minutes or until center springs back when lightly touched. Remove pan to a wire rack until completely cool.

4. White Chocolate Glaze: Melt the butter, shortening, and chocolate in a bowl that fits snugly over a pan of 120-degree water. Stir until glaze is smooth and liquid.

5. Using a 1½-inch round cutter, cut out rounds from the cake in the baking pan. Transfer the cake cut-outs to wire racks, spacing them 1 inch apart. Place racks over a jelly roll pan to catch drips when glazing. Ladle about 2 tablespoons of the glaze over each pastry, masking it completely.

6. When no more glaze remains in the bowl, pour glaze from the jelly roll pan back into the bowl, and reheat over hot water. It's useful to pour the glaze through a sieve before reheating, since some cake crumbs may have fallen into it during the masking.

7. After all the pastries have been coated, move each pastry gently from its base with a small metal spatula so that any drips are cut from its underside while the coating is liquid. This neat finish also keeps the pastries from sticking to the rack.

8. Melt the semisweet chocolate in a small bowl set over a pan of 120-degree water. Stir ¼ cup of the remaining glaze into the melted chocolate. Replace bowl over hot water and stir until smooth and liquid.

9. Half fill a small handmade paper cone with the dark chocolate glaze. Before the white chocolate glaze sets on the pastries, pipe several tiny polka dots on the minicakes with the darker chocolate glaze.

10. When the glaze has set, carefully lift pastries, one by one, with a small metal spatula, and transfer them to a foil-lined cardboard container, such as a cake box. Store, covered, in a cool room up to 1 day. When ready to serve, place the pastries in small paper cases, if you prefer.

Polka Dot Minicakes

Cranberry Almond Cake

Fold ½ cup fresh cranberries into the almond cake batter. After baking and cooling the cake, sprinkle with powdered sugar instead of the white chocolate glaze with polka dots.

Limoges Petits Fours

When you remove the almond cake from the oven, cool 10 minutes, then invert onto a rack to cool. Set rack over a jelly roll pan.

Prepare the white chocolate glaze as directed above. Heat ¼ cup currant jelly just until warm and smooth. Spoon into a small handmade paper cone and set aside. Pour glaze onto center of cake and spread evenly using a metal spatula. Sides of cake need not be glazed. Snip off tip of cone, and pipe thin lines of jelly between ¼ and ½ inch apart diagonally across the glaze. Set cake aside at room temperature until the glaze sets, at least 1 hour.

Transfer cake to a cutting board and trim the edges with a long, sharp knife. Using a ruler and the knife, cut into 1-inch squares. To make squares neat, dip the knife blade into hot water and wipe it with paper towels after each cut. Makes 4 dozen 1-inch square petits fours.

Polka Dot
Minicakes

Punsch Cakelets

Here's a perfect way to use the trimmings from the Almond Cake (page 316), Butter Cake (page 307), Genoise Sheet Cake (page 289), and Chocolate Almond Cake (page 304). I always freeze the scraps of cake in a sturdy plastic container until I have enough to make this recipe.

This is my version in miniature of the Punschtortes I've tasted in Germany and Austria. As the name suggests, these are bite-sized punch-flavored cakelets. Cake cubes are tossed with a punch of orange and lemon juice, jam, and dark rum. When assembling this no-bake cake, a simple technique compresses the mixture in a foil-lined pan to make it easy to remove the multicolored layer cake cubes before topping each one with a glistening red raspberry.

Makes 4 dozen 1½-inch squares

CAKE

8 cups cake trimmings, loosely packed

PUNSCH FILLING

8 small sugar cubes	⅓ cup strained apricot jam
1 orange	⅔ cup fresh orange juice
1 lemon	2 tablespoons fresh lemon juice
½ cup water	2 tablespoons dark rum
⅓ cup (65 grams) granulated sugar	1 cup (½ pint) fresh raspberries

DECORATION

1 cup (½ pint) fresh raspberries	3 tablespoons red currant jelly

1. Cut cake trimmings into ½- to 1-inch cubes and transfer to a 3-quart bowl. Line a 9- × 13-inch pan with aluminum foil.

2. Punsch Filling: Rub each side of 4 sugar cubes against the orange skin to capture the flavor from the fruit's oil. Rub each side of remaining 4 sugar cubes over the lemon. In a 3-cup heavy saucepan, combine the sugar cubes (to produce a more intense citrus flavor) with the water and granulated sugar over low heat. Stir occasionally, washing down any sugar clinging to the sides of the pan with a brush dipped in cold water, until the sugars are dissolved. Increase the heat and cook the syrup, without stirring, until it reaches 230 degrees on a mercury candy thermometer. Stir in the apricot jam and remove from heat to cool. Stir in the juices and rum.

3. Using a rubber spatula, toss raspberries with cake pieces. Gradually add ³/₄ cup of the punsch filling, tossing to coat and moisten the cake cubes. Continue to add more punsch filling just until cake pieces feel moist but not wet.

4. Spread moistened cake cubes and fruit in the pan. Fit a sheet of aluminum foil on top of the cake mixture, and set a pan the same size as the one below on top of the aluminum foil. Put a 5-pound bag of sugar or something comparable in weight on top to condense the mixture. Refrigerate, keeping the weight in place, for at least 8 hours or until the cake is firm and compact enough to slice without crumbling. During this period, the mixture absorbs the punsch filling evenly to form into a moist cake layer.

5. To serve, use a knife and ruler to cut cake into 1¹/₂-inch cubes.

6. Put raspberries in large bowl. Heat currant jelly just until smooth and liquid but not hot. Pour jelly down one side of the bowl and, using a rubber spatula, gently toss just to coat the berries. Top each small cake cube with a raspberry. Using a small offset metal spatula makes lifting each piece out of the pan easy. Before serving, place each cakelet into a paper mini muffin cup, preferably aluminum foil or silicone-treated.

BAKING NOTES

- Different cakes soak up varying amounts of punsch filling. For example, a spongy texture absorbs more of the filling than a buttery pound cake. For this recipe, 8 cups of leftover sponge cake (about 17 ounces) works well.

Punsch Cakelets

- Unlike a cake from a batter, which may include flour, eggs, ground nuts, or even chocolate to build its structure, these small cakes remain fragile since only the moisture from the filling holds the unbaked mixture together.

VARIATION NOTES

- Punsch Cakelets are delicious as a filling for Chocolate Thimbles (page 166). After preparing the Chocolate Thimbles, cut the cakelets to fit.

Punsch Balls

A German variation of this recipe is to form walnut-sized balls from the cake-fruit mixture. Scoop up small portions with a spoon and form into compact balls with the palms of your hands. Dip the Punsch balls into Dark Satin Chocolate Glaze (page 307), and let sit on aluminum foil until the chocolate sets up.

Punsch Cakelets

Part V

Making Miniatures Ahead, 1 to 100 Dozen

$\mathcal{W}$hether you cater on a regular basis, bake professionally, or simply entertain occasionally, you will find that everyone loves to be served miniatures. They are perfect for a congenial group of ten, a celebrating crowd of one hundred, or as accompaniments to a restaurant's regular desserts. For most miniatures, almost everything can be done in advance: mixing the doughs, baking them, even decorating them to a great extent.

These procedures are designed to make the most efficient use of your time, ensuring that your miniature making will go smoothly. The suggestions apply to the recipes in this book as well as to your own.

KEEP SCORE.

- When I plan to bake any more than three different miniature recipes for a large event, I draw up a simple chart to organize the process.

    First, I list the recipes I have chosen to bake. Then, along the top of the page, I create three thin columns, headed *D, B,* and *A,* for Dough, Baked, and Assembled. Each time I have completed one of these three crucial steps for a particular recipe, I make a check in the appropriate column next to its name. I often find it easier to bake assembly-line fashion, doing all the mixing of the dough first, then all the baking, then the assembly and decoration, rather than going from start to finish on one miniature at a time.

    On the other half of my sheet of paper I write a list of specific tasks I need to complete in order to create the miniatures. The list includes the fillings and glazes I need to make, and special techniques like peeling or blanching nuts and fruits or tempering chocolate. These items get crossed off as they are completed.

PREP EARLY.

- Gather and measure ingredients for all the miniatures you plan to make at one time. You can even do this the day before mixing them. Be sure to label setups to distinguish each miniature recipe.

MIX SEVERAL DOUGHS AT ONE TIME.

- After organizing the setups, mix one dough after another. When ingredients for doughs are similar, instead of washing bowls, wipe them thoroughly with paper towels to avoid unnecessary cleanups.

FORM DOUGHS INTO CIRCLES, ROLLS, LOGS, AND/OR BRICK SHAPES AHEAD OF TIME TO BAKE LATER.

- For example, roll out dough between two sheets of waxed paper to form circles as recipes specify. Stack circles on baking sheet and store as recipes specify. Take time to label and date each dough.

USE TIME-SAVING TECHNIQUES TO SHAPE DOZENS OF MINIATURES QUICKLY AND SIMPLY.

- Whenever possible, bake on parchment. It's reusable and baking sheet cleanup is minimal.
- To flatten balls of dough on a baking sheet uniformly at once: Evenly space dough balls on the sheet, flour the underside of another baking sheet with similar or identical dimensions, and press down gently but firmly on balls. Carefully lift the top baking sheet.
- A cookie press or a pastry bag fitted with a decorative tip shapes cookies quickly, easily, and uniformly.
- Miniatures made from bar cookies or sheet cakes allow you to make dozens at once.
- Spread batter over a plastic stencil (see page 9) to form miniature shapes quickly and uniformly.

- To form dozens of tartlet shells at once, see Rose Tartlets (page 214), Garnet Tartlets, (page 210), and Caramel Carmenitas (page 207). Each method is different, and quicker than pressing dough in tins with fingertips, one at a time, as for Chocolate Starlets (page 186).
- Roll pastry or cookie doughs thinly, cut shapes such as 2-inch rounds for tartlets, and store in plastic containers with tight-fitting lids and plastic wrap between layers to keep shapes apart. Freeze until needed.

STREAMLINE BAKING.

- To bake many batches of miniatures and make the best use of your time, try a baking relay system: Line four baking sheets with parchment just to fit. Set miniatures on each sheet of parchment, ready to bake. When one batch comes from the oven, lift the parchment with them to a cooling rack. Immediately place another parchment-lined baking sheet of unbaked dough in the oven.

  You usually need only four sheets for any baking relay since most baking sheets are cool enough to handle in 10 to 15 minutes. One or two baking sheets are in the oven, while the others are cooling.

USE DECORATIVE TOUCHES LIKE THE PROFESSIONALS.

- Applying a streusel to cookies before baking, as in Cornmeal Batons (page 66), shortcuts decorating. A baked-on garnish saves time and decorates without any additional handling for glazing or piping later.
- Prefabricated decorations, such as Buttercream Bees (page 293), are invaluable. Such planning ahead frees you to finish other miniatures.
- Stencils make it possible to brush a dash of design and color over each miniature, decorating quickly and easily as for Pecan Strudel (page 265).
- Use perfect pecan halves, as in Little Gems (page 44).
- To make sandwich cookies look neat and finished, flip cookies baked-bottom-side up on a tray. Dot each with jelly and sandwich a plain cookie on top, as in Apricot Medals (page 50).
- To make miniatures appear neat and trim, press nuts with fingertips into melted white chocolate to secure them in place, as for Java Sticks (page 46).

STORE MINIATURES WISELY.

- When stacking miniatures, select storage containers in which they fit snugly with little air space between them and the lid. Otherwise, the air stales the miniatures and affects their taste. Take care that lids fit tightly too.
- Store decorated miniatures in jelly roll pans and cover with foil or select shallow cardboard boxes, such as cake boxes or shirt boxes, and line with aluminum foil. The smaller the air space between the miniatures and the lid, the better the flavors are contained, keeping miniatures tasting their best.
- When stacking miniatures in containers, place sheets of plastic or aluminum foil between layers to prevent breakage.

DEVELOP A BAKER'S TIMETABLE.

- Set up a countdown to the serving day: Draw a simple chart on graph paper to organize yourself. Across the top, form columns by writing: "Several weeks before" (fill in actual dates), "Two to three weeks ahead," etc. Down the side, write the names of the miniatures you select. Fill in your timetable as each recipe specifies.
- Several weeks ahead: Prepare and freeze doughs.
- Two to three weeks ahead: Bake, wrap for long-term storage, and store.
- Up to two days ahead: Bake miniatures from doughs and batters.
- Day ahead or on the serving day: Decorate and store.

ADOPT SMART MINIATURE PLANNING.

How many miniatures to serve per person?
Count on three per person, unless miniatures are the only dessert you're offering. Then the number is raised to five or six per person. Keep in mind that the larger the assortment, the more you have to bake. People love to taste at least one of each type of miniature.

How many cookies in a batch?
When you need to determine how many cookies to expect from any cookie dough, use the following procedure.

- Mix the dough, then weigh the entire batch and record the weight on the recipe.
- Shape several cookies just as the recipe specifies. Place just enough shaped cookies on the scale to register one ounce; record that number next to dough's total weight.
- Multiply the number of shaped cookies in an ounce by the dough's total weight in ounces. For example, the Little Gems dough (page 44) weighs 22 ounces. Five cookies register one ounce on the scale; therefore, the recipe's yield is 110 cookies, a little over 9 dozen.
- Dough rolled between waxed paper to form circles, like the Drei Augen (page 48), is calculated the same way. Find the weight of each rolled-out circle, then cut out cookies until you have an ounce. Remember you must reroll and cut the scraps in order for your calculation to be correct.

How many pastries from a dough?
- You can estimate about how many tartlets, turnovers, or other shapes from any pastry dough if you use the method described above.

Learn how to form dough circles consistently the same size from a specific recipe.
When I need a large quantity of cookies, I multiply a favorite reliable cookie recipe. Here's a quick way to roll dough circles.

- First make the single recipe. Weigh the dough and make a note of the weight on the recipe.
- As the recipe specifies, divide the dough before rolling it. Weigh just one portion and mark that weight on the recipe.
- Roll out that portion between two sheets of waxed paper just the shape and thickness as the recipe specifies.
- Measure diameter and mark that on the recipe.

Now you can multiply any favorite recipe, and roll portions of dough one after the other quickly and easily. Just refer to your notes on the recipe for the weight of a single portion. Roll each portion to the correct diameter and you can be sure it is exactly the size the recipe specifies.

Making Miniatures Ahead, 1 to 100 Dozen

Quick Miniatures Reference

To help you select which recipes to bake, I have separated the miniature recipes into categories based on the method used to form them. Next to each one is its size, shape, and page. Texture is indicated only for cookies, since the textures of pastries and cakes are familiar. These categories will come in handy when you plan to bake a number of different miniatures. When I bake more than one or two kinds of miniatures, I make sure to provide a variety of shapes, textures, and flavors—and perhaps even a miniature with a touch of folly.

Miniature Cookies

ROLLED/CUT-OUT

	Size/Shape	Texture	Page
Harlequins	1½″ star	shortbread	42
Drei Augen	1½″ round	shortbread	48
Apricot Medals	1¾″ round sandwich	shortbread	50
Pineapple Pockets	1½″ flattened cone	shortbread	52
Lemon Sunflowers	1½″ petal	shortbread	76
Spicy Twin Thins	1½″ star-shaped sandwich	spicy shortbread	137
Springerle	1½″ by 2″ rectangle	spicy chewy	147
Speculaas	1½″ round	spicy shortbread	150
Lebkuchen Circles	1″ round	spicy chewy	154
Biberli	1½″ rectangle	spicy chewy	157
Tiffany Rings	1½″ round	chocolate shortbread	180
Chocolate Coins	1¼″ round	chocolate shortbread	182

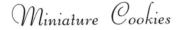

BAR

	Size/Shape	Texture	Page
Gianduja Cubes	1½″ square	chewy	83
Dacquoise Cheesecake Squares	1½″ square	chewy	88
Panforte di Siena	1½″ square	chewy	90
Glazed Almond Weave	1″ by 2½″ stick	chewy	94
Viennese Triangles	1″ triangle	chewy	96
Pecan Diamonds	1½″ diamond	chewy	98
Florentine Squares	1½″ square	crispy	110
Creamy Ginger Squares	1½″ square	spicy chewy	135
Pains d'Amande	1½″ square	spicy chewy	140

DROP

	Size/Shape	Texture	Page
Almond Confetti	1½″ wafer	shortbread	78
Tuiles	1½″ disc	crispy	109
Black Walnut Genoise Wafers	1¾″ round sandwich	crispy	112
Cognac Wafers	1″ round sandwich	crispy	116
Cigarettes	1½″ roll	crispy	118
Nougatine Cones	1½″ cone	crispy	120
Miniature Krumkake	2″ cone	crispy	122
Chocolate Fringe Cups	1¾″ cup	crispy	128
Chantilly Fans	1½″ wedge	crispy	131
Dutch Minicakes	1½″ cupcake	chocolate chewy	168
Chocolate Pistachio Cigarettes	1½″ roll	chocolate crispy	194

HAND-FORMED

	Size/Shape	Texture	Page
Little Gems	1½″ round	shortbread	44
Sweet Seashells	1⅛″ by 1¾″ scallop	shortbread	57
Chevron Twists	1½″ spiral	shortbread	60
Almond Teardrops	1½″ teardrop	shortbread	62
Macadamia Crescents	1½″ crescent	shortbread	64
Cornmeal Batons	1½″ stick	shortbread	66
Autumn Acorns	1½″ acorn	shortbread	70
Eight-Spice Twists	1¼″ by 2½″ twist	spicy shortbread	139
Hahnpfeffernüsse	1″ ball	spicy chewy	144
Chrabeli	1½″ leaf	spicy chewy	149
Double Kisses	1½″ kiss	chocolate shortbread	164
Chocolate Thimbles	1½″ cup	chocolate crispy	166
Chocolate Mint Nuggets	1½″ round	chocolate shortbread	192

REFRIGERATOR

	Size/Shape	Texture	Page
Shortbread Cameos	1¼″ by 1¾″ oval	shortbread	39
Cocos	1¼″ round	shortbread	58
Daddy Long Legs	2″ stick	shortbread	74
Gingersnaps	1½″ round	spicy crispy	152
White Blossom Circles	1½″ round	chocolate shortbread	188
Cocoa Cavaliers	1½″ triangle	chocolate shortbread	190

Making Miniatures Ahead, 1 to 100 Dozen

333

PIPED

	Size/Shape	Texture	Page
Java Sticks	1½″ stick	shortbread	46
Maple Butterballs	1¼″ spherical sandwich	shortbread	68
Mimosa Rosettes	1½″ rosette	shortbread	72
Meringue Bubbles	1¼″ round	chewy	86
Macaroon Trios	1½″ rounded triangle	chewy	92
Swiss Japonais	1¾″ round	chewy	100
Maple Japonais	1¾″ round	chewy	104
Ladies' Wafers	1½″ round	crispy	114
Crispy Corkscrews	2″ spiral	crispy	124
Champagne Biscuits	3″ finger	crispy	126
Sesame Spice Chips	1½″ round	spicy crispy	142
Chocolate Macaroons	1½″ round sandwich	chocolate chewy	161
Chocolate Shadows	1½″ round	chocolate shortbread	196

COOKIE STRIPS

	Size/Shape	Texture	Page
Lemon Macaroon Diamonds	1½″ wedge	shortbread	54
Neapolitan Wedges	1″ wedge	chocolate shortbread	170

Miniature Pastries

FLAKY MINIATURES

	Size/Shape	Page
Sweet Cheese Puffs	1½″ puff	240
Pumpkin Pastries	1½″ round	242
Eccles Tarts	1″ by 2″ barquette	244
Heartovers	1½″ half heart	246
Shreveshire Tarts	1″ by 2″ oval	248
Eva Deutsch's Almond Slices	1″ slice	250
Four-Star Rugelach	1½″ crescent	252
Cinnamon Twists	2″ stick	254
Sweet Ravioli	1½″ square	256
California Rolls	1¼″ roll	258
Dried Fruit Pastry Strips	1″ by 2″ slice	260
Flaky Windmills	1½″ pinwheel	263
Pecan Strudel	2″ by 1½″ slice	265
Miniature Caramel Cream Vol-au-Vents	1½″ round	268
Fig Pastry Rolls	2″ by 1½″ slice	270
Florentine Pastry Strips	1″ by 2″ rectangle	275
Streusel Pastry Strips	1″ by 2″ rectangle	277
Phyllo Accordions	2″ roll	279
Flaky Cheesecake Turnovers	1½″ triangle	281

Making Miniatures Ahead, 1 to 100 Dozen

	Size/Shape	Page
Chocolate Tulips	1½″ round	177
Chocolate Starlets	1½″ round	186
Caramel Carmenitas	1½″ barquette	207
Garnet Tartlets	1½″ round	210
Chocolate Cherry Chaps	1½″ round	212
Rose Tartlets	1½″ oval	214
Double Chocolate Tartlets	1½″ round	216
Mazarine Tartlets	1½″ round	218
Lemon Meringue Tartlets	1½″ round	220
Scheherazade Tartlets	1½″ round	222
Pumpkin Tartlets	1½″ round	224
Jade Buttercups	1½″ round	226
Poirettes	1½″ round	228
Lemon Drops	1½″ round	230
Raspberry Lemon Tartlets	1½″ round	232
Swiss Bettinas	1½″ round	234
Midas Cups	1½″ round	235

Making Miniatures Ahead, 1 to 100 Dozen

337

Freezing and Storing

Storage, if not taken lightly, is the final key to beautiful and delicious miniatures. Proper storing and freezing methods preserve the quality and freshness of miniatures by maintaining their correct textures, thereby maintaining their correct tastes.

The following chart lists, by texture, the best storing and freezing methods for all the miniatures in this book. Most of the miniature doughs can be made in advance and stored unbaked. Since fillings and decorations are the most perishable parts of miniatures, it is often a good idea to bake cookies, pastries, or cakes, store until close to serving time, and then add the finishing touches.

Miniatures that require a filling keep longer unfilled because most often the filling is quite perishable, as with cream cheese mixtures, or apt to stale quickly, as in frangipanes, and because a filled miniature, as with fresh fruit and whipped cream, given time to sit may become soggy.

Whether decorations are perishable like whipped cream, lemon curd, and fresh fruit, or nonperishable like jellies and sugar glazes, their appearance becomes less attractive with age. For example, jelly loses its shine and a sugar or chocolate glaze also will become less shiny and fresh looking. In short, the less adorned a baked good is, the longer it will keep. Use the chart to plan your baking, perhaps freezing a dough until an opportune moment, baking on a quiet week night, then decorating the day you plan to serve the miniatures.

A note about the recommended containers for storing miniatures of different textures: Airtight sturdy plastic containers keep moisture in so that miniatures remain chewy, while airtight metal containers keep moisture out so that crispy miniatures retain their texture. Though this is especially relevant for storing miniatures at room temperature, they may be frozen in these containers also.

Making Miniatures Ahead, 1 to 100 Dozen

Proper defrosting is just as important as proper wrapping and labeling. Transfer from the freezer individual packages of dough, such as Sour Cream Pastry (page 239), or an assortment of stacked dough circles, such as Drei Augen (page 48) and Almond Teardrops (page 62), that are already on a baking sheet directly to the refrigerator at least 8 hours before using. This gives the doughs time to defrost gradually without absorbing excess moisture.

To defrost already baked miniatures, remove labeled containers from the freezer to room temperature. You can keep most miniatures in the container until serving. If you're going to decorate them further, remove them to a shallow container with a cover.

I advise bakers to store decorated miniatures in a single layer because there is no point in going to the trouble of making your creations beautiful if you are going to risk smudging the sticky or shiny ones or crushing the delicate ones under the weight of the others. To store in one layer, place the miniatures in a jelly roll pan, then cover with aluminum foil. A cake box or similarly shaped cardboard box is also spacious enough to hold a single layer of filled, assembled, or decorated miniatures before serving.

Freezing and Storing Chart*

	Dough or Batter 3 days to 1 month	Baked, unfilled 1 week to 1 month	Baked, filled† 1 week to 10 days	Assembled and Decorated 1 to 2 days
Shortbread	Refrigerator or freezer	Airtight metal container Room temperature or freezer	Airtight metal container or cake box Room temperature or freezer	Airtight metal container or cake box Room temperature or refrigerator
Chewy		Sturdy plastic container Room temperature or freezer	Sturdy plastic container Room temperature or freezer	Sturdy plastic container or cake box Room temperature or refrigerator
Crispy		Airtight metal container Room temperature only	Airtight metal container Room temperature only	Airtight metal container or cake box Room temperature only
Spicy Shortbread	Refrigerator or freezer	Airtight metal container Room temperature or freezer	Airtight metal container or cake box Room temperature or freezer	Airtight metal container or cake box Room temperature or refrigerator

*General storage guide. Please refer to recipe for specifics.
†If filling is perishable or contains moisture like fresh fruit, whipped cream, or buttercream, refrigerate.

Freezing and Storing

	Dough or Batter 3 days to 1 month	Baked, unfilled 1 week to 1 month	Baked, filled 1 week to 10 days	Assembled and Decorated 1 to 2 days
Spicy Chewy		Sturdy plastic container Room temperature or freezer	Sturdy plastic container Room temperature or freezer	Sturdy plastic container or cake box Room temperature only
Spicy Crispy		Airtight metal container Room temperature only	Airtight metal container Room temperature only	Airtight metal container or cake box Room temperature only
Chocolate Shortbread	Refrigerator or freezer	Airtight metal container Room temperature or freezer	Airtight metal container or cake box Room temperature or freezer	Airtight metal container or cake box Room temperature or refrigerator
Chocolate Chewy		Sturdy plastic container Room temperature or freezer	Sturdy plastic container Room temperature or freezer	Sturdy plastic container or cake box Room temperature only

	Dough or Batter 3 days to 1 month	Baked, unfilled 1 week to 1 month	Baked, filled 1 week to 10 days	Assembled and Decorated 1 to 2 days
Chocolate Crispy		Airtight metal container Room temperature only	Airtight metal container Room temperature only	Airtight metal container or cake box Room temperature only
Tartlet	Refrigerator or freezer	Airtight metal container Room temperature or freezer	Airtight metal container or cake box Room temperature, refrigerator or freezer	Cake box Room temperature or refrigerator
Flaky	Refrigerator or freezer	Airtight metal container: room temperature Sturdy plastic container: freezer	Cake box Room temperature, refrigerator or freezer	Cake box Room temperature or refrigerator
Cake		Cake box Room temperature or freezer, well wrapped	Cake box Room temperature, refrigerator or freezer	Cake box Room temperature or refrigerator

Index

Numbers in **boldface** indicate the pages on which a recipe appears.

Index

346

C

Index